M.

This b

RC

-24

1

LOC -2. AU

28 JUL

-6 SEP

FOOD CONTROL IN ACTION

Institute of Food Science and Technology Summer Symposium, held at the University of Surrey, Guildford, UK, on 25–27 July 1979.

FOOD CONTROL IN ACTION

Edited by

P. O. DENNIS
Chief Chemist, Brooke Bond Liebig

J. R. BLANCHFIELD
Food Industries Research Manager, Bush Boake Allen Ltd

and

A. G. WARD
Emeritus Professor, Procter Department of Food Science,
University of Leeds

APPLIED SCIENCE PUBLISHERS LTD
LONDON

APPLIED SCIENCE PUBLISHERS LTD
RIPPLE ROAD, BARKING, ESSEX, ENGLAND

British Library Cataloguing in Publication Data

Institute of Food Science and Technology. *Summer
Symposium, University of Surrey, 1979*
Food control in action.
1. Food industry and trade—Quality control—
Congresses
I. Title   II. Dennis, P O   III. Blanchfield,
J R   IV. Ward, Alan Gordon
664'.07   TP372.5

ISBN 0-85334-894-4

WITH 12 TABLES AND 12 ILLUSTRATIONS

© APPLIED SCIENCE PUBLISHERS LTD 1980

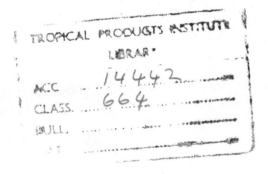
The selection and presentation of material and the opinions expressed in
this publication are the sole responsibility of the authors concerned.

Printed in Great Britain by Galliard (Printers) Ltd, Great Yarmouth

Preface

Early in 1974 Ralph Blanchfield, then Secretary of the Institute of Food Science and Technology of the UK, focused attention on the professional aspects and role of the Institute, particularly as a qualifying body. Towards the end of the same year a working party led by Professor Alan Ward drew up plans for a qualification which included examinations, the passing of which, combined with considerable and suitable practical experience in the food manufacturing industry at postgraduate level, conferred the title of Master in Food Control on successful candidates. It was an ambitious project and demanded ambitious candidates because nothing less than the complete activity of ensuring that wholesome food reached the consumer was the area covered. Since 1978, when the examination was introduced jointly by the Institute of Food Science and Technology of the UK, the Royal Institute of Chemistry, and the Institute of Biology, thirty-three Masterships have been awarded.

The control of the characteristics and quality of manufactured food is a topic of direct concern to agriculturalists, to all those involved in food production and distribution, to those who teach food science and technology, to Government Agencies and the Enforcement Authorities, and, finally, to informed consumers and those—nutritionists, dietitians, home economists, etc.—who advise or educate them about food. This volume, which is based on a symposium of the Institute held in July 1979, is the first to elaborate on the principles and practice of total food control as applied to food manufacture and distribution. It meets the needs especially of technologists in the food industry and in food distribution taking part in control operations. It is required reading for the Mastership in Food Control examination.

The reasons and a framework for overall control in food manufacturing and distribution operations are elaborated from the food technologist's point of view in the first paper, entitled 'Philosophy of Food Control'. There follow a series of interlinked papers, for each of which the author was given a strict editorial brief delineating his subject. Nevertheless, the reader will find some repetition of subject matter and ideas but presented from different viewpoints. The Editors have deliberately allowed this overlap because it demonstrates the inter-relationships among the various parts and aspects of control and the integration necessary to produce the total control function. No attempt has been made to impose an arbitrary common nomenclature upon the authors, particularly with regard to the term 'quality' and industrial functions. The terms and definitions they use reflect no more than the practices within their own companies. As time passes we hope that as the term 'food control' becomes better known it will become more widely used, with a commonly accepted meaning.

My part in bringing about the collection of the papers was that of task-master for the briefs set, a role undertaken with some initial apprehension. I should not have feared: the authors' ability to control within the constraints of the market place was exemplary notwithstanding that their products were being given away. After each paper there appears a discussion. This was led and recorded by the person whose comments are given first in the text. For the cheerfulness and patience with which the authors and recorders endured the slings, arrows and mind-bending editorial activities of myself and my colleagues we are all very grateful.

P. O. Dennis

Contents

1

Philosophy of Food Control

J. Ralph Blanchfield

President, Institute of Food Science and Technology, Food Industries Research Manager, Bush Boake Allen Ltd

'Philosophy' may seem an unduly grandiose term to introduce, but I use it to indicate an intention to go beyond and behind the 'nuts and bolts' of food control, and to pose in relation to it the sort of age-old fundamental questions about meaning and purpose and rationale that philosophers pose.

What I am *not* going to do is indulge in sterile argument about semantics or the supposed meanings and alleged relative merits of terms like 'quality control' or 'quality assurance' as differently interpreted by different people. I intend to concern myself with the substance rather than with the terminology.

I am using the term 'food control', not because it is a whim of mine to do so, but because the term was adopted, after a very careful and lengthy consideration, by the Institute of Food Science and Technology of the UK, not only to describe a function and a field of activity wider and more comprehensive than is normally encompassed by terms such as 'quality control' or 'quality assurance', but also to designate a Mastership—the first and at present the only postgraduate, post-substantial-experience qualification signifying proven ability to accept top responsibility for this function in a manufacturing context, namely the Mastership in Food Control.

Let me start by indicating some of the things which 'food control' is not.

It is *not* the restricted area of food legislation and its enforcement, though I am well aware that the term is sometimes used in official and regulatory circles as a convenient verbal shorthand to refer to that area. For example, Alain Gerard, in his '*An outline of food law*',[1] written for the FAO, stated:

'In the broad sense food control is often understood as comprising all

1

those measures, of whatever kind, which the government sees fit to introduce with a view to protecting consumers of food. In the strict sense, however, food control consists of all those institutional and procedural arrangements whereby the effective observance of the food regulations by producers and tradesmen may be verified and enforced'.

Verbal shorthand can be useful provided everyone concerned understands and remembers that it is verbal shorthand. Even Dr. Gerard's broader definition is on a par with saying that the nature and character of your progress along a road is 'controlled' only by traffic laws and the actions of traffic police. They are certainly part of the picture, but how can one ignore the influence of such factors as the kind and condition of your car? Or your ability as a driver? Or the skill and assiduity with which you continually monitor and evaluate the complex of data being fed back to you through your instruments and your senses about your car's behaviour, about road conditions, about other traffic, and so on? Or the efficiency and promptness with which you continuously take appropriate consequent actions?

Certainly, the food controller has to know about food legislation and its enforcement, has to operate within legislative and other constraints, and has a professional responsibility to contribute to the proper development of legislation. But food control is concerned not merely with establishing whether what has been done and produced conforms or conflicts with legal requirements and dealing appropriately with infringements and transgressors, necessary as those activities undoubtedly are. Food control is also concerned—and I submit much more centrally concerned—with the technical measures taken before, during, and after production to ensure that the products comply, not only with all the legal requirements, but also with many other requirements which the law does not and often cannot specify. This primary task must rest squarely with responsible professional food scientists and technologists exercising the function in industry. The official inspection/sampling/testing is secondary and supplementary—which is not to deny its necessity and importance. So food control is not synonymous with legislative enforcement but is much wider in scope and with its centre of gravity elsewhere.

Nor does food control limit itself to the statistical, chemical, microbiological, physical, and sensory methodology and techniques which are essentially the tools which food control uses to do the job—and are thereby part of the job but not the job itself. It is, of course, desirable to have a wide range of likely tools at one's disposal; it is vital to know how to select the most appropriate tool for a particular purpose and, having selected it, to know how to use it properly.

Again, food control is a much wider subject than that of the scientific and technological factors affecting food product quality. It would, of course, be impossible to carry out effective food control without thorough and extensive knowledge of the physical, chemical, biochemical, microbiological, nutritional, and other characteristics and behaviour of foods, and of the principles and practices involved in the conversion and stabilisation operations and processes comprising the technology of manufacture, storage, distribution, etc., of finished food products. Without it, how could one translate required product properties into raw material and packaging specifications, ingredients formulation, processing and storage procedures, conditions, and precautions? How could one establish the connections and relationships between properties required and parameters selected for specification and measurement? How could one establish what tolerances may be acceptable on particular parameters? How could one decide (other than by rule of thumb) what modifications and adjustments to formulation or to processing conditions will produce what qualitative and quantitative effects, when control results indicate that something should be done? How would one understand how to exercise control so as to produce consistent products from inherently variable biological materials? How could one possibly take on board products and processes with which one has had no previous experience?—and that is essential in these days of product diversification, mergers, takeovers, and technologist mobility among companies and even among sectors of the food industry.

No doubt some will have noticed the use, a few moments ago, of the naughty word 'quality'. I am not going to argue with anyone about what it means or ought to mean. It suffices if I tell you what *I* mean when *I* use it today, so that you will know what I intend to convey. The classical definition is:

'the composite of those characteristics which differentiate between individual units of product and which also have significance in determining the degree of acceptability of that unit to a buyer'.

That definition has been around a long time and may be sanctified if not fossilised by age. Provided that one understands cost as being one of the characteristics, one would not quarrel unduly with the definition except perhaps on grammatical grounds. I would, however, prefer to paraphrase and clarify it as:

'a multi-component measure of the extent to which the units of a product, which a seller is willing and able to offer at a price, consistently meet the requirements and expectations of the group of buyers willing and able to buy that product at that price'.

I do not claim the above as an authoritative or superior definition, but I like it because it explicitly covers all such aspects as my friend's dissatisfaction with his Fiat 128 which admits water into the boot when it rains; my own complete satisfaction with my own well behaved Fiat 128, which, however, would not satisfy one of my neighbours because for him it's the wrong colour; or another neighbour who prefers a Ford at a similar price; or another who, at the same price, prefers a secondhand sports car; or another who likes a Fiat but needs the larger boot of a 132 model; or another whose price limit stops at a Mini; or another who prefers to travel by bus and spend his money on hi-fi stereo instead of on a car; or those of you whose tastes and incomes run to Rolls-Royces; or the unreasonable fanatic who will only buy a car if accompanied by a cast-iron 100% absolute lifetime guarantee against accident.

At any rate, my definition is given as my explanation of what the reader should understand me to mean when I use the shorthand term 'quality'. This definition also indicates, as indeed the reasons outlined for the essential importance of knowledge of the relevant scientific and technological factors equally indicate, why food control is not limited to monitoring what goes on in the production area, although that monitoring, with rapid feedback of data and advice on which appropriate action may be taken, is an essential constituent of food control. The totality of control must, however, be considered as extending much further in both chronological directions; from participation in all aspects of the design of the product and methods of ensuring that it is capable of being achieved in practice; through the monitoring/feedback process to ensure conformance with design, supplemented by checks on a representative proportion of product units to ensure compliance with legal and company standards; to the subsequent behaviour of the product, its quality characteristics when it reaches the consumer, and the consumer's reaction thereto.

Thus the scope of food control, as a function, is extremely wide, but nonetheless limited, not least by the four major constraints within which it has to be performed, as well as by the fact that it has to be performed in a real-life complex system in which other functions also operate and exert their intentional or fortuitous influence on product quality.

When reference is made to constraints, many people's hackles rise—but unjustifiably. A guard rail around a dangerous chasm is a constraint, but a valuable safety aid. The lane markings on a road, intelligently used, will help you keep to your desired route instead of inadvertently being led astray, to say nothing of minimising the risk of head-on collisions. So a constraint is not necessarily a malevolent restriction on freedom of action. Nowhere is that better illustrated than in the first of the four constraints indicated, the quality requirements of the market.

What is the point of developing and manufacturing a supposedly 'better' product which people do not want to buy or consume? We can all think of products which have appeared and disappeared through failure to comply effectively with that constraint. Important considerations for our present purpose, however, are the steps taken to define the market aimed at, to obtain and evaluate information on its requirements, and to establish quality of design and practical methods of conformance, with participation of the food control function in so doing.

The second constraint is that of cost. This also springs clearly from the requirements of the market, for the cost allowable in the production of a product must be related to what amount can be sold at what price. In maintaining a balance between product quality and product cost it is important to keep costs down to standard as well as to keep quality up to standard. Many factors involved in cost are outside the direct influence of the food control function, but others can and should be influenced, directly or indirectly. The Study Guide for the Part III examination for the Mastership in Food Control sets out the main influences of food control on product costs on a continuing basis as follows:[2]

1. Raw materials—by specification and buying sample evaluation, assisting the purchasing function to obtain both the right raw materials and value for money; by evaluation of bulk deliveries ensuring that they conform to specification and/or buying sample.

2. Production—providing the effective means whereby production can consistently conform to product standards, thereby not only maintaining consumer satisfaction but also minimising costly rejection or reworking of sub-standard product.

3. Risk prevention—minimising the risk of defective products reaching the consumer or becoming the subject of a prosecution (the cost of which, in harm to the manufacturer's reputation, may far exceed any fine).

4. Incentive schemes—recommending that any incentive bonus scheme aimed at maximising quantity of production has an effective inbuilt quality factor which penalises any sacrifice of

quality below the agreed standard, coupled with being alert for
bonus-earning unauthorised 'short-cuts' by operators causing
otherwise inexplicable quality defects.

Elsewhere, the Study Guide refers to the need to bear in mind such factors
as raw material prices, wage rates, and energy costs when choosing raw
materials and process specifications, while recognising that subsequent
inflation of such costs is entirely outside the influence of the food control
function.

In addition to all these aspects of the interaction of food control with the
cost constraint, there is of course the cost of the function itself. Whether a
company treats that cost as a cross it has to bear, whether it regards it as an
insurance premium, whether it regards it as an activity which probably
more than repays its cost but unquantifiably so, or whether it attempts the
somewhat dubious task of justifying the cost of control in terms of
quantified savings it produces, the cost is still part of the overhead that the
products will have to bear. This raises the question of how a company
decides what scale of control function to mount and maintain. Too little is
probably money and effort down the drain; beyond a certain level, the laws
of diminishing returns and of Parkinson both come into play, plus the
generation of unwarranted complacency. Somewhere in between those two
extremes? But where, precisely? This also concerns the constraint of 'the
organisation', which is discussed later. The manager of the food control
function is the most competent person to advise the company on value for
money in control effort, but even an established reputation for responsible
professionalism may not entirely outweigh a maybe totally unjustified
suspicion of empire building. In these circumstances both the manager and
the company may prefer to seek an additional and independent opinion
from a consultant. There is, however, no doubt that the efficiency and
productivity with which the function is organised and carried out has a
tremendous bearing on what can be achieved with a given amount of
resources, and greatly depends on the skill and ability of the food control
manager.

The third constraint, that of legislation, has already been mentioned.
Both the design of products and their conformance with design must
comply with the legislation of the country in which they are made or the
country in which they are to be sold (in some instances, both) as regards
vertical and horizontal legislation affecting composition and ingredients, in
some instances nutritional characteristics, hygiene and environmental
conditions under which they are manufactured, and the nature and form of

information which must be provided to the purchaser about them. Mention has also been made, however, of the responsibility of the food controller to contribute to the proper development of legislation. Food legislation has not been, and is not, a static immutable edifice; on the contrary, it is in a state of continuous development, reflecting the changing needs of society, technological developments, and newer knowledge in fields such as nutrition and toxicology. In many countries, and certainly in the UK, the legislation-making and modifying processes provide ample opportunities, at several stages, for the food controller to contribute. These opportunities have been made use of effectively in the past and present, where the food controller has acted as the technological spokesman for the company or for a group of companies comprising a trade association of a section of industry. Such contributions clearly cannot disregard the interests of the company or industry concerned, but from long personal experience I would say in general that they are made in a way that also reflects the personal integrity of the individuals concerned. Moreover, it can be claimed, without fear of contradiction, that food legislation has evolved over the years more effectively, less ambiguously, more realistically, and more workably, and indeed more in the public interest, through just such contributions; conversely, one can call to mind some of the nonsensical draft legislation documents (for example, some of those emanating from Brussels) prepared by worthy and well meaning drafters who had obviously never been involved in the manufacture of anything nor seen the inside of a factory. Nevertheless, valuable though contributions from the technological spokesmen of industry have long proved to be, and continue to be, they do tend to be regarded—and reasonably so—as 'representations' of sectional interests, along with representations by other sectional interests such as consumerist bodies and various enforcement bodies. In recent times, however, an entirely new feature has appeared on this scene, at any rate in the UK. This is the consequence of the emergence of a clearly defined profession of food science and technology, and of the Institute of Food Science and Technology as its incorporated professional qualifying body. Consisting as it does of members in industry, in teaching in higher and further education, in research establishments, in enforcement, and in government, all bound to adhere to its Code of Professional Conduct and its particular requirements concerning wholesomeness of food, when the Institute speaks in consensus it does so, and may be clearly seen to do so, grinding no sectional axe, and offering not 'representations' but objective advice and comment.

The fourth constraint affecting the food control function is that of 'the organisation'. The function is carried out within an organisation, a company manufacturing and/or distributing food. The food controller is not a free agent but is constrained by a variety of matters relating to the organisation. How much practical importance do company policies attach to product quality? What kinds and quantities of resources and facilities are put at the disposal of the function to perform its work? To what extent does the function have authority and responsibility? To what extent does it rely on advising and convincing other functions—and to what extent is the manifest attitude of directors and top management conducive to the willingness of other functions to cooperate? To what extent does the Board or top management listen to and act on the advice and recommendations of the food control function when receiving contrary (and sometimes more comfortable and apparently more lucrative) advice and recommendations from other quarters? Obviously to anyone with experience of industry, circumstances, organisational structure, and the position of food control in those structures vary widely from company to company. Indeed, even in apparently similar sets of circumstances, differences in effectiveness will derive from the maturity and forcefulness of the food control manager and the skill with which he or she copes with the constraints of the organisation, the functional interfaces, and the management of the function and those within it.

Reference to functional interfaces highlights the fact that food control is only one function among others involved in the complex activity of manufacturing and distributing food products. Each from its own viewpoint sees itself as central, and understandably so, but this hardly matters so long as they appreciate the fact that they are interdependent. The proper understanding of food control therefore crucially involves an understanding of the important interfaces with other functions, and much of the effectiveness of the control function lies in the way in which those carrying it out operate, collaborate, and secure collaboration across those interfaces.

The general nature and character of those interfaces can be described but the precise detail will obviously vary with the organisational structure of the company. The principal interfaces of food control with other functions are those with product and process development, with materials purchasing, with production and productivity, and with the distribution function all the way from the end of the production line to the consumer. These are quoted not in order of importance but merely in chronological sequence.

There is indeed an interface between food control and product and process development as functions, regardless of whether they are treated as organisationally separate or whether, as in some companies, they are organised as sub-divisions of an overall technological function. What is of great importance is that the food control function and management should have the opportunity from the outset to participate in and agree the product and process design, the specifications for materials and for processing methods and procedures, and the design of the initial control system for the new product.

Reference has already been made to materials specifications, buying samples, and checking of incoming deliveries and stocks as topics for the interface with materials purchasing. To this must be added the vitally important liaison with suppliers' technologists. To be fully effective this has to be direct technical-to-technical communication and not through one or even two layers of intervening non-technical people, and yet must be done without offending or leaving in the dark or usurping the roles of either the materials purchasing function or the supplier's sales function.

References have already been made to the interface with production. While the central theme is that of providing processing specifications and of monitoring conditions and key parameters, with rapid feedback of data and advice on which appropriate action may be taken to keep or return the process within control limits, it should also extend to other helpful activities, such as advice on varying treatment (or pretreatment) of different batches of raw material to minimise end-product variation; advice on ways of utilising and, where possible, rectifying defective product, being alert for 'unofficial' variation from standard procedures, and general 'trouble-shooting'.

Part of the interface with production concerns productivity, the continuing effort to maximise efficiency in the use of people, machines, materials, energy and time, i.e. to obtain the desired result with the least possible input expenditure. Unless there is close and continuing liaison between the food control function and those concerned with pursuing productivity, there could be a very real danger that methods may be adopted or modified regardless of—indeed in sheer ignorance of—the effect on the quality or even on the safety of the product.

Insofar as 'quality' involves meeting the requirements and expectations of buyers and, in the case of food products, that is put to the crucial test mainly at the time of consumption, the interface of food control with distribution must be concerned with all the varied activities involved in the progress of food products from the end of the production line, through perhaps several stages of warehousing, storage, transport, handling, display, sale, and even storage and preparation in the home, specifying what should happen and monitoring for compliance therewith in all aspects which the manufacturer can control or influence, building into the product and its packaging sufficient tolerance and protection to enable it to encounter foreseeable vicissitudes and mishandling in phases outside the manufacturer's direct control and yet still reach the consumer in acceptable condition, and providing the consumer with adequate information and

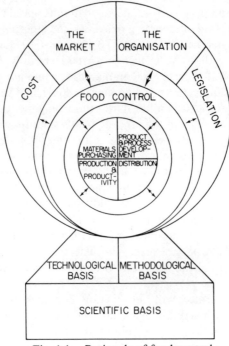

Fig. 1.1. Rationale of food control.

advice on storage and preparation. This interface also involves the handling of customer complaints. Apart from the value of satisfying the customers concerned and helping to preserve the manufacturer's reputation, investigation and identification of the cause of a customer complaint may sometimes point to a way in which methods or control, or both, could be improved.

So, we arrive at a rationale, a structure, a framework of food control (Fig. 1.1).

The primary foundation is the *scientific knowledge* of the nature, behaviour and interaction of food materials; the two secondary bases, each of which depends on and derives from scientific knowledge, are the *technology* of manufacture of foods and the *methodology* of examining, measuring, and testing what is happening before, during, and after production.

While resting on those bases, food control has to operate within certain *constraints* and, in doing so, has to operate not in isolation but *interfacially* with other industrial functions.

The management, effective practice, and operation of the food control function, like any other, requires a managerial skill and ability, especially in dealing with people and organising activities. It will be seen that it also necessarily involves a combination of knowledge and understanding of its bases, of how to operate, collaborate, and obtain collaboration across the functional interfaces, and of how to interact effectively with the contraints.

To study any complex subject it is necessary to isolate individual facets, but it is all too easy to forget that in real life they are not isolated but inter-connected and inter-reacting such that the whole is far more than the sum of the parts.

The Institute has adopted three measures to avoid that pitfall. The first measure is this Keynote Address, providing a framework corresponding to the structure of the Symposium, and highlighting the inter-connections among topics dealt with by the authors. The second measure concerns the papers themselves. Each was written to a precise and detailed brief by a selected author, and all were checked by an Editorial Board to ensure avoidance of excessive replication of subject matter. Nevertheless, as participants will have noted when reading the preprints, a significant degree of overlap was deliberately retained, not only to allow a theme to be illuminated from various angles, but also to emphasise the inter-connections among the different facets. The third measure was to arrange four papers in the final session under the general title 'Putting It all Together' or 'A Day in the Life...' (see Session IV—Practical Applications). These were *not* intended to cover a wide range of technologies or end-product groupings—indeed, that was not the purpose of this Symposium. Four widely differing real-life industrial contexts were selected, and the four papers show how the facets of control covered in earlier sessions are put together in each of these contexts, and, moreover, reveal how some parts of the manner of putting together are apparently independent of while other parts are greatly influenced by the nature of the industrial context.

The Institute held a major national Symposium under the title 'Quality Control in the Food Industry' in April 1967. Its purpose and scope were not completely identical with those of this Symposium, but there was a large area of overlap.

Of course, there have come into the field large numbers of scientists and technologists who were not there then. That in itself would justify repeats of the Symposium from time to time; but this is not merely a repeat performance and not just a question of a new audience. So what else has happened in the intervening 12 years?

The economic context in which food manufacture operates has changed substantially from what in retrospect might be seen as the halcyon days of the 1960s. There have been changes and developments in the market itself and the marketing of food. There have been developments in scientific knowledge, in technology, and in methodology. There have been very far reaching developments in legislation, particularly in the EEC, and not merely in actual legislative changes but in the manner in which legislation develops.

It is also true to say that we have developed a deeper understanding of the concept of food control. This is not to criticise the organisers, speakers, or participants in the 1967 symposium. We stand on the shoulders of our predecessors and for that reason alone should be able to see further. But there is the additional fundamental factor that professional developments in recent years have caused us deliberately to sharpen our minds and bring together experienced groups for purposeful study of food control concepts. Indeed, this Symposium is a further stage in that process, which is why the papers were preprinted for prior considered study, and why most of the time was devoted to discussion.

I suspect, however, that it will be imperative to hold the next major Symposium on food control far sooner than 12 years hence, for it would be remiss to omit from this philosophical overview, as we move into the era of the microprocessor, which is likely to affect our lives in many ways, its likely specific influence on food control. This is likely to be manifest firstly in the production field itself, minimising the erratic effect of human operators and human intervention, and increasing the effectiveness and precision with which process conditions may be designated and adhered to; secondly in the area of monitoring and feedback, greatly increasing the extent to which processes may be continuously monitored at appropriate stages, the data being instantly, automatically, and continuously fed back to maintain or adjust an earlier stage of the process so that the process is in effect self-controlling; and thirdly in increasing the extent of and reducing the cost of rapid automatic instrumental carrying out cf complex analyses for routine control purposes.

The advent of the microprocessor is unlikely, however, to affect the ways in which food legislation is developed or interpreted, the availability, variability, choice, and specification of raw materials, the principles of conversion and preservation on which food process and product design are based, the need for interfacial relationships with other industrial functions, or the need for skilful professional management in food control. But this is speculation and deduction based on crystal-gazing, and I am sure we shall need to make a factually based assessment of the impact within the next 2 or 3 years.

All the changes of the past 12 years are significant, but most significant are the professional developments to which I have referred. Winding-up the 1967 Symposium, the second President of the 3-year-old infant Institute of what was only just beginning to emerge as a profession, felt constrained to defend the very formation of the Institute, differentiating it from other bodies by its combination of entry standards and its multi-disciplinary membership. He and others could, I know, envisage in broad terms the shape of things to come, but many stepwise developments were needed before they could gradually be brought about.

In contrast, the tenth President, opening this Symposium, can point to the well-established incorporated professional qualifying Institute of a profession, the increasingly well defined and well established nature of which is itself substantially the consequence of the existence and effort of the Institute, an Institute recognised and respected by Government, an Institute fully complying with all the stringent professional criteria established by the UK community of scientific and technological professional Institutes, and respected and accepted by all of them as an equal partner, an Institute well on the way to becoming the professional qualifying body outside which any self-respecting food professional will regard it as unthinkable to remain. In that very great progress, the two giant steps have been the Code of Professional Conduct (see page 283) and the Mastership in Food Control (MFC). The former, and its associated Professional Conduct Guidelines, are of great significance in many other ways that do not directly concern food control; but the provision of the Guideline on 'Wholesomeness of Food',[3] which is the keystone of the whole Code, is of the greatest possible relevance to food control. The development by the IFST, and the launching by a partnership of the IFST, RIC and Institute of Biology, of the Mastership in Food Control as a postgraduate, post-substantial-experience qualification signifying knowledge and experience-proven ability to manage all aspects of technical control in the manufacture and handling of foods, besides providing a yardstick of food control management expertise, will in time result in the much wider extension of application of and a general raising of the standard of competence and effectiveness of technical control of food; and if (or, perhaps, when) legislators decide that public safety requires a closer and more comprehensive control and assurance of food quality, this would provide a practicable and acceptable self-certification by responsible experts within the industry instead of control from without by government inspectors and veterinarians. This is not the occasion for an outline of the MFC. A full account has been given elsewhere,[4] and participants will have received the MFC folder containing its Regulations, Syllabuses, and Study Guides. Suffice it to add that the Professional Conduct Guideline on 'Wholesomeness of Food' and the MFC have together created a whole new dimension in food control. Indeed, it was the drafting and discussion of the Syllabus and Study Guide for MFC Part III which revealed the need for this Symposium for the benefit of all concerned with the quality of food in manufacture and distribution, whether in ensuring it, enforcing it, teaching it, or learning how to do it and manage it; a Symposium intended not merely to record the 'state of the art' but also as an instrument for further progress.

REFERENCES

1. Gerard, A. (1975). *An outline of food law*. FAO, Rome.
2. *Mastership in Food Control; Regulations, Syllabuses and Study Guides*, IFST, 1978.
3. *Professional Conduct Guideline No. 1, 'Wholesomeness of food'*, IFST, 1975.
4. Blanchfield, J. R. (1978). 'The Mastership in Food Control', *IFST Proc.*, **11**(3), pp. 174–178.

SESSION I

The Components

2

Scientific Basis of Food Control

JOHN HAWTHORN

Professor of Food Science and Head of the Department of Food Science and Nutrition, University of Strathclyde

INTRODUCTION

Food is processed to increase its value, and value is measured by the price the purchaser is prepared to pay. If the value is higher than the cost at the point of sale, a surplus has been created which may be used to increase either personal or national wealth. If the value is lower than the cost, a deficit arises which decreases either personal or national wealth.

Since neither people nor nations seem to want to become poorer, and since the above statements are true of both managed and free economies, the achievement of greatest value for a given cost is the objective of any economic enterprise.

The controls applied to a food enterprise are therefore aimed at maximising the margin between value and cost. Traditionally, the primary control is that of the accountant and his activities are directed to the accurate measurement of this margin. It is widely believed that he can influence the size of this margin, and in a short-term technical sense this belief is not without justification. In the long term, however, value reflects the quality of the product and in this sphere the influence of the accountant can only be indirect.

VALUE AND QUALITY

If value be measured by the price the purchaser is prepared to pay, it must represent the summation of the product characteristics the purchaser requires. For a given cost, the greater the sum of these the higher is the value. Furthermore, if a first purchase satisfies, an expectation is produced.

17

If that expectation is not realised on a second purchase, that is to say, if the summation of quality factors varies in a way detectable to the purchaser, successive purchases become less and less probable. This brings the second factor of constancy into the equation. But a food purchase involves quality factors which may not be obvious to the purchaser. For social reasons the food must be both safe and nutritious within its frame of reference. To protect the purchaser on these important matters, governments establish legislative processes aimed at achieving these desiderata, and this is the third factor.

Food control is therefore aimed at achieving the best value, that is to say, the optimisation of the quality factors desired, for a given cost and within the framework of legal requirements. This is a complex equation to solve. Enterprises rise and fall depending on the individual solutions achieved. The purpose of this introductory paper is to examine the kind of scientific resource required, first to measure and thereafter to control these variables, within the marketing and legislative framework associated with the product. Since it is concerned with the scientific basis of *all* aspects of food control, this paper must necessarily refer to topics which will be dealt with in detail later in this Symposium.

The starting point in this task is the variability of foodstuffs. To the biochemist, no two ears of wheat are identical. To the miller, no two shipments of wheat are identical. To the baker, there are subtle but sometimes important differences between each flour consignment. To the purchaser, today's loaf should be the same as yesterday's. In practice this is not always achieved, but successful bakers produce bread at a level of acceptable quality and with day-to-day variations of such a minor character that they are rarely apparent to the purchaser, and indeed may often only be detected by laboratory tests.

THE DEFINITION OF QUALITY FACTORS

The every-day terms used to describe food qualities lack precise meanings and therefore cannot be used directly by the food scientist. Nouns such as goodness, freshness, purity, tastiness, and richness, and adjectives such as mouth-watering, flavoursome, creamy, crispy, and the like, reflect subjective reactions to food situations. They must be translated into a less emotive environment and broken down into measurable or potentially measurable variants before science can react with them. This interface can be a source of confusion and error.

THE SCIENCES WE USE

Let us turn to what can be said about food in terms of the traditional imperatives of science—measure, generalise, and validate by prediction. We start with mathematics.

Whatever mathematicians may say, mathematics is really about counting things. It deals with continuities (curves, for example) by dividing them into a very large number of very small bits and manipulating them from there. But it also deals with the relationships between the bits, either singly or in groups. Foodstuffs, either raw or processed, are made up of bits —milk in bottles, peas in pods, eggs in baskets, bread in slices, sides of beef in freezers. The food controller deals in numbers. But peas, eggs, bread slices, and sides of beef all contain chemical constituents at levels which can be expressed in numerical terms. These levels often vary, and find practical expression in quality variations detectable either by the purchaser in terms of such things as colour, texture, and flavour or by the Public Analyst in terms of legislative trespass. No one, it seems, wishes to purchase green beef, red-yolked eggs, yellow peas, or pink bread, yet all of these are possible under certain circumstances. We are therefore now moving in thought from concepts such as freshness and purity towards expressing characteristics in terms of numbers which have a more precise meaning.

All this is easy and obvious, but if we express all that we can measure about a single grain of wheat in numerical terms we shall have pages of figures to cope with. When we deal with 100 tonnes of wheat the situation becomes unmanageable, if we merely log data. Clearly, we must select the significant, that is to say, the factors which are important to our objectives. Selection implies judgements. Gentlemen, according to Miss Marilyn Monroe, prefer blondes. A judgement has been made. In wheat, we prefer what?

We cannot escape this matter of exercising judgement. I know, as a matter of subjective experience, that I prefer vanilla ice-cream. As a matter of practical observation I also know that some eccentrics prefer coffee, strawberry, or raspberry ice-cream. To me, these preferences are irrational; to them, I am irrational. Somewhere there must be a numerical referee. If I manufacture ice-cream, I must know the proportions of my customers who prefer one or another flavour. But tastes are not constant. Occasionally the vanilla addict may capriciously order strawberry. Statistics offer an answer.

In addition to counting preferences, we must also count things, weigh things, measure volumes, and measure variances in our countings, weighings, and measurings, and the relationships if any between these. If the net profit on a 28-oz loaf is 5 % and I make my loaves at 29 oz, my profit almost disappears. This seems a simple problem to overcome, and so it is if I hand bake 100 loaves per hour. It becomes more difficult if I machine bake 100 loaves per minute. Being able to count is the beginning of wisdom for food control, and for making judgements about the characteristics which are to be controlled.

Next we come to physics, which is about the nature of things, from satellites to sausages. It deals with the invisible—gravity, energy, electricity, and the like—and the visible and audible—fluids and solids, heat and sound. Foods have physical properties—mass, density, freezing points, melting points, boiling points, heat transfer coefficients, viscosity, vapour pressure, etc.

It is therefore obvious that the physical properties of food must be appreciated by the food controller. But physics goes further than the food itself: it extends to the environment in which the food is produced, processed, packaged, transported, stored, sold, prepared, consumed, masticated, digested, converted to bone, muscle and energy, and even to the excretion of the undigested residue. It also is basic to the engineering that we use to process food.

Next in this catalogue are chemistry and biochemistry. To a chemist foods are mixtures of chemicals which are of such complexity that even now, after 140 years of study and research (I date food chemistry from the work of Justus von Liebig), there is much that we only glimpse through a glass, darkly. But to the biochemist, these individual chemicals are interrelated in subtle and diverse ways, the ways of the living plant or animal which they are or from which they were derived.

Superimposed on this is another world, that of the micro-organisms—the bacteria, yeasts and moulds which are the prime causes of food spoilage, and the phytoplankton of seas and lakes upon which all marine sources of food ultimately depend for their existence.

Food is for consumption. To understand its function in and disposal by the human frame, there must be appreciation of at least some elementary physiology as well as its specialised offshoot, the science of nutrition. This is a particularly difficult area because of the problems, both ethical and practical, of conducting nutritional experiments on human beings. We probably understand the nutritional needs of pigs, cattle, and poultry much better than our own. We may speculate, we may even have strong suggestive evidence, but we do not know with certainty the optimal nutritional needs of man. The very word 'optimal' raises doubts. Optimal for what?—growth of a human baby? Here we have a fair idea of what is needed and it is natural to assume that high growth rates are good. But if long life be the criterion, there is some evidence to suggest that maximum growth rates in infancy may be a bad thing. Optimal for health gives us the problem of defining health. Is it merely freedom from organic disease, or is it something more? We do not know. The existence of a relationship between diet and disease is clearly established for some but remains obscure for others, despite tantalising demographic and epidemiological evidence.

Mathematics, physics, chemistry, biochemistry, microbiology, physiology, nutrition, and the links between food and health make a formidable catalogue. But three further steps have to be taken before we are finished. One we have already hinted at. Food processing involves machinery to move the food from point to point, to prepare it, to grind or cut it to size, to heat it or to cool it, to fill it into containers, and finally to wrap and pack it. Twice armed, then, is the food controller who knows enough of the elements of engineering to put his needs accurately and clearly to the engineer who designs and runs the equipment. To this end he must at least understand the basics of size reduction and separation, heat transfer, mass transfer, distillation, temperature and volume controls, the limitations of packaging materials and equipment, and, above all, the properties of materials of construction, and especially their resistance to corrosion because corrosion increases costs. It also introduces hazards to the food when the products of corrosion are either toxic or influence the quality of the finished product.

All this also involves the further requirement of attention to the legal restrictions within which the food controller must work. Standards of identity, safety, quantity, quality, and labelling in this country for internal sale or the legislative framework of other countries to which the food may be exported all play their part. These standards are imperatives, lack of knowledge of which may lead not only to error but to substantial financial loss.

Finally, and in many ways the most difficult problem, the food controller must understand the basics of food selection. The user buys the product because he likes the appearance, the texture, and, above all, the flavour which it offers him. The measurement of these subjective reactions is associated with psychology rather than the more precise physical and biological sciences which have been our previous concern. Yet this brings us full circle to the starting point of this paper—the relationship between value and quality. We must now attempt to measure, and this is the scientific basis of food control.

FOOD CONTROL FROM DEVELOPMENT TO PRODUCTION

Let us start with the assumption that a new product is to be developed and put into production. The first questions to be asked are, 'Is there a home market, is there an export market, do similar products already exist on these markets, and what size are the markets?'. Strictly these are questions for the marketing department of a company rather than for the laboratory, but the earlier the laboratory is brought into the picture the easier is the task of developing the product and putting it into production. To begin with, similar products usually exist and the nature and size of the market are therefore known, if not precisely then at least in terms of a rough annual figure. For marketing, as for food control, the first task is to examine the product already available both in marketing and in quality terms.

The next question to consider is the possibility of making a new product which has clear advantages over existing products. These advantages may take one or several of the following forms: improved convenience, more attractive organoleptic properties and better shelf-life, or alternatively a product essentially similar to those already on the market but produced to sell at a lower price.

Of course, occasionally a completely different situation may arise through, for example, a technological development which permits a new type of product to be offered. The problem of assessing the market size is often (in the early stages) little more than guesswork associated with high hopes. In the later stages market surveys and test marketing may allow more accurate forecasts, but the product has to be produced first, albeit on a small scale, before reasonable estimates are possible. Such situations, however, are comparatively infrequent.

Practice and procedures vary from company to company depending on internal structures and organisation, but whether the product is a sparkling new concept or the adaptation of an existing one, at least five sections of the company must be involved from the start if the development and launching process are to be carried out with minimum costs and maximum effectiveness. These are marketing, product development, engineering, the technical control function, and the cost accountant. Details of marketing and costing functions are outside the scope of our present consideration, but it is necessary to consider the situation which exists between product development and the control processes which will operate when full production is achieved.

The concept of the new product may have had its origin either from marketing or from the product development unit. Assuming that the preliminary market appraisal has been satisfactory and that a development project is undertaken, the work must progress against a background of liaison between the development function and the control function. Development tends to proceed in stages and to progress by a series of approximations. This is best illustrated by a simple example. Suppose a new canned soup is to be produced which is based on a traditional recipe. This means that potential customers already have a mental expectation of what this product is like.

The British do not much favour fish soups, although in other countries they are popular. However, in the north east of Scotland there is a delicious traditional fish soup known as Cullen Skink which is occasionally offered in expensive hotels but more often made at home for purely domestic use. At the time of writing and to the best of my knowledge this soup is not canned, so an imaginary exercise based on a proposal to can it will not invade commercial privacy. Its recipe is simple—smoked fish, preferably haddock, potato, milk, onion, cream or butter, salt and pepper. Some housewives will vary the recipe with a hint of cinnamon or clove together with a touch of sugar—not enough to make it sweet but just enough to produce the suggestion of sweetness. Those who do will perhaps use a heaped teaspoonful to a pot of soup to serve six portions (or about 2 litres).

The flavour is affected by the levels of fish, milk, onion, and seasoning, and the texture by the amount of potato used. As a first approximation assume that four levels of fish, three levels of milk, five levels of onion, five levels of butter, and twelve variants of seasonings will give a soup recognisable as Cullen Skink, but each detectably different from the other. It will take therefore $4 \times 3 \times 5 \times 5 \times 12 = 3600$ experiments to try out the whole range of variants even in this simple recipe. But if we find that smoked whiting or eel are alternatives, if we accept that dried milk and dried onions may be more convenient to use than the fresh products, we introduce further variants which brings our experimental total to 14 400. To try all these variants would be hopelessly expensive and in the end, how would one decide which was the best? Clearly some process of simplification to restrict the alternatives is required at the outset.

Product development is relevant to food control in so far as the processes are linked. Here the control team will advise in the light of the subsequent raw materials and process controls on the alternative raw materials in terms of quality and uniformity and the scientific control measures required to ensure these. In this particular case dried onions, butter, and dried skim milk are recommended on grounds of availability to firm specifications at prices competitive with fresh milk, raw onions, and cream. This cuts the number of trials considerably. Smoked fish is the next consideration and again price and availability provide a basis for reducing the number of alternatives. A further reduction in alternatives arises from experience of seasonings on the well established principle that unless there are good reasons against, 'simplest is best' if the fish flavour is to come through. Finally, knowing the ingredient costs, it is a comparatively simple matter to calculate the range of ingredient costs or even to improve on it. On this basis a manageable experimental programme can be put in hand to derive a suitable recipe and method of manufacture.

However, the problem of selecting the ideal formulation from these alternatives has to be met in terms of flavour, colour, and thickness. The ideal answer is to try out all possible combinations on a sufficiently large number of ordinary consumers as will make the results significant, but such a large number is needed for this that the process is rendered impractical. In practice, a tasting panel must be introduced to weed out the unacceptable and reduce the alternatives to a manageable number. The process of selecting and training such a panel, the methods to be used to present the samples to it, and the statistical treatment of the results comprise a subject in its own right and cannot be dealt with here. Suffice to say that by its use a final elimination of alternatives is made and the product is ready for public appraisal by marketing. Let us now assume that this is successful and a product launch is to be made.

During all these processes of experiment and selection, the food control unit is or should be in constant touch and working on its own problems, the solution of which will be put to the test by the launch. The specification of the raw materials must be decided in chemical and microbiological terms and provision made for detecting variants in flavour from batch to batch which might affect the finished product.

Thus, by the time the product goes into production the control laboratory has the following reference points at its disposal:

1. A stock of standard cans of the product to be stored at low temperature so that direct comparison between the production runs and the agreed product can be made as needed. If storage conditions are chosen with care, these reference samples (in this instance) can be held for up to 2 years.

2. A knowledge of exactly how the product is to be made, that is, its formulation, the production rate, the machines, tanks and vessels to be used, the raw material supply position, the can size, date and line codes to be used, the can fill, the sterilisation conditions, the

labelling arrangements,† the conditions of warehousing and distribution, and the product shelf-life under these conditions.

3. A knowledge of the product characteristics based on taste panel experience during the development stages. This will have been systematised into a flavour, colour and texture specification understood through a common vocabulary of descriptors shared by the product development unit and the food control laboratory. The systems used for this are varied and for further information specialised sources should be consulted. Usually some sort of score sheet emerges against which standards are set and day-to-day variations measured, all with the stock of standards to refer to as required.

4. A knowledge of the variations to be expected in the raw materials used. In this case it will be assumed that the other ingredients—milk, butter, onions, thickening agent, and seasonings—can be purchased to a specification sufficiently close as to avoid detectable variation from these sources. In contrast, the fish is subject to variation and means of controlling this must be found and applied.

During the development stages, small parcels of fish were frequently purchased for experimental purposes and stored at 2–3 °C until required for use. At an early stage it was noticed that there was considerable variation in character from batch to batch as follows.

1. The bacterial load on the fish was often high and always variable.

2. The smoke colour varied from different suppliers, as also did the smoked flavour. Some smokehouses, it appeared, used artificial colours to provide the golden brown appearance their customers wanted without at the same time generating too heavy a smoke flavour.

3. Before smoking the fish were normally brined (the brine containing the colour where this was used) and, depending on the ideas or caprice of the commercial smokehouses, a variable level of salt was to be found in different samples.

† The design of labels for pre-packed foods is a topic in itself and the details cannot be considered here. For the present purposes the label would carry the following information: the name of the soup, the name and address of the canner, the weight of the contents, and a list of the ingredients used in descending order of quantity. These are legal requirements. In addition, the label will give instructions for preparation indicating whether the soup is ready-to-serve or pre-concentrated for subsequent dilution and any further statement which accurately reflects the product's properties (such as 'free from artificial colour and preservative').

The control unit was therefore faced with the decision as to whether to accept these normal market variations and to adjust the formulation depending on the fish, or to attempt to contract with one supplier to provide fish cured and smoked in as near standard a fashion as could be achieved. Examination of the first alternative showed it to be fraught with difficulties. The colour was one of these. Cullen Skink should be a creamy white and the range of variation found in the open market produced one or two samples which gave an unacceptable dark colour to the soup. Flavour was a further problem, since the panel could easily detect flavour differences in the development samples when fish from different sources was used in experiments. The salt levels also varied widely, depending on the brining systems used by the smokehouses and this in turn raised the unpleasant possibility of having to vary the salt additions to the soup with each batch of fish. During these studies a useful circumstance was discovered. The control laboratory used gas–liquid chromatographic (GLC) profiles for controlling another product and during development of Cullen Skink samples of headspace gases from the cans were presented to the GLC equipment, not in any attempt to identify the volatiles but rather as a finger-print to look for variations in them. The equipment recorded a complex pattern of peaks (as would be expected), but at around a retention time of 13 min under the standard conditions used two large peaks were always observed close together. A comparison of tasting panel results on flavour showed a good correlation between flavour score and the total area under both peaks. Thus, an objective means of selection had been found.

At this point it was observed that the fish from one particular smokehouse gave more consistent results in terms of the two peaks in question than did the others, but that the artificial colour used by this producer gave too dark a colour to the final soup. Discussions with the supplier led to an agreement whereby fish were brined and smoked without any addition of colour and by carefully standardised procedures. GLC and a salt determination on each consignment would establish whether the situation was being sustained. Previous observations of fish storage had established an appreciable deterioration after 9 days at 2 °C. Arrangements were therefore made for thrice-weekly deliveries when possible. Storms and variable catches produced an element of uncertainty but experiment established that continuity of production could be maintained by using frozen fish provided that the period of frozen storage was 6 months or less. A buffer stock was therefore held in case of breaks in supply.

One final factor had to be determined. The character of the traditional recipe requires that the finished soup contains recognisable portions of fish, the fish being first steamed and thereafter crumbled into small broken flakes of flesh by hand before incorporation into the soup. Mechanical means of doing this in such a way as to simulate the domestic process were necessary. Some experiment was required to produce the desired result which was eventually achieved using a silent cutter (bowl chopper) with deliberately blunted knives and an altered ratio of cutter speed to bowl speed.

The potato serves both to modify flavour and to control texture. However, a true Cullen Skink contains some recognisable fragments of potato, usually about the size of a pea, as well as of fish. The sterilisation required had been established (by the usual combination of heat penetration studies followed by incubation tests) as 35 min at 240 °F, and this was enough to disintegrate the pre-boiled potatoes called for by the traditional domestic recipes. It was therefore necessary to add part of the potato in the form of diced raw cubes to the soup immediately before the can-filling operation to obtain the traditional texture, the proportion of pre-boiled potato acting as a rather coarse-grained thickener. In this way, a canned product closely resembling the domestic soup could be obtained.

THE CONTROL REQUIREMENTS

With these facts established, the control requirements can now be listed.

Raw Materials
Fish

This is the most critical ingredient. Sample each delivery, check total bacterial count, salt content and marker peaks by GLC. Check also by smell for traces of off-flavours.

Milk

Bought as dried skimmed milk to specification. Less effect on quality than the fish. Confirm that deliveries meet specification in terms of moisture, pH, and solubility (curdling is a problem if these are incorrect).

Onion

Bought on specification. Should give little trouble. Visual inspection combined with occasional analytical checks.

Potatoes

Not critical, but firm-textured waxy varieties are preferred. Visual checks for freedom from mechanical damage, rots, mould infections, wireworm, etc., are sufficient.

Butter
Supplies normally consistent and reliable. Analytical check against specification on each consignment.

Condiments and Flavourings
Supplies normally consistent and reliable. Inspection of each consignment with analytical checks if called for.

Process
There is some choice of possible processing steps in this case. Without discussing all the variants, it is possible to make a general statement of procedure. Any process is characterised by critical steps or points at which faults may be introduced. In general, these are associated with weighing or measuring, pre-cooking and mixing, can filling, closing, and sterilisation and cooling.

When the details of the process are known, the critical control points are listed and appropriate action is taken (a) to establish permissible limits of variation at each point and (b) a system of observing variations as they occur together with the action to be taken when the limits are exceeded. It is at this point that a basic understanding of the physical, chemical, and microbiological considerations involved is essential if the controls are to be effectively designed and applied. Furthermore, since the results will generally be numerically expressed, numeracy, and especially an appreciation of statistical variation, is required on the part of the person responsible for establishing the control system.

The word 'system' is used advisedly. Not only must there be control observations, but these must be recorded systematically so that a quality record pattern is established for each production run. The principle is the same for batch, semi-continuous, or continuous production, although the nature of the controls will vary depending on the system used. The correct choice of control method depends again on a scientific appreciation of all the factors involved in the system being used. More will be said about the detailed techniques in later papers.

Product Inspection
If the raw material and process controls have been correctly applied, the finished product will mirror the specification and no further controls should

be necessary. However, with the complex nature of food products and the possibility of errors in even the most carefully designed control system, it is advisable to carry out some form of finished product inspection by systematic sampling of the product and examining it to confirm that it meets the required standards. At this point the records are brought together of raw material controls and process controls. The more effective these prove to be in practice, the lower can be the sampling rate. However, for canned products, incubation and bacteriological examination are also needed as confirmation of the sterilisation process applied. Only when these have been completed to the satisfaction of the quality controller can release certificates be signed to permit despatch of the product.

The case quoted as an example is a particularly simple one and is intended merely to illustrate the principles of a control system and the scientific background necessary to implement it. For most products the requirements are more complex. Furthermore, a food company of size and standing is usually involved in the simultaneous production of several or many products, involving large stocks of hundreds or even thousands of tons of different raw materials, any one of which may be used not for one but for a range of different products. It is therefore an organisational problem of complexity to establish, assemble, staff, and co-ordinate all the lines of control in such a series of operations. It is work for a good scientist who adds to his science an appreciation of the organisation necessary to establish and make the system work. The importance of a basic knowledge and understanding of the scientific principles of food control, as opposed to detailed familiarity with a given process, however useful that may be, is the capacity to apply the principles in diverse circumstances. Most food companies operate a range of processes. The food controller of the future must be able to switch from the familiar to the new with confidence and knowledge. Many food companies are international. He must therefore be able to switch from one country to another. The local circumstances may change, and change at short notice. The principles remain the same.

The exercise of judgement was referred to earlier. A control system has to be staffed, supplied with test equipment and laboratory facilities and, if the system is carelessly designed, it may interfere with and even slow down production. The system itself becomes part of the cost of the product or products. Clearly, the control system must itself be controlled in terms of cost–benefit. Effectiveness without waste of effort is the criterion and data accumulation for data's sake can be a hazard. As experience with a new product grows, so should its control system be tightened or eased as the situation demands. This paper started with a statement of the relationship between cost and value, and what is true of the final product is equally true of the controls that are applied to the process which produces it.

DISCUSSION

Professor E. F. Williams (University of Nottingham) said that he found some slight difficulty with the paper largely because in the introduction the word 'value' appears to be used without qualification or definition. Without qualification or definition, 'value' has many meanings, some of which were complex and obscure. He asked Professor Hawthorn to clarify this point. He was also unclear what was meant in the first sentence of the paper which stated that food was processed to increase its value. He asked if this meant an increase in value to the manufacturer, or to the consumer, or the retailer, or increased nutritional value. To the best of his knowledge there is no evidence to suggest that processing increased the nutritional value of foods. Perhaps Professor Hawthorn was referring to cost?

It was inferred in the paper that scientific control involving mathematics, physics, chemistry, biochemistry, and microbiology was necessary to produce consistently high-quality processed foods. This is not necessarily so, but it does enable the manufacturer to make uniform products which may or may not be of high quality. It also enables the manufacturer to comply consistently with legal standards which may only be minimum ones. It may also enable him to use raw materials of lower quality which, with changes in technology, may result in only a marginal loss of apparent quality. These factors alone or in combination may possibly lead to a slow but continued downward trend in quality with time and this was already happening to some kind of food products. ·

It could not be denied that good scientific control led to uniformity of production and reduction in waste, but it would be unfortunate if uniformity resulted in the disappearance of the various crafts in the food industry and the degree of variability which often made foods more attractive. In this context there is still a considerable proportion of food processed with little or no scientific or technological control to give products of high, albeit variable, quality based on craft experience. He did not attempt to define those products in which a high degree of uniformity had resulted in mediocrity, but was sure we were all aware of the situation. He was well aware of food manufacturers' problems associated with raw materials, processing methods, the present economic climate, and very small profit margins; but we should not overlook the fact that most people eat for pleasure and not for what they may believe to be nutritional value.

He observed that in the paper the quantitative aspects of scientific control are stressed and in this context asked Professor Hawthorn for his views on microbiological standards. He was well aware that Professor Hawthorn had a marked appreciation for pheasant when it was 'high'. In a quantitative sense what did he consider high to be and how high would he consider the safe level for acceptance or rejection, and in fact did it matter? The question of microbiological standards has been argued for many years and he himself always opposed quantitative standards because of the difficulties of interpretation, sampling methods, methodology, temperature control and sample history.

Mr. M. D. Ranken (British Food Manufacturing Industries Research Association) noted the distinction between Newtonian and Einsteinian sciences and the application of this to food science. In Newtonian terms every action had a cause and you could measure them both. Einstein's contribution to science was to say that at the ultimate level you cannot measure everything and your knowledge must contain uncertainty. Once this is accepted enormous advances became possible.

Mr. D. E. Blenford (Hildon Associates, Consultants) said that Professor Hawthorn in his paper and Professor Williams in his remarks had brought out a very important fact inherent in striving towards scientific quality control. Consumers sought safety, value for money, quality, and variety. Scientific quality control would always produce uniform products of pre-determined quality. He asked how this could be prevented and scientific quality control be adapted to provide the variability of food that 'mother used to make' which was never identical on repeated occasions of preparation which was part of its appeal. The attraction of 'chef' food lay in the chef preparing food to a standard which was not sharply defined to meet his interpretation of the quality of the finished product.

Dr. R. Spencer (J. Sainsbury Ltd) pointed out that Professor Hawthorn, in dealing with the scientific basis, had restricted himself to the 'hard' sciences, chemistry, physics, microbiology, mathematics, etc. The food controller, armed with these services was no doubt *well equipped* to do his job but this did not necessarily mean he would be *effective* in the environment in which he found himself. The 'soft' sciences such as social sciences and management sciences might aid him.

Professor J. B. M. Coppock (Surrey University) said that Professor Hawthorn referred to the Cullen Skink. Another Scottish delicacy, the Speldin consisted of a sun-dried dab or small plaice kept until it had rotted so far as to be phosphorescent. It was then lightly cooked and eaten. Like the pheasant to which Professor Williams referred, microbiologically this product also was undefinable but it was a delicacy. He wanted to know how to ensure that such products of art and craft were preserved in the form we knew them. In our concept of food control we were perhaps omitting to build up a dictionary of art and craft, for without definition the hope of preserving the traditional characteristics of our foods may well be irretrievably lost.

Professor J. Hawthorn, in replying to the discussion, explained that in his paper he used the term 'value' in the economists' sense of being measured by the price a person was prepared to pay for goods or a service. This varied with circumstances. The 'value' of a litre of drinking water is higher in the middle of the Sahara Desert than in the middle of Manchester. When his paper states that food is processed to increase its value, he simply meant that, in general, people are willing to pay more, for example, for a cake than for the ingredients from which it is made. This difference is often referred to as the 'added value'.

Professor Williams had made an extremely important point when he suggested that strict scientific control when wrongly directed may produce a 'domino' effect. This happens when a series of cost-cutting steps is taken successively over months or even years. This may be done in such a way that no single step produces a reduction in product value detectable to the average customer, but the cumulative effect of many such steps ultimately leads to a less attractive and less acceptable product.

When commercial preparation was dominated by craft skills, this situation was less likely to occur although it did happen. The same dish prepared by the same chef will vary from time to time, but unless it measures up to his own judgement of 'standard', the good chef will refuse to serve it. Scientific quality control attempts to remove the element of personal judgement and replaces it with objective criteria. There can be no doubt that it has achieved much. One has only to compare the quality of the retail milk supply of 1919 with that of 1979 to note the advances which have taken place in this one product alone. But no system is free from abuse, not even scientific food control.

In raising the question of microbiological standards, Professor Williams put us in his debt. To the simple-minded, the enumeration of bacteria in a sample must reflect its hygienic quality. Therefore, so the reasoning goes, standards should be established in the form of a kind of national or international numbers game. This is an area in which a little knowledge is very dangerous and much knowledge can be frightening. By and large, microbial counts are for interpretation by microbiologists. Legislators will only make a hash of it. He could think of one or two special cases where such standards in expert hands may be very useful. In general he was opposed to them.

He appreciated Mr. Blenford's question, but did not think that scientific quality control could produce the food that 'mother used to make'. That is not its function. An African student, writing an essay on organoleptic testing which he had marked, hit the nail on the head when he wrote, 'Food tastes better if it's cooked by someone who loves you'. No laboratory could beat that!

He thanked Professor Coppock for drawing Speldin to his attention. It is a Scottish dish he had so far left untasted; now he must try it! In the discussion, references to the old craft skills had come up several times. He had learned to respect them as a young man working in the traditional field of bread-baking, but he found them also in the newer industry of canning. At that time, he thought that science could beat them at their own game, and in one sense it has already done so. He did not want to reverse the clock in the dairy industry, in the canning industry, or in the freezing industry. Dangerous foods and risky processes had been made safe in many areas. However, he would love to see the British eat more bread. To go to France or Switzerland and eat craft-produced bread and pastry was a gustatory delight. If we are to eat more bread in the UK, he suspected that an increasing proportion of our production must be on traditional lines from the kind of craftsmen who, for example, bake barm bread by a sponge and dough process. It is expensive but a real treat. To taste it is to make a meal of it.

3

Technological Basis of Food Control

ROLAND S. HANNAN

MIDAS Liaison Officer, ARC Meat Research Institute

INTRODUCTION

Although the successful food controller must have a wide knowledge of food science and technology, his specific interest is not in the generality of food processes. His main concern is with one or more designated processes and he has primary responsibility for ensuring their correct working. He must study them in detail, monitor the relationship between actual performance and specified performance, and provide corrective action if they show evidence of moving out of control.

He must do this, moreover, against a background of complexity of even the simplest of processes. In most cases they will involve a number of separate operational steps and these may follow each other in simple sequence or be arranged in complex network relationships. They may incorporate varying degrees of manual and mechanical operation and may operate on a batch or continuous basis. Each may affect the performance of the whole and there will usually be so many possibilities of variation and interaction that local characteristics are the norm rather than the exception. This can be advantageous in a single factory producing a regional or traditional product with unique character but can be a disadvantage where the aim is to manufacture a product of standardised quality in a group of separate factories.

Each process, therefore, must be treated as an individual and there is no substitute for direct observation on the way it operates in practice. This must be combined with continual reappraisal in the light of new knowledge and experience. The ultimate may be to specify performance in terms of multidimensional mathematics, leading to automatic control by computer, but present-day knowledge makes this a practical proposition in only

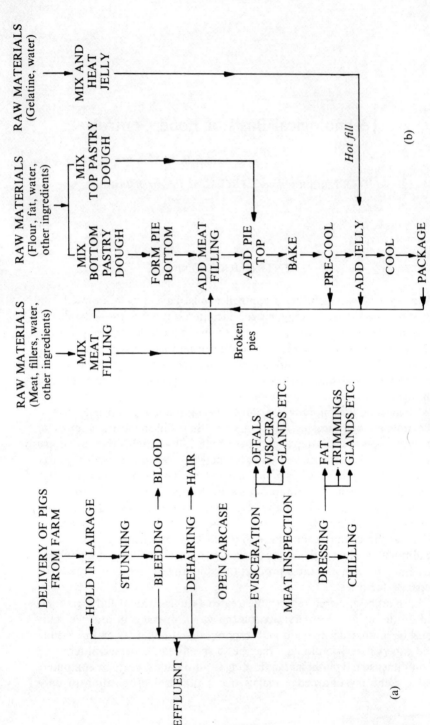

Fig. 3.1. (a) Typical pig slaughterline; (b) typical basic pork pie line.

special cases. The controller of today must usually settle for a more primitive solution.

THE FLOW DIAGRAM

Most processes are based on a progressive flow from raw material to finished product. A flow diagram is, therefore, a major aid to understanding. Two examples from the meat industry are shown in Fig. 3.1.

Pig slaughter (Fig. 3.1a) is essentially a linear sequence of operations in which a single raw material—a live animal—is converted into a primary finished product—a cooled carcase. The main processing line may be supplemented by ancillary lines for processing by-products and such operations are characterised by increasing complexity as the product passes through the plant.

Pork pie manufacture (Fig. 3.1b), on the other hand, is a complex of three converging processing lines which come together at different stages of the overall process. Various types of operations are involved, including heating and cooling, and, as the diagram shows, there is an example of the use of re-work in the return of broken pies to an earlier stage of the process. Procedures such as this can create feedback loops which can be a source of biological and other types of instability, as will be discussed later. The flow diagram should be used to highlight such inter-relationships and help to locate procedures which have a potential disproportionate effect on the product or process.

The simple flow chart, however, has many limitations. A full operational scheme will need to specify the detail of operational procedures and must take account of events which occur outside the main processing plant, including variation in the production of raw materials and unusual performance of the finished product in the field.

UNIT OPERATIONS

The first requirement in expanding the flow chart is to examine the individual component operations. Table 3.1 summarises some of the more important examples, some of which are common to many types of process and can be considered in more detail.

The relative importance of the various unit operations will vary from product to product and process to process. Different methods of handling

TABLE 3.1
Some typical unit processes

Processes	Examples
(a) *Processes mentioned in text*	
Selection of raw materials	
Preparation of raw materials	Cleaning, grading, sorting, peeling, de-hulling, conditioning, grinding, sieving
Preservation	See Table 3.2
Raising temperature	
Heating	Heat conduction (solid, gas, liquid), convection, radiation, electrical resistance
Thawing	
Lowering temperature	
Cooling	
Chilling	Heat conduction, evaporation
Freezing	
Size reduction	Cutting, comminution, crushing, grinding
Size increase	Moulding, pressing, reforming
Reduction of water content	Concentration, drying, distillation, membrane processes
Increase of water content	Injection, mixing, soaking
Mixing	
Holding at defined temperature	Cooking, storage, maturation
Packaging	
Storage	
Despatch	
Treatment of by-products	
Treatment of effluent	
(b) *Other processes*	
Change of: atmospheric composition, osmotic pressure, pH	
Centrifugation, crystallisation, emulsification, extraction, extrusion, filtration, irradiation, massaging, tumbling	

and different overall disciplines will be required by perishable and shelf-stable products and by liquids, dry powders and solids, and the methods of control will be correspondingly different.

Before looking at individual unit operations, it should be noted that single operations will not necessarily be equivalent to the workings of a single machine. Many machines perform one or more operations, simultaneously or in sequence, and recognition of this fact may be basic to full understanding of the process.

Raw Material, Selection, and Preparation

The nature and quality of raw materials can vary according to the overall objectives and the degree of flexibility of the process. Some processes may be aiming at an end-product with unique properties and may require selected raw materials. Others may have been designed from the outset to use residual materials and have high tolerance to variability. It is important, therefore, to establish which properties in the incoming raw materials are vital for effective operation and arrange for substandard materials to be rejected or channelled into special applications.

Many raw materials require pre-processing preparation such as cleaning, grading or mixing before they can be committed to the process proper. Leaf vegetables will need washing, potatoes will need peeling, sausage casings will need soaking, and dry materials will need mixing to overcome the effect of layering in transit. With a demanding process, it may be necessary to exercise constant vigilance over many features of the raw materials. In others it may largely be a question of monitoring one particular property such as the presence of heat-resistant micro-organisms in seasonings intended for a canning operation.

In some instances, the need for controlled quality may be sufficient to justify intervention in the production of the raw material. Milk supply in bulk from farm to factory and transit of animals to the slaughterhouse in a potentially stressful manner are examples of sensitive procedures which can have a dominant effect on subsequent processing quality. Problems with a raw material twice removed may even be involved, such as shortcomings in the quality of a cereal filler due to wet harvesting of the original grain.

Water is an essential raw material for most products and varies widely from factory to factory. Gross variation can occur, particularly in respect of 'hardness' constituents, but minor contaminants may often be more important. Bacteria in can cooling water or unwanted nitrate in a meat processing plant are examples where chlorination and ion-exchange treatment, respectively, may be called for. Other raw materials include perishable raw foods, prepared foods, additives, processing gases, and packaging materials. The list is too long for itemisation in detail, and each is a study in itself.

Preservation Processes

Many processes have preservation as their direct objective and the operational steps which introduce the preservative action are therefore most important. A single operation such as change of temperature may be involved or a combination of two or more changes.

The commonest procedures are shown in Table 3.2. They include two levels of raising temperature (cooking and canning), two of lowering temperature (chilling and freezing), drying, change of pH or osmotic pressure, and addition of substances with a preservative action. In all cases, the general objective will be clear and the main need for the Controller will be to study the tolerance of the system and, particularly, the effect of marginal treatment. Addition of biologically active substances such as

TABLE 3.2
Some preservation processes

Process	Typical conditions
Cooking	Temperature above 65 °C
Canning	Temperature above 100 °C under pressure
Chilling	Temperature below 10 °C
Freezing	Temperature below -10 °C
Drying	Water content less than 10 %
Increased osmotic pressure	Addition of salt or sugar
	Partial removal of water
Change of pH	Below pH 4·5 is inhibitory for many organisms
Addition of preservatives	Sulphite, nitrite, sorbate, etc.
Controlled atmosphere	Reduced oxygen content
	Increased carbon dioxide content
Irradiation	Treatment with ultraviolet or ionising radiation

nitrite and sulphite must conform to strict legal requirements, which will usually only be realisable with good manufacturing practice. Some processes such as canning and freezing can be carried out according to strictly defined physical considerations whereas others are traditional in character with a theoretical background which has not been fully elucidated. Manufacture of fermented 'dry' sausages is an example of the latter.

Raising of Temperature

An increase in temperature is inherent in many processes and many methods of heating are available. The problems are simplest when heating liquids or gases, where efficient and rapid heating is possible. With bulky heterogeneous solids, such as meat, there can be many difficulties if the temperature is raised by heat conduction. Some methods, such as oven-type processes, involve a measure of heat transfer by radiation, whereas others rely entirely on heat conduction from solid (e.g. metal) surfaces, liquid (e.g.

water), or gaseous media (e.g. air or steam); heat transfer from liquid or gaseous media may be assisted by free or forced convection. The problem for the controller is to identify the rate of heating which is ideal for the product and the length of time that specific temperatures must be maintained, and control accordingly.

Cooking processes will usually involve achievement of a minimum temperature of 65 °C for cured products or 75 °C for uncured products at all points in the product, to achieve adequate microbiological destruction and enzyme inactivation, and thus preservation. This may not, however, be sufficient to develop an adequate cooked character. Tenderising sinewy meat, for example, may require a long process of 'stewing' at higher temperature.

Where the process aims at eliminating all micro-organisms which can develop in the product, the temperature must be raised substantially above that which suffices for mere 'cooking' and a minimum combination of time and temperature must be achieved, usually at pressures in excess of atmospheric.

The greatest care is essential with the latter processes (i.e. canning), since this is a classical example of the potential problems of under-processing. Inadequate heat treatment can remove common spoilage organisms but not dangerous pathogens such as *Clostridium botulinum*. The significance of the reservation above, that is 'micro-organisms which could subsequently develop', is illustrated by canned cured meats in which the curing agents reduce the need to give the normal heat treatment for *Clostridium botulinum* and by canned fruit in which the acidity serves a similar purpose. In contrast, the heat treatment for some canned meat products may exceed that needed to control any danger from *Clostridium botulinum* because of the presence of thermophilic spoilage organisms able to develop during storage. A high degree of monitoring and control of temperature is essential and processing records should be retained for reference in the event of failure of packed stock.

Some types of heat treatment are normally combined with other operations such as drying or smoking, and these can produce a unique combination of conditions at surfaces which may be essential, for example, for correct development of flavour at the surface of products such as bread and roast meat.

Lowering of Temperature

Many of the considerations which apply to heating processes apply in reverse to cooling, particularly if the cooling operation follows heat treatment. Very high rates of cooling are theoretically achievable with liquids and gases, while solids can be cooled by use of liquid nitrogen or evaporative cooling under vacuum. Cheaper, less efficient methods are likely to be preferred with most products and, where possible, the choice of cooling medium is likely to fall on air at ambient temperature or water at mains temperature. Lengthy cooling times can result from such methods with bulky products and the temperature can dwell in an intermediate incubation range for many micro-organisms. Such processes are greatly affected by the ambient temperature and must be kept under close observation in hot summer conditions. Mechanical refrigeration has obvious advantages but economic factors will not always allow its use.

Permissible cooling rates may also be subject to an upper limit on technological grounds. Need to avoid localised freezing is a common limiting factor but pre-rigor meat provides an example of more specialised effects; too rapid cooling before the onset of rigor can cause toughening due to cold-shortening.

Freezing and Thawing

A special case of temperature change occurs in processes which involve a change of state from liquid to solid or *vice versa*. Freezing or thawing of water-containing products is the commonest example.

The technology of freezing is well developed and less complication is likely than with most other methods of preservation. In many instances the rate of freezing determines the crystal size and the resulting quality of the product and must be controlled. On the whole, the main need is to ensure that the available equipment has sufficient heat extraction capacity.

Thawing, on the other hand, is a much neglected process. With normal retail packs of frozen foods it takes place in the home and is not included in the factory process. Increasing use of frozen raw materials such as meat is occurring in the processing factory. With bulky products, the rate of thawing by commoner methods is limited entirely by the rate of conduction of heat from the outside to the inside, and raising the temperature of the thawing medium does not provide a simple answer, as the outer layers thaw much quicker than the centre and become susceptible to bacterial spoilage. Thawing with air, therefore, must usually be restricted to air temperatures no higher than 10 °C, often with associated thawing times of 24 h or longer. Thawing by cautious use of microwaves is one solution. Another is to adapt the original process to use the frozen raw materials without thawing.

Water-containing products are not the only users of solidification processes. It is often essential to control crystal size with fat-based products for optimum textural properties, and a high degree of temperature control is necessary, for example, by cooling in a scraped-surface heat exchanger.

Size Reduction and Increase

Reduction of the size of pieces of food has been common practice since the invention of the knife. Many types of procedure are now available, including cutting, slicing, mincing, shredding, crushing, and grinding. The original product may be solid, semi-solid or liquid and the effectiveness of size reduction may depend on an intricate balance of rheological factors. Sharpness of cutting edges, speed of cutting, generation of heat and adventitious incorporation of air must all be taken into account and each procedure will merit intense study. Size reduction will often be accompanied by some other process such as mixing and gross breakdown of texture, the classical example being the common food mincer or grinder, where the product is 'worked' in a screw press before final subdivision.

The degree of size reduction will often be basic to the desirable characteristics of the end-product. A simple slicer must produce clean slices of product, often of accurately known dimensions and without breakup. A chopping operation may need to leave the product in a characteristically coarse condition.

Increase in size may often follow an initial size reduction. The overall objective may be to simulate the texture and general characteristics of the original product but in a more reproducible or convenient form (e.g. reformed products). In other cases, the objective will be to develop new products with novel properties, such as the wide variety of bakery products which can be made from wheat flour. The main need in this technology is to recognise which components of an ingredient mix are responsible for the binding and textural characteristics and ensure their presence in the right amount and the right form. Vegetable proteins are among the newer available materials for this purpose, while the characteristics of the fat play a crucial part in some bakery products.

Removal and Addition of Water

Water may be *removed* from foods in many ways and for many reasons. Removal may take place at elevated temperatures, under vacuum or at low temperatures direct from the frozen state. The objective may be to produce a concentrated or partly dried product with enhanced keeping qualities or a shelf-stable dried product containing only a small percentage of water. Again, the technology will vary according to the physical form of the material to be dried. Flash drying of liquids will often be possible without significant damage and the main need will be to avoid losses of volatile non-aqueous ingredients. These methods are substantially inapplicable to products such as meat, for which normal practice is to use freeze-drying or lengthy exposure to cool dry air.

Water can be *added* for a number of reasons. In gravies it can be an essential ingredient of a composite product. In curing brines, it can act as a medium for introducing preservatives and in many products it can, in association with binding or emulsifying agents, contribute to the desirable physical characteristics. It can be introduced by direct addition or by injection procedures and the latter, in cured meats, are frequently associated with massaging or tumbling. The details of these processes may affect the final water content of the products, a topical subject and currently a controversial one for discussion.

Mixing

Most processed foods are mixtures of numerous ingredients. Some must be incorporated as uniformly as possible. Others, such as smoke, may be highly localised in their placement in the product. Again, it is essential to know whether the uniformity of distribution is an important quality factor and to control the process accordingly.

The mixing process may often be the single most important operation, for example, in compounding a mixed dried food where the individual components may need to retain their separate integrity and suffer minimum damage during mixing. On the other hand, it may be an inherent part of some other operation such as size reduction (e.g. the use of a bowl chopper for meat) or introduction of energy (e.g. the manufacture of dough). It may involve incorporation of a few parts per million of a functional additive or large amounts of a major component such as curing brine.

Addition of air may be deliberate, as in light-textured ice-cream, or incidental to an agitation process. Trapping of air can affect quality in a number of ways. It can 'lighten' the eating texture, encourage oxidation, and expand or come out of solution on heating. It must be watched for and controlled. If it is a problem, one approach is to carry out the primary mixing under vacuum or include a vacuum mixer in the line. If oxidation alone is the danger, operation in an inert atmosphere may provide an alternative, particularly if an operation under vacuum could lead to a loss of volatile components.

One of the extreme forms of mixing is production of emulsions. These may be of the water-in-fat or fat-in-water types and may be wanted or unwanted. Some are true emulsions in the language of the physical chemist.

Others, e.g. 'meat emulsions', are often no more than gross mixtures of fine particles set in a stable matrix.

A common feature of most mixing operations is that they can distribute micro-organisms throughout a product and this can have many consequences for process stability and product quality, particularly if the mixing process also raises the temperature into the incubating range. Cleanliness and constant monitoring are essential, particularly if a multi-purpose mixer is used with various products of differing microbial status. The common mincer/grinder is the classical example of equipment which can find multi-purpose use.

Holding at Defined Temperatures

Traditional processes often involve lengthy holding periods and the resulting product characteristics are identified with desirable eating quality. Maturation may continue for years (vintage wine), weeks (cheeses), or days (beef carcases) and will usually involve subtle changes of chemical, enzymic, and microbiological origin. The basic science of such processes is often only partially developed and the controller must rely on empirical assessment, particularly in deciding whether there is any practical substitute for time. Economic pressures, alone, are a continuing influence towards shortening time and the controller must be alert to the possible consequences. He must, in particular, know the importance of temperature since this, for example, can be the deciding factor in establishing the correct balance of microflora and resulting quality and safety of the product. These considerations normally prevent satisfactory acceleration of maturation by the simple means of raising the holding temperature, as this modifies the balance between the various changes.

Control of overall temperature in processing areas is also becoming more common, especially with perishable products. Related to this question is the need for the controller to take account of company obligations for employee safety and comfort, an area which is increasingly subject to legislative control and Trades Union agreements.

Packaging

Many types of packaging are in common use and their purpose differs widely. The simplest may merely be decorative and provide a medium for product identification. Most, however, are also protective, if only in excluding gross contamination, and many play a functional role in holding the product under sterile conditions or in a controlled atmosphere. The material of the container may be flexible or rigid, metallic, plastic, glass, or paper and it may be applied manually or by machine. The appearance of the product will often be heavily dependent on the efficiency of the packaging operation, and close control over intricate machinery may be required. Much of this operates at high speed and the packaging materials must be in the correct physical condition for smooth, uninterrupted running.

Weighing or measurement of volume will often be associated with packaging and will need to operate to closely defined legal limits. The technological problems, particularly on high-speed lines, vary greatly from product to product.

Storage and Despatch

Products are commonly classified as perishable, semi-perishable or shelf stable but none of these terms is sufficiently precise for control purposes. The controller will usually be aiming to achieve a clearly defined marketing objective in terms of method of distribution, length of pipeline and expected total 'shelf-life'. Hot summer conditions will often be the testing time.

An important question is whether the product is intended for immediate distribution or buffer stock. Product which has been dispersed is no longer available for confirmatory checking and this has immediate implications for the controller. Operations which work on this basis, moreover, may often meet fluctuation of demand by varying production volume, with corresponding further complications.

Other problems will arise from the increasing requirement for printed declaration of expected shelf-life on packages especially when embodied in EEC labelling requirements. Supporting data must be obtained by direct experiment and monitoring of performance 'in the field'.

By-products

Most operations are designed to produce a range of primary products which complement each other in making effective use of the available raw materials. Residuals from one process will be used in another, but inevitably materials arise which cannot be used economically or effectively in main-stream products. These will be disposed of as by-products for use by other operations and the role of the controller will be to check that they are of acceptable, and usually agreed, marketable quality.

Effluent

Disposal of effluent, including exhaust gases, is a further ancillary activity which must be controlled, usually against the background of locally controlled standards of increasing severity.

INTEGRATED PROCESSES

Individual unit operations of the types which have been described can be put together in many ways to produce many types of end-product. They can, however, rarely be considered in isolation from each other. Interplay between one operation and another is common and the various components of a process may respond differently to some external influence.

The controller has a special part to play in recognising relationships of this type since they may not be immediately apparent to production colleagues whose responsibilities are for individual operations. A few brief examples will indicate what is involved.

Interaction

Interaction can be of many types. It can involve microbiological, physical, or chemical effects and it can be beneficial or disadvantageous. One of the problems is that it can be difficult to spot if cause and effect are separated in time and space. It may remain unnoticed until trouble arises.

Feedback

A special case of interaction has already been mentioned, namely feedback from late to early stages of the process. As with electronic circuitry, this can be a stabilising or destabilising influence. Resistant micro-organisms which have survived a marginal heat treatment should not be fed back to the beginning of a process, but organisms which give desirable mature characteristics to an end-product are often used as 'starter' cultures.

Cross-contamination

Feedback will often be a side-effect of some intentional operation. It can also result from cross-contamination, for example through movement of operatives or via the air or water supply.

Gross cross-contamination can leapfrog several stages of a process in either direction and especial care is needed to prevent the large number of micro-organisms in many raw materials from finding their way into the finished product. With meat products this has led to EEC Directives which call for separate rooms for most parts of common processes, but this is not necessarily the only or most effective solution.

Effect of External Influences

Change in ambient temperature is a typical influence which can affect different parts of a process differently. There is an increasing tendency towards air-conditioned factories, but even this cannot guarantee steady-state conditions.

Effect of Temperature

Variations of ambient temperature can affect the balance of flora in a product and the overall numbers of micro-organisms present. It can change viscosity and chemical stability, and it can produce indirect effects if overloaded refrigeration equipment breaks down in summer conditions. The effects of inadequate heat treatment can be magnified by slow cooling.

Accumulated records of temperatures at all stages of a process can often provide an explanation for unusual effects, particularly if they show that raw materials or product in process are held for any appreciable time in the incubation range (15–45 °C with many undesirable organisms).

Holding Times

Long holding may form part of a process (e.g. maturation of cheese) and it may be used to provide buffer stocks of partly processed materials. Close study of time/temperature relationships may be needed. Even frozen storage may be limited in duration if temperatures in the 'tempering' range of 0 to −10 °C are used to prepare a product for further processing.

Special problems can arise from holding product for relatively short periods during breaks in production. Overnight holding can usually be accommodated without difficulty and advantage may be taken to clean the plant during down-time. Shorter meal breaks during the working day and the longer breaks at weekends, however, can cause problems with partly finished product. Production of perishable processed products on Mondays will often require special precautions.

Continuous processes are one answer to the problems of shorter interruptions and are being adopted increasingly where volume permits. Where this results in production of a single integrated piece of machinery, however, the controller may find that he has to deal with uncertainties of a different type since the product may not now be accessible for testing at intermediate stages of the process.

Vulnerable Operations

Experience will usually show that one or more operations in a process are especially important from the point of view of quality or efficient working.

It may be a simple question of sharpness of cutter blades, correct seaming of open-top cans, or hygiene standards at a vital point in the process, but special control at these points will almost always be rewarding.

Environmental Conditions

The effects of temperature have already been mentioned. Humidity can also be important with many processes since, depending on the conditions, it can cause drying out, condensation, or surface spoilage. Foreign odours or odour-producing compounds can find their way into the product at any stage of the process and minor contaminants in the air or water can have many effects. The presence of copper, with associated oxidative side-effects, is an example, arising from the use of copper and brass pipework. Air-borne yeasts and moulds may be a seasonal problem or may originate from a neighbouring factory.

Factory layout and organisation will play a major part in controlling these effects and one trend is towards open-plan factories where an integrated approach to control is possible. Prevention of cross-contamination needs special care, especially if multi-purpose production lines are involved.

Role of Management *vis-à-vis* Technology

Many processes include a large content of manual operation. Staff training and discipline are essential for correct working. It is relatively easy to relax apparently outmoded disciplines in the interests of short-term economy, only to discover later what part they were playing in the process.

The controller also needs to be on guard against the natural tendency of involved management to explore the limits of any technology, particularly under economic pressure. Experience will often have taught them that new processes contain built-in safety factors developed on a predictive basis from small-scale testing. Accumulating evidence from large-scale working will show where these precautions can be relaxed, and evolution of the technology in this way is part of the natural inventive process. Problems can arise, however, when too many people take the law into their own hands and, in general, radical changes should only be made after cross-checking with earlier findings. Nevertheless, ideally all operators as well as management should be consciously involved in the control operation. The attitude of senior management and of the controller and his staff can greatly influence the extent to which this is achieved.

THE TECHNOLOGY OF CONTROL

Process Understanding and Specification

Effective control can only be based on a sound understanding of the technology of the process and all its nuances. Desirable procedures should be specified and adequate provision made for the strengths and weaknesses of the system and the predictable interactions. Background knowledge, accumulated experience, and evidence from outside sources should be brought to bear in setting up specifications and they should be kept continually under review. Experience with an apparently similar process in an apparently similar factory may be useful but may not necessarily be directly applicable.

Process Monitoring

Once the process has been established, arrangements must be made to monitor its important features, and this is a technology in itself. The variability of raw materials and processes must be recognised, together with the realities of detecting small changes with a feasible rate of sampling. Some parameters may be recorded continuously, particularly where a gaseous or liquid material is involved, but others can only be checked on a discontinuous basis.

There will often be a choice between a simple test method which can be applied to a large number of samples in the production department or a sophisticated method which can only be carried out in a remote laboratory. Many factors must be taken into account in deciding which to use, particularly the degree of expected variation and the intended use of the information.

Test methods which are used for immediate adjustment of a process must necessarily be rapid and capable of providing on-the-spot information. Measurements of temperature, pressure, and weight or simple visual assessments fall into this category. The ultimate is in-line automatic testing linked to direct control of the process.

Tests which are largely retrospective in character and are used for adjustment of the process in the light of recognisable trends need not be so rapid. The commoner microbiological procedures are of this type since they often take a day or more to complete. Taste panels, also, are essentially cumbersome and slow in operation.

The methods used in any given process must therefore be carefully selected to give the optimum combination of speed of feedback with required degree of accuracy, to achieve control within the desired limits, and the control procedures must be designed to accommodate the timing necessary to carry out the checks.

Rate of Sampling

In some cases a product quality may be sufficiently important to justify 100% sampling. Achievement of specified minimum weight is a typical example, usually justifying provision of a check weigher. Checking for misshapen packs or otherwise unusual appearance will also usually justify some form of 100% inspection. Methods which are used at a high rate of sampling must, of course, be non-destructive.

The usefulness of lower sampling rates will depend entirely on the individual circumstances and the relative importance of variation of the process. Action limits should only be established on a valid statistical basis but the disciplinary value of taking even one reading a day on a regular basis should not be underrated.

Trouble Shooting

The typical process contains so many possibilities of variation that anticipation of all possible problems is a virtual impossibility. Adequate monitoring, however, should reveal trouble before it takes a firm hold and provide clues to its possible cause. From this point onwards, each investigation will take its own course. Some may be solved by simple deduction based on accumulated evidence. Others may devolve into a classical sequence of hypothesis and confirmatory experiment and may shed new light on the whole process. It is important that knowledge gained in this way should be recorded and used to minimise repetition of similar trouble in the future.

Ancillary Procedures

Most of the control effort must clearly be concentrated on the primary products which leave the factory and must follow them 'in the field' to keep a check on their performance under normal and adverse conditions.

The degree of effort which can be justified in broader aspects of technical management will vary from factory to factory. Close control over effluent and recycling of waste products are typical of the areas where the controller of the future must be heavily involved and more knowledgeable than most of his predecessors.

Continuing re-education is part of the job.

DISCUSSION

Mr. K. G. Anderson (Brooke Bond Liebig) said that in the application of technology to food control, we must define what we want to control and why, and the accuracy required. We must understand the scientific principles involved and then find, develop, or invent the technology to apply the control method.

He asked Dr. Hannan to comment upon the application of evolutionary operations techniques to food control systems, particularly to cost and formulation, and to elaborate a little on the technology of packaging, packaging materials, and packaging operations and their control.

He was pleased to see the trouble-shooting aspects of control brought out because in the first place one can only seek to control foreseeable problems. The first time a problem arises the response can only involve trouble-shooting. Once the problem has been identified and solved it may be possible to put in a control system to prevent a recurrence. Machinery aspects are important. For example, the cost and time involved in knife sharpening can be balanced against the quality of cut and its value.

Reaction from the factory floor can be useful. Sometimes an operator really does know a better way of doing something and to take this up helps to increase the credibility of the control function and encourages good communications.

Variations occurring in ostensibly the same product when made by a large number of local units are interesting in relation to control. He believed that a consumer in Edinburgh expected to buy a branded tea with exactly the same characteristics as he would find in the same tea in the West Country the following week. He asked if centralisation causes problems for companies in the control of their products made in a number of areas and suggested that Professor Coppock might comment on this later with regard to bread making, in relation to the constraints caused by the decentralisation of an industrial operation.

He suggested that the last paragraph in the paper under *Effect of Temperature* should be extended to say that processing records should be *checked and confirmed* as soon as possible after processing and retained for reference.

Dr. Hannan asked Mr. Anderson to explain what he meant by evolutionary operations. Mr. Anderson said that EVOP† is a technique for assessing the effects of controlled minor alterations of identified variables

† Box, G. E. P. and Draper, N. R. (1969). '*Evolutionary operation*'—*a statistical method for process improvement.* New York: Wiley.

upon the process to provide the basis for optimising the system continuously. The presumption is, of course, that the true optimum is never actually achieved. Dr. Hannan said that from what he had heard of this technique, he thought it a splendid thing to be able to do. However, in his experience of dealing with biological materials he found the privilege of using deliberate changes was rare. The real problem was to see what nature was doing already, to explain what had happened, and to control it; but certainly for a process totally under control deliberate changes can be introduced to see what happens.

Packaging aspects were very well documented already and much information was available from the packaging industry.

Individuality of products made in different factories is a fundamental point. If a factory is producing a very different product it might be sold as a premium brand. Ham production is a good example of this, where an individual factory has built up a unique spectrum of microflora over many years to give a characteristically flavoured product. Similarly, no two factories were likely to have identical machinery in them and the problem was to decide whether to try to standardise to the degree of bringing them into line, or to accept that a difference existed and try to turn it to commercial advantage. One should also have regard to characteristic regional products and the changes which might be induced in product character when processes or equipment were changed.

4

Methodological Basis of Food Control

ANDREW BOLTON

Company Quality Assurance Manager, Batchelors Foods Ltd

INTRODUCTION

The food control operation has the objective of establishing and maintaining standards, and in considering the implication of this it is appropriate to remind ourselves of the relationship between quality, cost, and volume. Commercial success is not achieved without these aspects being complementary and no company Board will succeed unless it is totally committed to selling a consistent and reliable quality product at the right price and in the right volume. It is imperative that quality standards, whatever their place on the quality scale, should be fully defined and communicated.

The task of any food control operation is to achieve the cost, quality and throughput objectives. The commitment of a Board to its quality standards will dictate the relationship between quality management and production management, a subject dealt with later in this Symposium. Suffice it to say that both departments should be working to the same objectives! Quality management is concerned with ensuring that this happens, with measuring the success of the food control operation in achieving these standards, and with the identification and rectification of areas of quality failure and non-conformance. The confidence and effectiveness with which staff carry out their duties directly relates to the attitude at the top of the company.

But how are these objectives created and defined?

SETTING THE STANDARDS—THE SPECIFICATION SYSTEM

At the out-set of a project the legal requirements relative to the product area need to be clearly defined by the company experts concerned.

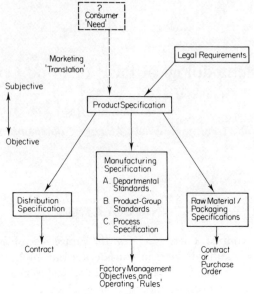

Fig. 4.1.   The specification system.

Subsequently, Product Development and Marketing Departments will develop product concepts to the marketing brief and will test their relevance by market research tests with consumers. When satisfactory results have been achieved, the product attributes need to be translated into operating standards against which the company can manufacture—this is done through the specification system (Fig. 4.1).

A concise practical specification system is an effective way of recording and communicating standards, and it forms the basis of an evaluation system to determine how well production quality has met its objectives.

The Product Specification

The product specification should specify:

—What the product is, including legal and nutritional standards.
—The organoleptic characteristics.
—The formula and quality standards.
—Analytical and microbiological standards, including acceptable tolerances about the mean.
—A packaging specification and standards.
—A reference to the manufacturing specification.

Additionally, product standards can be communicated through the use of pictures showing the permissible limits, through reference samples, etc.

Raw Material Specifications

Clearly, product quality is governed to a large extent by raw material quality, and it is necessary to define the acceptable standards of critical parameters of ingredients and packaging materials. Developing these can involve much bench work by product development specialists and by analysts, but thorough ground work at this stage can make a significant contribution to conformance of quality. These standards are expressed in the raw material specification, which typically will consist of the following:

The general description;
Organoleptic properties;
Physical and chemical standards, including additive and contaminant levels;
Bacteriological standards;
Packaging format.

Such a specification having been set, appraisal methods including statistical considerations, needs to be developed in order to control the raw material quality.

The specification should be agreed with the supplier and form the basis against which he is appraised for his conformance to that specification.

Effective supplier assessment schemes quickly identify good suppliers and unreliable suppliers, and the skill of the Quality Assurance Manager will enable him to concentrate on the latter with the objective either of improving a supplier's performance, or removing the offender from the list of a company's approved suppliers.

Manufacturing Specifications

It is necessary that the process conditions and procedures are defined such that products conforming to the product specification will be produced, and it is essential that acceptable tolerances are defined if standards are to be met with maximum throughput and minimum cost.

Ensuring that product standards and process capability are compatible is one of the key roles of the Quality Assurance Manager, who should ensure that effective process control is introduced so that key product attributes are achieved.

Distribution Specification

Most products, especially fresh, chill cabinet, and frozen products, require particular conditions during distribution if they are to reach the customer in good condition, and it is necessary that requirements are clearly defined.

MEETING THE STANDARDS

Quality Assurance or Quality Control?

It is appropriate here to consider the two basic ways of organising a manufacturing control operation (Fig. 4.2).

The traditional quality control route involves production with detailed technical control being provided by the independent Quality Control Department. In this respect *quality control* may be defined as:

'the regulatory process through which we measure actual quality performance, compare it with standards and act on the difference'

and can be likened to a statistical net in the production operation with quality control sieving out non-specification items using a series of tests at sampling rates which relate statistically to throughput. Defective material is rejected or reworked.

The advantages or disadvantages of the approach are as follows:

Advantages	*Disadvantages*
Control exerted by technically trained staff, disciplined to working to a standard	Control is off-line and is dependent upon its effective communication with production management
Test frequency statistically relevant to the process	Control implies a consistent (high?) level of cost
	Production not necessarily motivated by quality consciousness
	Responsibility is not clearly defined

Quality assurance, on the other hand, involves the Production Department in carrying out their own detailed process control, with the quality assurance function involved in the activity of:

'Providing to all concerned evidence to establish confidence that the quality function is being adequately performed'.

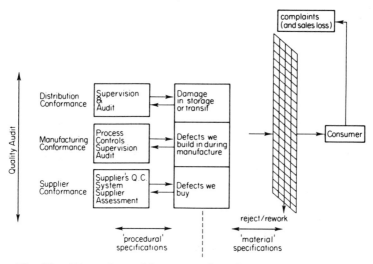

Fig. 4.2. Ways of organising a manufacturing control operation.

This is done using the quality audit team, who are the independent investigators who satisfy themselves by routine and non-routine audit procedures that product standards and manufacturing specifications are being met. Another key role is to identify areas of quality hazards and to take steps to rectify them.

An innate strength is required by quality assurance management to ensure that emphasis on cost does not override the use of effective process control measures. This is always a danger when manufacturing costs are under pressure.

The system then is dependent upon three feedback loops which assure supplier conformance, manufacturing conformance and distribution conformance, and success with this approach is dependent upon:

1. A good relationship with suppliers and a mutual understanding of each other's requirements and processes.
2. Production management being technically competent.
3. Production operators being in a state of self-control, i.e.:
    a. The operator knows what he is supposed to do.
    b. He knows what he is doing.
    c. He has means for regulating what he is doing.
4. Quality assurance management demonstrating flexible application of resource to identify and eliminate areas of quality hazard.

It is appropriate here to consider how the various parameters can be defined, before going on to consider the problems of commissioning and process control.

DEFINITION AND CONTROL OF PRODUCT ATTRIBUTES

Defining and measuring the various attributes of a food product is by no means as tangible as the measurement of the length of a screw or the pitch of its thread, and it is appropriate to examine the various assessment methodologies available to the food scientist.

Perceived Quality

Sensory evaluation of colour, flavour, texture and appearance is usually carried out by trained panels using defined scoring scales, 5-point up to 9-point scales being most common. Figure 4.3 is a scoring scale for dehydrated peas. They can be used to define required product characteristics, evaluate different sources of raw material, alternative product formulations, consumer acceptability, flavour changes in storage, etc.

The design and conduct of taste panels are particular skills involving training of panel members, and the use of different types of test dependent upon the objective of the panel, e.g. paired, comparison, triangle test, ranking test, and acceptance tests.[1]

Instrumental methods are becoming more frequently available to measure some of the parameters, e.g. colour can be measured:

—analytically, e.g. extracted colour of tomato;
—physically, e.g. tristimulus colorimetry;
—comparatively, e.g. Lovibond.

Flavour can be measured chromatographically. Texture can be measured with instruments such as the Instron, by viscometry, etc., e.g. a simple viscometer to control gravy consistency in canned meat products.

However, most instrumental methods are laboratory methods more appropriate to the establishment of standards and the auditing of finished product quality. On-line process control of these parameters usually is simple, e.g. use of standard reference samples, colour standards, photographs, and Munsell chips, although simple fixed-wavelength spectrophotometers and viscometers are used.

Thus panel techniques can be used to define the preferred level of an attribute and instrumental methods can be used to quantify that preference by a tangible measurement and contribute to effective process control. It is important that these criteria are always related back to consumers' preferences to ensure the factory is producing the right product.

Composition of Ingredients and Products

A capability to analyse raw materials and finished product is essential to:

—establish specifications;
—confirm that goods received are within specification;
—confirm that finished product is within specification, particularly where statutory compositional requirements have to be met.

The basic need is to determine moisture, fat, nitrogen (protein), ash, and carbohydrate, and it is appropriate to examine the methods available for their determination.[4,5]

Moisture

The basic accurate method is that of *Karl Fischer*, suitable for products with moisture content below 15%, e.g. confectionery and dehydrated vegetables. The most commonly used methods in the food industry are methods evaluating loss in weight—*the drying methods*—and it is important to remember that that is the parameter being measured, so that the result may not necessarily be the true water content. The methods are used comparatively and are accurate to 0·1%. The concept is to dry to constant weight, and the period of drying therefore varies for different materials. An air oven at 100 °C is commonly used, although for products that decompose a vacuum oven at 60 or 70 °C is more appropriate.

It is important to compare only results obtained under identical drying conditions.

In a production situation it is not possible to wait for results, however, and it is common to use either infrared lamps or electrical moisture meters, be they capacitance or resistance types. This is satisfactory provided that they are regularly calibrated against an oven method, and that it is accepted that they are accurate only to ±1%.

Nuclear magnetic resonance techniques are now used in advanced laboratories.

Fat

Fat is most simply extracted from a dried, ground sample with light petroleum—the Soxhlet method. Liquid materials can most easily be

COLOUR	SCORE
Practically uniform bright green colour with not more than 5% slightly paler than the bulk. Not more than 2 stained or partially bleached peas. No brown or completely bleached peas.	5
Colour slightly pale or dull or slightly lacking in uniformity with not more than 10% slightly different from the bulk. Not more than 4 stained or partially bleached peas. No brown or completely bleached peas.	4
Colour pale, greyish green, or lacking in uniformity. Not more than 6 stained peas. No brown and not more than 10 completely or partially bleached peas.	3
Colour pale, greyish green or lacking in uniformity. Not more than 8 stained peas. Not more than 2 brown and not more than 15 completely or partially bleached peas.	2
Colour pale, greyish or dull or badly lacking in uniformity. Not more than 10 stained peas. Not more than 6 brown and not more than 20 completely or partially bleached peas.	1
Colour very pale or greyish and completely lacking in uniformity. Not more than 10 stained peas. More than 6 brown and 20 completely or partially bleached peas.	0

FLAVOUR	SCORE
Sweet natural flavour of tender fresh peas. Free from off-flavours and odours.	5
Flavour good but not as strong or sweet as tender fresh peas. Free from off-flavours and odours.	4
Flavour weak. Free from off-flavours and odours.	3
Flavour weak. Slight off-flavours.	2
Flavour very weak and lacking in sweetness. Slightly scorched or moderate other off-flavours.	1
Lack of pea flavour and sweetness. Strong scorched or other off-flavours.	0

Fig. 4.3. Grading of dehydrated peas.

TEXTURE	SCORE
Uniformly plump and soft but not mushy or mealy. Skins may be firm but not tough. Not more than 5 unpricked peas (other than very small).	5
Rather firm with not more than 10% slightly tough or slight trace of mealiness. Skins firm but not tough. Not more than 10 unpricked peas (other than very small).	4
Uniformly firm or appreciably mealy, or texture varying within these limits with up to 5% tough. Skins firm but not tough. Not more than 15 unpricked peas (other than very small).	3
Uniformly firm or appreciably mealy, or texture varying within these limits with up to 10% tough. Skins slightly tough. Not more than 20 unpricked peas (other than very small).	2
Generally hard or mealy or varying in texture between these limits. Skin tough. Not more than 50 unpricked peas (other than very small).	1
Very hard. Skins very tough. More than 50 unpricked peas (other than very small).	0

Fig. 4.3.—contd.

extracted by repeated shaking with solvent. Protein can interfere with extraction, and acid treatment (*Werner–Schmid*) or alkali treatment (*Rose–Gottlieb*) is appropriate to remove the protein, the latter method being most appropriate in the presence of sugar. A common volumetric method, particularly for dairy products, is the *Gerber* method, in which the fat is centrifuged off, following acid treatment.

Nitrogen
   The basic method is that of *Kjeldahl*, involving acid digestion in the presence of sodium or potassium sulphate to release nitrogen, which is converted into ammonia sulphate. This is made alkaline with sodium hydroxide and the ammonia is distilled into standard acid and titrated. The protein level is given by multiplying by a factor.

Various semimicro developments of the method are documented and automatic equipment capable of dealing with many samples is now available.

Ash

The total ash of the foodstuff can be a general measure of quality. An alkaline, low water-soluble ash can indicate previous extraction, and the acid-insoluble ash is often a measure of the sand present. Thus the ash content is particularly relevant to vegetables, herbs and spices.

Carbohydrate

Carbohydrate is often determined by difference, but there are more specific methods available. The microscope provides the best qualitative method of identifying *starches*, since each type of starch has particular characteristics.

Individual carbohydrates have specific physical characteristics, e.g. specific rotation and melting point, and the refractometer is a useful means of determining the sugar content of syrups of known composition. Chromatography is useful for identifying sugars in low-carbohydrate products.

Total sugars are determined by the method of Lane and Eynon, and reducing sugars by that of Munson and Walker. Sugars reduce Fehling's solution under standardised conditions, releasing copper (I) oxide, which is then weighed.

Glucose and sucrose can also be determined enzymically.

Filth and Crude Fibre

The filth test is a means of evaluating rodent and insect contamination and the fibre figure is a measure of the effectiveness with which raw materials have been milled or processed.

Nutrients and the Nutritional Value of Foods

Here we can consider computation and analysis. The labelling laws of the country specify how *energy claims* shall be calculated, i.e. 1 g of carbohydrate, protein, and fat shall be deemed to contribute 3·75, 4 and 9 kcal, respectively.

Basic nutritional data have been assembled for a large range of materials and products.[6,7]

Analysis for vitamins and trace elements is a specialised analytical area. Methods have been published[4,5] and atomic-absorption spectroscopy is now used in sophisticated laboratories, as also is mass spectrometry.

Additives and Contaminants

These include preservatives, antioxidants, heavy metals, and pesticide residues. In all cases the analyst needs to effect a good extraction and separation and then apply a suitable detection method. The methods are very detailed[4,5] but more modern methods, e.g. spectrophotometry and atomic-absorption spectroscopy, are making these methods less cumbersome and more accurate.

Packaging Materials

In common with any raw materials, tests are needed to ensure that packaging materials conform to the correct specification, and that they perform correctly.

Structural tests will include physical measurements, strength, oxygen, water, light and fat permeability as the case may be, lamination strength, print stability, and register.

Performance tests include tensile strength, seal strength, effective closures, compression tests, drop tests, and bursting strength.

Properties of Food Products and Ingredients

The behaviour of materials and products during manufacture, storage, and distribution can be important. Many can and do change chemically and physically, e.g. dehydrated foods pick up moisture, fats oxidise, and frozen foods thaw out. These undesirable changes have to be minimised and controlled during distribution and storage.

Choice of the right specification of packaging material, e.g. use of moisture barrier or oxygen barrier, is often the solution to these problems, but it is appropriate to confirm the effectiveness of decisions by carrying out transit and storage trials.

Storage testing involves placing the finished product in its packaging in the envisaged environment in which it is to be distributed. Samples of test material together with controls are withdrawn at time intervals and evaluated analytically and by a trained taste panel using a routine scoring scale. The experiment is run until either the product is shown to be acceptable after the required storage period or until it fails to meet the product specification.

Failure to maintain the requisite standards will require investigation and rectification, e.g. use of better quality ingredients, reformulation, change of packaging material. When satisfactory test data are available, distribution and storage specifications can be confirmed.

TABLE 4.1
Typical bacteriological data, per gram

Material	T.V.C.	E. coli	S. aureus	Salmonella	Cl. perfringens	Moulds	B. cereus
Cooked frozen meat	10^5	1	100	Absent	—	—	—
Raw frozen chicken	10^6	—	10^3	—	—	—	—
Free flow frozen prawns	5×10^4	10	10^3	Absent	—	—	—
AFD prawn	10^5	10	10^3	Absent	10	—	—
Pasta	10^4	10	50	Absent	1	200	—
Butter powder	5×10^4	1	10	Absent	1	—	—
Full cream milk powder	10^4	10,	50	Absent	—	—	50
Dehydrated vegetables	10^5	10	50	Absent	10	500	—

Microbiological Techniques

Commercial food products need to be extremely safe microbiologically, since any failure could cause a number of consumers to be ill, with serious commercial consequences to the manufacturer. It is important, therefore, to pay considerable attention to the microbiological quality of raw materials, intermediates, finished products, packaging, manufacturing plant, and the factory environment.

An essential element is that the microbiological standards for all materials and processes are clearly defined, in common with analytical standards. Typical data for some raw materials are given in Table 4.1.

Working details of specific tests can be found in the standard works,[8,9] but it is appropriate to consider the application of tests, and particularly the interpretation of results.

The *total viable count* (T.V.C.) gives an indication of the overall quality of raw material or product and could be described as an indicator of good manufacturing practice. If the starting material is poor, or processing conditions are inadequate, this count will be high, i.e. 10^7–10^8. There are two forms of the test—pour plate and the droplet techniques.

Escherichia coli or *total coliforms* are used as indicator organisms since they are found in the intestinal tract, and their presence in excess indicates possible faecal contamination and the possibility of presence of pathogenic organisms. These tests can be done by plate count or by the most probable number (M.P.N.) method.

Staphylococcus aureus occurs on the human skin and produces toxin capable of causing food poisoning if it grows on food. It is thus an indicator of mishandling. Since the toxin is heat stable, it is appropriate to test prior to heating, i.e. look at ingredients and early parts of a process. The test method is a plate count on a selective agar.

Clostridium perfringens and *Bacillus cereus* can cause illness when present in large numbers and it is appropriate to test fish and dairy products for these organisms. Both tests are plate counts on selective media.

Moulds and yeasts should be monitored on fruit materials and products, and their presence in dehydrated materials indicates inadequate drying or the fact that the load had got wet during distribution and dried out naturally.

Salmonella can cause typhoid fever (*S. typhosa*) and food poisoning (*S. typhimurium*). The latter usually originates from consumption of unheated meat. Beef, poultry, and egg powder are particular sources and the mere presence of *Salmonella* in products requires immediate action by factory management. The detection method involves actually growing the organism in the laboratory, which requires a high level of discipline, particularly concerning the sterilisation of all equipment.

Appraisal of the pattern of test results will indicate whether the materials and products are of satisfactory microbial quality. Any drift from the norm needs to be investigated thoroughly.

In addition to raw materials and products, it is wise to appraise the state of equipment and the buildings in order to monitor the effectiveness of the hygiene and cleaning procedures and to ensure that no pocket of spoilage organism can develop and contaminate the product. Regular swabbing of key points in the process is an effective way of doing this. Efficient use of detergents and sanitising agents is necessary to maintain a food factory in a hygienic state.

Particular precautions are necessary to control spoilage and pathogenic organisms, particularly in meat plants.
Personnel should:

—wear protective clothing properly and change it when soiled;
—wash hands regularly, particularly after meal breaks and using the toilet, and use barrier creams.

Factories should have:

—adequate hand-washing facilities in production areas;
—effective cleaning and sanitisation procedures;
—an arrangement such that raw meat and cooked meat operations and operators are separated.

A fundamental contribution to this problem can be made when buildings are designed, equipment chosen, and plant layout is established.

Food Safety

There are two aspects of food safety—contaminants and foreign matter and safety in toxicological terms.

The food hygiene regulations make it clear that it is an offence to sell any product containing a foreign body. It is thus prudent that a manufacturer should protect his product by the use of pneumatic and gravity separators, stone traps, magnets, and metal detectors as necessary, supported by general vigilance by all operators.

Precautions should be taken that the heavy metal content, e.g. lead, tin, arsenic, mercury, and cadmium, is within the limits prescribed by regulations, and pesticide residues should be monitored similarly.

Toxicological safety is controlled through the allocation of an ADI for ingredients, defined by the Scientific Committee for Food as follows:

'An ADI represents an estimate of a daily intake of a substance which, taken throughout the human lifespan, would not result in obvious harm to health'.

In arriving at an ADI, the 'no effect level' is determined by administering a range of dose levels to each species of test animal (often 0.1, 1.0, and 10% of the diet) and observing the results physically and histologically.

A reported 'no effect level' could thus be a tenth of the dose known to produce an effect—in itself a substantial safety factor. The ADI is then calculated by extrapolating the result to humans. A safety factor of 100 is commonly used but experts will vary this depending on the quality of the data, the type of material being considered, etc. The safety factor allows for sensitivity differences between animals and man, and within the human species.

It is interesting to note the comment of JECFA (WHO/FAO Joint Expert Committee for Food Additives)—'an ADI is intended as a guide and may be exceeded after consultation with experts if there are important advantages in so doing. An ADI provides a sufficiently large safety margin to ensure that there may be no undue concern about occasionally exceeding it, providing average intake over large periods of time does not exceed it'.

Environmental Factors

The prime concerns are water quality, effluent quality, and the atmosphere.[10,11]

The base standard for drinking water has been laid down by the World Health Organisation (WHO), involving the following criteria:

Physical: appearance, colour, turbidity, odour, taste and temperature, pH, conductivity.

Chemical: alkalinity, temporary and permanent hardness, iron, copper, zinc, lead, and toxic elements, e.g. arsenic, cadmium, chromium.

Bacteriological quality is indicated by the presumptive coliform test (absence in 100 ml of chlorinated water). *Clostridium welchii* can be used as an indicator of remote pollution since it is a spore former.

Most Local Authorities will aspire to the WHO standard, but some industries need particular requirements over and above this and treatment plants are necessary, e.g.:

1. Dairy products need low nitrate and ammoniacal nitrogen levels.
2. Canned vegetables are affected adversely by hard water, and if recirculated water is used for can cooling it should be chlorinated to the level of 3–5 ppm of free chlorine.
3. The soft drinks industry requires a particularly high-quality water and in plant treatment it is essential to control clarity and product quality.

Particular attention has to be paid to the control of boiler waters, both infeed and outfeed, not only to maximise the efficiency of the boiler but also to minimise corrosion of feedpipes and tubes. Solids, total hardness, and alkalinity are monitored to define the treatment necessary before the water enters the boiler, and phosphate and sulphite levels are monitored to control anti-corrosion treatment. About 85–150 ppm of sodium phosphate is needed in the water to precipitate the hardness.

Most Water Authorities impose strict limits on the volume and quality of effluent and impose severe financial penalties for exceeding those limits. It is appropriate to monitor biological oxygen demand (BOD) (5 days at 20 °C), suspended solids, grease and oil levels, temperature, pH and permanganate value.[10,11] An alternative test to BOD is chemical oxygen demand (COD).

Control of the atmosphere can be important from several viewpoints. Dust can be a health hazard and an explosion hazard, so extraction systems are valuable for appropriate situations. Air-conditioning systems are used to control humidity, e.g. dry mix plants and processes using hygroscopic materials, and gas packing and storage in controlled atmospheres are also common, e.g. fruit stores and potato stores.

Metrology

The important point to remember concerning the measurement of length, area, volume, and weight is to consider the accuracy to which you need to make the measurement and to use equipment capable of working to that accuracy.

Particular care is needed to ensure that scales are set up properly and that they are kept clean. Modern weight measurement systems use electronic balances which require careful servicing. Traditionally the nation has worked to the minimum declared weight system, in which the manufacturer has to guarantee that everything is above his declared weight. He will also have his own commercial target weight to achieve, and this control has been

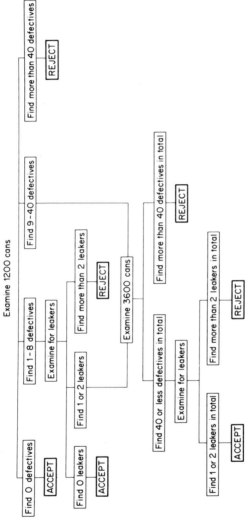

Fig. 4.4. Quality control shipment inspection—double sampling scheme.

exercised through use of charts depicting target levels and warning and action limits. Average weight legislation is soon to be introduced, in which an average weight has to be declared and weight maintained within specified tolerances. Control of range of fill becomes important and range charts will be appropriate. However, modern electronic equipment with computed programmes takes the labour out of the operation and provides accurate on-line information very quickly.

Statistical Concepts[12]

Many of the methodologies discussed above are applied to samples. In taking those samples we need to be satisfied that they are representative and in interpreting the results to have a feeling for the variability about the mean. Computation of the standard deviation of a set of results will indicate how variable the results are and how well the parameter is in control. Often it is desirable to appraise different sets of results for any significant difference. This can be done by the t-test and the chi-squared test, which express the results at different levels of confidence.

Sampling plans are based on the concepts of lot quality protection and average outgoing quality protection, relating to consumers' risk and producers' risk. In single sampling plans a random sample is drawn from the batch and if the number of defectives exceeds the acceptance number the batch is rejected. Tables relating sample size, lot size, and acceptance level at various levels of process average percent defective are available. The consequences of failing a batch is that it should be 100% inspected—often a formidable task—and double sampling plans in effect allow a second opinion to be taken. An example is given in Fig. 4.4, which represents a higher outgoing quality level than is usual due to nature of product and process.

Single sampling plans require one large sample and provide more information from a single group of units. Double sampling plans take a smaller initial sample and give a quicker decision on whether the number of defectives is either small or large. Whichever system is employed it must relate to the outgoing quality level required.

COMMISSIONING WORK AND PROCESS CONTROL

It is imperative that new products and processes should be thoroughly commissioned using the production facilities before planned initial production runs commence. There are several objectives:

1.   Establish the process capability and define the process controls.

2. (Confirm) identity areas of quality hazard and confirm the safety of the process.
3. Establish that the product specification can be achieved and confirm that cost and volume targets can be met.

Process Capability/Process Control

An acceptable process capability is one which delivers a product that meets the standards and tolerances defined in the specification. It is therefore necessary, using the methodologies already outlined, to sample each stage of the process adequately to be satisfied that the key attributes of the product are within the acceptable tolerances. An appropriate way of doing this is to confirm that ± 3 standard deviations about the target is within the specified tolerance.

There are examples where raw material quality is the essence of a product and little process control is needed. For example, harvest peas are subjected to waste and stain appraisal together with a canning test and the bulk directed to canned processed peas or to packet peas depending upon the result. Effective sample control and batch control are the key to the operation. More usually, however, key process control is an integral part of the process.

An illustration for a dry mix product is given in Fig. 4.5.

Finally, the complete packaged product should be evaluated against the original specification. If there is a failure in any respect then the process or process conditions need to be adjusted. Alternatively, it may make

Operation	Control
Raw materials	Laboratory confirmation that they meet specification.
Batching	Confirm weighing accuracy is adequate. Institute weight record sheet (automatic printout from equipment) to confirm accuracy of batching and weighing.
Mixing	Confirm mixer type and time of mixing. Sample several batches and analyse for key attributes, e.g. vegetable content, salt content, etc., and confirm that they are uniformly spread.
Filling	Sample and weigh on an accurate balance. Confirm that ± 3 standard deviations in weight is within tolerances set, and confirm that product quality at the limits is acceptable. Establish Shewart chart to provide weight record and weight control mechanism.
Packaging	Confirm the machine settings and closure mechanisms necessary to give adequate seals, closures, etc., and to confirm that they are of adequate strength.

Fig. 4.5. Dry mix process control.

economic sense to adjust the specification to accommodate the process capability, i.e. achieve a cost-effective balance between marketing needs and manufacturing ability.

The most desirable way of achieving process control is to build it into the equipment capability, but often it is necessary to put control into the hands of the operator.

We should not forget the three criteria of *operator self-control*. If he is to do the job properly, an operator needs to:

—know what he is supposed to do;
—know what he is doing;
—have the means of regulating what he is doing.

For this he needs to be given thorough training and be supplied with equipment that has an accuracy appropriate to his needs.

Ideally, meaningful control tests should be on-line and arranged on a feed-forward basis, i.e. the control signal should be generated before the event and not after. If feedback control is necessary or tests have to be off-line, then results should be fed back to the operator quickly so as to have the maximum effect. The accuracy of the test method should relate to the accuracy of the process and the acceptable tolerance in the specification. There is no point in a highly accurate analysis if the process cannot respond.

At the commissioning stage it is prudent to evaluate and remedy all areas of potential quality hazard and to confirm the safety of the process, both to operators and in terms of a safe product. It is imperative that all sterilisation processes are thoroughly checked in the production equipment to ensure that specified procedures are correct and that safe and adequate heat treatments are applied. Hygiene and cleaning procedures also need to be confirmed.

Records and Process Audit

It is wise, and in some cases legally necessary, to keep detailed records of process conditions in order to:

1. Document process conditions.
2. Provide evidence of good process control, for example retorts.
3. Enable quality and production management to audit processes, identify out-of-control situations, and then to rectify them.

The most efficient method is to use records prepared by the operator and in this respect proforma, range charts, and cusum charts are relevant, and we should not ignore the use of programmed calculators to process numerical data and printout summaries. In whatever form the summary is prepared, it is the data upon which judgement is made concerning the efficacy and consistency of the process and through which management can identify items where improvement is necessary. This is another key role for the quality function.

FINISHED PRODUCT QUALITY

It is important to confirm that finished product quality meets with requirements of the product specification. There are a variety of inputs to this judgement:

1. Factory management will sample and appraise finished product quality against the product specification, using suitable scoring scales, analytical test data, etc., as necessary. Evidence of significant non-conformance will lead to a review of the manufacturing specification.

2. A detailed technical analysis of customer complaints on a regular basis can be revealing and rewarding. No manufacturer will satisfy all his customers all the time, but by routinely monitoring complaint patterns it is possible to identify significant areas of quality defect, be they due to unsatisfactory product concept or manufacturing error.

3. Audits of product from factory, warehouse, and store will further add to knowledge of conformance to standard, and comparison with competitors' products on an objective basis is always prudent.

Quality assurance management will review these numerous pieces of information and discuss necessary action with marketing, technical, and factory management in the light of the quality and cost issues involved.

CONCLUSION

We have seen that an effective food control operation is dependent upon an effective, practical administrative system for communicating and defining product manufacturing and distribution standards. The various methodologies available to aid this objective have been reviewed.

It must be recognised that the food control operation is an integral part of a dynamic system (Fig. 4.6), and as such has to react to the pressures

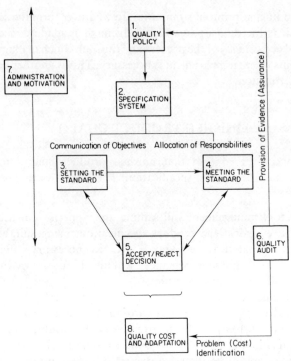

Fig. 4.6.   Food control operation.

prevalent in a business. Amended policies, cost pressures, and a host of other reasons can cause changes. The system has to react to new standards and have the ability to show that the revised standards have been met.

However, a methodical approach can only succeed if correct attitudes have been engendered in employees at all levels towards *conformance* with practical standards and acceptance of responsibility to the consumer. Methodology is a back-up to good manufacturing practices on the factory floor, performed by people well trained in the skills and technologies that they operate and supervise.

BIBLIOGRAPHY

1. IFST Symposium (1977). *Sensory quality control—practical approaches in food and drink production*. Proceedings of symposium held at University of Aston.
2. Herschdoerfer, S. M. (Ed.) (1967, 1968, 1969). *Quality control in the food industry*. Vol. 1–3. London: Academic Press.

3. Juran, J. M. (1962). *Quality control handbook*, 2nd edn. New York: McGraw-Hill.
4. Pearson, D. (1976). *The chemical analysis of foods*. 6th edn. Edinburgh: Churchill Livingstone.
5. *Methods of analysis of the Association of Official Analytical Chemists*. (1970). 11th edn. Philadelphia, Pa.: AOAC.
6. Paul, A. A. and Southgate, D. A. T. (1978). *McCance and Widdowson's The composition of foods*, 4th edn. London: HMSO.
7. Osborne, D. R. and Voogt, P. (1978). *Analysis of nutrients in food*. London: Academic Press.
8. Collins, C. H. and Lyne, P. M. (1967). *Microbiological methods*. London: Butterworth.
9. Mackie and McCartney (1960). *Handbook of bacteriology*. 10th edn. (A. Cruickshank (ed.)). Edinburgh: Churchill Livingstone.
10. *Approved methods for physical and chemical examination of water*. Institute of Water Engineers.
11. *United States standard methods for examination of water*. American Public Health Association.
12. Moroney, M. J. (1978). *Facts from figures*. London: Penguin.

DISCUSSION

Mr. E. I. Williams (Spillers Ltd) said that it is essential that any standard set for food control should be realistic, meaningful, and capable of achievement. The methods of test should allow the provision of information on quality to those actually in control as early as possible.

He considered that a common defect in specifications and standards was over elaboration of analytical requirements which often miss out unidentified but often critical parameters. A standard in terms of performance, such as a baking test, is often a useful addition. Quick and simple tests within the capability of production operatives, coupled with much greater use of automatic process controls, could be of major benefit. Examples of the latter are moisture control systems and dough consistency control, both commonly used in the milling and baking industry.

Referring to Mr. Bolton's distinction between quality control and quality assurance, Mr. Williams said that in some organisations, quality assurance embraces and is not dissociated from quality control. The basic compositional parameters may only have relevance for certain commodities. For instance, the statement that total ash is a general measure of quality could be misleading. The higher ash of, say, wholemeal flour compared with other types of flour does not indicate a lower quality.

Referring to microbiology, Mr. Williams said that control is essential not only in relation to health hazards, but also in avoiding the production of organoleptically unacceptable products.

Regarding the specific classes of organisms mentioned, Mr. Williams commented as follows:

Total coliforms: the method of test is important in that misleading results can be obtained with cereal and vegetable products containing *Erwinia* species which are coliforms of non-faecal origin.

Staphylococcus aureus is an indicator of mishandling if on *cooked* foods. It occurs naturally, as on raw meats.

Bacillus cereus in cereals, particularly rice, has caused problems and should be looked for when evaluating quality.

Moulds may indicate a mycotoxin risk.

Salmonella species: there are more than 1000 serotypes, many of which cause food poisoning other than *S. typhimurium*—*S. agona* for instance, originated from imported fishmeal. Cocoa powder, desiccated coconut, and pork may be mentioned as other materials associated with the *Salmonella* problem.

There is now an increase in microbiological examinations to detect the presence of other food poisoning organisms such as *Vibro para-haemolyticus* in fish products and *Campylobacter* species in raw poultry.

Finally, Mr. Williams said that the publications of the International Commission on Microbiological Specifications for Food, commonly known as the Thatcher Committee, were worth mentioning at the Symposium, since the important new concepts proposed regarding microbiological standards appeared to be gaining acceptance in many areas.

Mr. A. Turner (Cadbury Typhoo Ltd) said that it is often better to be roughly right at the time than precisely right when it is too late to take action. He also queried Mr. Bolton's statement that 'flavour can be measured chromatographically'. Flavourings, i.e. flavour constituents, may be measurable but chromatography cannot give a true indication of complex perceived flavours.

Mr. E. Druce (Rank Hovis McDougall Ltd) said that often insufficient consideration was given to the 'scale of scrutiny', i.e. the breadth rather than the accuracy of useful measurement. Too much attention was paid to the precision of methodology and the literature neglects the innovatory methods meeting requirements relating to scales of scrutiny applied to production and in use.

Dr. R. G. Booth (Consultant) commented that there are many food products and some food ingredients for which scientific skills and measurements do little to establish their quality. Scientific tests applied during manufacture of these kinds of materials are mainly, if not entirely, irrelevant to the ultimate quality (particularly the fine detail and financial value) of such products, the quality of wine being an example.

Mr. J. R. Blanchfield (Bush Boake Allen Ltd) noted that Mr. Bolton had rightly mentioned sensory analysis as a tool in methodology. Although not so objective as chemical analysis, those engaged in the sensory analysis of wines, for instance, would no doubt be able to state very precisely the quality of this year's wine compared with last year's.

Mr. A. Dulin (Marks & Spencer Ltd) expressed interest in Mr. Bolton's clear differentation between quality assurance and quality control. In his experience these terms were rather loosely interpreted. Sometimes quality audit staff are called quality controllers and their work on the finished product is often emphasised as the major function of quality control. This dilutes the effort on the control of the manufacturing process. Possibly process control and quality assurance are better terms to use.

Mr. A. Bolton, in his reply, agreed with the need for practical standards and performance testing. The relation of quality assurance to quality control and to process control was of interest. He had not intended to imply that a barrier existed between process control and quality assurance. His experience was that the umbrella view provided by quality auditors, and the supply of their results to reinforce or improve the process control standards, gave good quality motivation. The point made about identifying the production team with 'process control' was constructive.

Whilst not having much experience of the ICMSF microbiological classification system, Mr. Bolton appreciated its potential usefulness. However, if microbiological standards are to be applied to plant hygiene and product quality, one should not be equivocal about it. In his opinion it has to be on the basis of numerical standards and any deviation requires investigation.

Mr. Bolton ended by acknowledging that Mr. Turner's point concerning chromatography and flavour was well made.

SESSION II

The Constraints

5

Quality Requirements of the Market

CHARLES A. SLATER

Grocery Products Research & Development Director,
Rowntree Mackintosh Ltd

INTRODUCTION

Any paper which purports to describe quality, and quality requirements, in relation to food must begin by explaining what is meant by the word quality. The quality of any product is, of course, in the eye of the beholder. What, then, is meant by quality as applied to the title of this paper— 'Quality Requirements of the Market'—and what is meant by quality in the practice of quality control? There is probably no better place to start than the Oxford English Dictionary, which defines quality as it is understood by the average person. The definition given in the Concise Oxford Dictionary is as follows: 'Quality—Degree of excellence, relative nature, or kind or character; general excellence'.

Up to a point that is what is meant by quality in terms of food. Quality is that which any product may have whatever ingredients are used, provided that those ingredients are wholesome and the best of their kind at the price the consumer is willing to pay. Gorsuch[1] sums this up well with the following definition: 'Quality is a measurement of the degree to which a product meets the expectations of the consumer'.

Good-quality ingredients, wholesome ingredients, will make a good-quality product which may be a cheap or an expensive good-quality product depending on the cost of the ingredients. Clearly, the highest quality ingredients will always cost more than poorer quality ingredients of a similar type. A poor-quality ingredient could still be a wholesome material, for example well grown peanuts, containing large quantities of harmless bric-à-brac, what the Americans call 'trash'. It is possible to obtain a high-quality ingredient by removing the trash from such peanuts in the manufacturer's factory. This, of itself, increases the price of the ingredient

83

so that in order to get the higher quality there is a price to pay. That price
may be paid to the supplier of the ingredient, when he will provide an
ingredient which is of high quality, or the cost may be incurred in the producer's own factory. Another aspect of the quality of ingredients is illustrated
by the following example. The ingredient may be clean and pure and
absolutely wholesome, but still not of high quality for a specific purpose.
Two samples of flour may be purchased for making biscuits. One of these
samples could have too high a protein content for a biscuit flour, and the
other could be perfect. The one with high protein content will give a less
satisfactory product, and therefore is not of high quality for this purpose,
whilst the other will give an excellent product and is therefore rated as of
high quality. Clearly, quality depends upon what, at the end of the day, is
required of the product and that is the object of this paper—the quality of
the product as required for the market.

The quality requirements of the market involve two major considerations. The first is the requirements of the consumer, which will have
been identified by the Marketing Department. The second is the UK law in
the 1955 Act, from which comes that phrase which must be on the tip of all
food manufacturers' tongues 'of the nature, substance or quality
demanded'. Combined, these requirements have to be translated into a
product specification jointly agreed by the Marketing, R&D and the Food
Control Departments.

THE REQUIREMENTS OF THE CONSUMER

The requirements of the consumer will be assessed by the Marketing
Department carrying out consumer research. In designing a new product, it
is first necessary to find out whether there is a place in the market for the
product being considered. Alternatively, the Marketing Department may
have identified a gap in the market and asked for a product to fill it. After
making a few prototypes, the heads of the Marketing and Product
Development Departments will decide whether any one of these looks like
the right kind of product of the right quality for the market. In other words,
a first guess will be made of the requirements of the consumer.

The next step is to take the product to the consumer for his comments. At
this stage a concept test is carried out as follows: a group of consumers is
offered a product and asked if they think they have a use for it, do they like
it, and do they think it should be modified in any way. Answers to these
questions having been received, the product can be modified to give a final

sample of the product the consumer seems to want, and samples of the best quality at a reasonable price can be made. The absolute quality will depend on whether the product is for the cheaper end of the market or for the more expensive end. In either case, the highest quality product will be produced within the constraints of cost. This product is then taken again for market research, and this time the consumer is asked whether he likes the product, whether he will buy it, is it good enough, is it what he wants, and does it fill his quality requirements at a price he is willing to pay.

Very little has been said about the techniques of market research, but it is perhaps pertinent to make a comment on the efficacy of this technique of finding out what the consumer wants. At best, market research is carried out with a few hundred consumers, every effort being made to obtain a suitable cross-section of the consuming public, but at the end of the day a few hundred consumers are all that will be consulted, and for some aspects of consumer research there may be as few as 10, 20 or 30 consumers. It follows, therefore, that there is no way in which consumer research can positively identify the product of the quality that the consumer requires. If in the research the consumers say unanimously it is a wonderful product or unanimously that is a poor product, then this gives some indication, not perfect, of what will happen to that product when it is put into the market place. The only way to test whether a product meets the quality requirements of the consumer at a price he will pay is to carry out a test marketing exercise in a suitable area of the country. When the product is sold and when people come back for more, the Marketing Department will be able to judge whether that product is likely to be a success.

'NATURE, SUBSTANCE OR QUALITY DEMANDED'

We must now turn to quality demanded for the consumer by the 1955 Act, in particular what is meant by 'the nature, substance or quality demanded'. Clearly the law has to be interpreted and over the years different interpretations of these three terms have been considered and discussed. Perhaps for the sake of this paper we should refer to O'Keefe's interpretation.[2] It will be obvious from this work, which cites many examples of cases brought under this section of the law, that legal experts over the years have not, themselves, been clear on the proper interpretation of this part of the Act.

O'Keefe suggests, and I would only partially agree with him, that 'apples or fish (etc.) not of the variety or kind asked for, are not of the "nature" demanded', and that 'articles not containing the proper ingredients or containing some added adulterant are not of the "substance" demanded'. If the consumer does not get a product of the nature or substance demanded, I would maintain that he is being misled and I suspect that the manufacturer would be guilty of an offence under the Trade Descriptions Act, but at the time of the 1955 Act the 'nature or substance demanded' covered this point.

O'Keefe's suggestion with regard to the use of the word 'quality' is in my opinion much less apt, but we must remember that he is suggesting the use of the various words largely to support an appropriate prosecution, whereas we are more interested in their use as guidance to food manufacturers for the provision of suitable foods to the consumer. Occasionally, of course, quality standards are defined by Parliament in Statutory Instruments and in such cases must be followed.

As food technologists we should not be too surprised that the word 'quality' in a legal sense is ill-defined. With all our expert knowledge we find definitions difficult, but I would certainly commend to O'Keefe, as I already have above, the definition given by Gorsuch quoted at the beginning of this paper.

Nowadays many constraints are put upon the food industry to maintain prices at a low level—as low a level as possible because the consumer will not pay a high price if he can get something which he believes to be of equal quality for a lower price. When the consumer comes to pay his money for the product which he intends to buy he will buy the one which to him is of a satisfactory quality at a price he can afford. If he sees two similar products side by side, one an own-label product for say 10p, the other an expensive market-leader branded product for say 14p, both having the same flavour as far as he is concerned, he must say to himself first (having decided, of course, that he wants that product), 'How much money do I have—I have 10p—is that 10p product of suitable quality for my requirements?'. It will be of a suitable quality for his requirements when it is going to be used in such a way that it will give him a finished product which satisfies him when he consumes it because he enjoys it and regards it as wholesome—it is of the quality demanded. Now, it may be that he prefers the cheap flavour in the cheap product anyway, in which case the 10p product is not only the right price for him, it is also the right quality for him. Notwithstanding all this, the more expensive product undoubtedly contains more expensive ingredients, may well be the more sophisticated, give a better mouthfeel, have a better flavour, smell better, look better, even appear to be more wholesome, but if he is not a sophisticated person why should he spend an extra 4p, 40 % more, on the branded product? It may not be of the quality demanded. On the other hand, the consumer may have decided that the more expensive product must be better, must be higher quality, must be more wholesome because it is more expensive, and he is not going to give his children anything but the best—so he buys the more expensive product. What, then, is the quality demanded? In marketing terms it is that quality which the consumer thinks he requires on any particular occasion.

In defining quality for our purposes, I think that we must always bear in mind the wholesomeness of the food. An unwholesome product can never be of the 'quality demanded' and can never meet the quality requirements of the market. Members of the Institute of Food Science and Technology, will have received a copy of the Code of Professional Conduct (see page 283), item vi of which refers specifically to the wholesomeness of food. Wholesomeness is a difficult word to define briefly, and I would therefore refer to Professional Conduct Guideline No. 1,[3] which explains precisely what is meant by this term.

CONTROL SYSTEM

Having defined what is meant by the quality requirements of the market, how do we arrive at that quality? Reference has been made to the important characteristics of any food product—appearance, smell, taste, texture, and wholesomeness. How do these characteristics rate in terms of importance from the marketing point of view? As far as the first four are concerned, the answer to that question will depend entirely upon the intended use of the product. However, there is one attribute which can never be ignored, whatever the intended use of the product, that is wholesomeness. At the end of the day, the real quality requirement of the market is that the food shall be wholesome.

What, then, of the control system, the system which will provide this wholesome product? This is the basis of quality control, the way in which the manufacturer provides the quality demanded by the market. It is the duty of the Production Department to control quality. The R&D and QC Departments must provide the basic methodology for the control of the quality of the product which the Production Department is expected to make, but the Production Department alone will control the quality. When it invents a new product, the R&D Department will provide a recipe and manufacturing instructions to enable the production man to make the product. Included in the recipe and the manufacturing instructions will be a series of quality checks. These will come at certain cut-off points in the manufacture. Even with a continuous manufacturing system there are always points at which a sample can be taken to check the progress from raw ingredients to good-quality finished product, and at those points it is up to the Production Department to make checks, checks which will have been laid down in my organisation by the R&D Department. The best way to explain what is meant is to refer to a suitable example, so let us consider peanut butter.

The recipe will provide for the product a list of the ingredients required, and will explain what has to be done to each ingredient to arrive at peanut butter, and the manufacturing instructions will point out the steps one by one through the manufacturing procedure. The first control check must be on the raw ingredients, in this case mainly peanuts. These, therefore, will be inspected and checked against specification by the Quality Control Department. A scientist in the laboratory will examine the peanuts, he will test them for certain parameters which will be described in the recipe, and he will accept or reject the nuts on the basis of their conformity with specification. The laboratory will also examine the other ingredients, which, being basically pure chemicals, will present very few problems. The nuts, having been accepted, will be passed into a roaster, which will cook them to a given colour, and this can be checked by the Production Department at the point at which the nuts leave the oven. Following this, the nuts will be passed into a blancher, which will remove the skins, split the nuts, and remove the hearts. They will then be visually examined to see whether all the skins have been removed, whether the hearts have been removed and whether any foreign materials remain in the nuts. The final removal of dark kernels, which are probably bad, and stones and pieces of bric-à-brac will be ensured by passing the nuts through an electronic sorting machine, on another belt for visual examination, and through a de-stoner which will remove stones and other such particles. Finally, the roasted nuts will be put through a mill together with the other ingredients, which will be metered using suitable equipment. Samples of the product being filled into jars will be taken and examined by the Quality Control staff to ensure that the correct level of salt and sugar and emulsifier have been added and once more to check that the product meets specification.

Now, if the product at this stage is incorrectly made, or is not wholesome, this is a production fault probably caused by not having properly controlled manufacture of the product. Two very important elements in this control system are supervision (management) and inspection. It is the duty of a supervisor to instil into every person working on that line the necessity for good hygiene and careful inspection at every stage. If the staff—all the staff from the man who sweeps the factory to the general manager—are quality conscious, then the product leaving the plant will be a high-quality product consistent with the cost and wholesomeness of the ingredients which have been used. If such a system operates in a food factory, in this case on a peanut butter line, then each jar of peanut butter that comes off the end of the line will be virtually indistinguishable from the previous jar, and if the Production and Quality Assurance Departments have done their jobs properly the consumer will not see any difference from one jar to the next. This is not to say, of course, that there are no small differences between one jar and the next, because in food one is invariably dealing with natural products and natural products vary. Only when you are putting into bags a pure chemical substance such as sugar can you ever expect a 99·9 % similar product time and time again. However, even with an ingredient such as peanuts, provided the Production Department works to the recipe laid down and the manufacturing instructions laid down, and provided that the simple tests which have been written into the instructions for manufacture have been followed, then, within well defined limits, all units of the finished product will be very similar at the end of the day.

The extent of variability will, of course, be defined by the Marketing Department on the basis of the requirements of the consumer and within any appropriate legal requirements. In the case of peanut butter the limits in terms of the colour, stability (that is, its ability or otherwise to separate into oil and solid material), saltiness, and sweetness of the finished product will be defined on the basis of consumer requirements determined by market research in the first instance. There is no real problem in keeping to the limits provided that everyone in the factory is quality conscious. Many of the constraints upon the defined limits come entirely from the price the consumer is willing to pay. Indeed, as the Marketing Department will realise, they can have, within this context, anything they like if they are prepared to pay for it.

The product required in the market place has been defined, and from that it follows, working backwards to the beginning of the process, that only by the use of materials of a certain specification will it be obtained. In order to arrive at the quality required for the market, that specification must be right and must be adhered to.

Not only must the ingredients be right, but the packaging materials must also be right, because on the packaging materials as much as on anything else will depend the way in which the product finally arrives in the hands of the consumer. Poor packaging materials could result in a good-quality product finishing up in the hands of the consumer as a poor-quality product. A cracked jar, a split bag, or a faulty lid and the consumer may finish up with a mouldy product, an inedible product (because of bad physical condition), an unwholesome product. It is up to the food manufacturer to provide a foodstuff of the nature, substance, and quality demanded.

Supervision and inspection have already been mentioned when the quality consciousness of the staff in the factory was discussed. Staff must also be conscious of a need for good hygiene, and again it is the duty of the management to instil this. Clearly, some foodstuffs will be more difficult than others to produce and sell in the market place in a wholesome state. However, a properly worked out control system is designed never to allow a lethal product to reach the market place and to enable a wholesome and pleasant product to do so, but a product will be neither wholesome nor pleasant unless hygiene is carefully watched. It is not part of my brief to discuss hygiene in depth, but it is an essential part of the control system and must be considered if a product of the quality required by the market is to be produced.

The overall system of control will result in the efficient manufacture of the product to high quality standards. However, since at the end of the day the cost of the product is of considerable importance, as mentioned above, the control system must also aim to improve the efficiency of manufacture of a wholesome end product. That is, the system must help to produce the same product more economically. This will be done only if the control system ensures the use of satisfactory ingredients and correct operation of the manufacturing process.

The efficient manufacture of a product to a high quality standard will also depend upon sufficient feedback from the Marketing and Sales Departments. These two Departments will provide the direct link between the consumer and the Quality Assurance Department. There are two major points to consider. Firstly, if sales have fallen to a low level and this information has not been fed back to production, then a stock-pile of the product concerned will result. It is then very necessary for the Quality Assurance Manager to ensure that the stock held does not exceed its shelf-life before it is finally sold. Clearly, for every day that the product stays in the depot or store it will deteriorate until eventually it reaches such a low standard of quality that when it is ultimately sold to the consumer the product will not be satisfactory to the consumer, nor indeed of the nature, the substance, or the quality demanded. Thus, it is essential that there be a proper link between the Sales Planning and Production Planning Departments, and that the moment sales fall production should be reduced or stopped in order to avoid stock-piling of product, which may ultimately become unsatisfactory. The second point is efficient feedback from the consumer to the Quality Assurance Manager, and this must come through the Marketing Department and through the complaints procedure. The majority of complaints will, of course, be of a technical nature in terms of poor manufacture, of foreign bodies in the product, of a product which has been badly kept by the shopkeeper. However, there is always a body of complaints concerning the nature, substance, and quality of the actual product. These will be an indication of the consumers' dissatisfaction with the product as such. Thus, if a large number of complaints are coming back from the consumer to the effect that the product is unsatisfactory because it is not reaching him as was intended by the writer of the manufacturing instruction, then the Quality Assurance Department must rapidly snap into action to find out why the Production Department is not making the product according to instructions.

Summing up, the quality requirements of the market are that the consumer shall receive for his money a product that meets his expectations in that it is nice to eat and is in all respects of the nature, substance, and quality demanded.

REFERENCES

1. Gorsuch, T. T. (1978). *IFST Proc.*, **11**, pp. 126–9.
2. Bell, W. J. and O'Keefe, J. A. (1968). *Sale of food and drugs*, 14th edition. London: Butterworths.
3. *Professional Conduct Guideline No. 1*, '*Wholesomeness of food*', IFST, 1975.

DISCUSSION

Mr. P. E. Stevens (Blackpool College of Technology and Art) said that while the last paragraph of the paper defined the ultimate requirement of the market as represented by the consumer, there was a critical need to identify accurately the nature of the market in which a specific product is offered. This nature has a major influence on the quality characteristics of the product and the standards set for them.

Quality Assurance (QA) staff find themselves operating between the marketing and production functions and in contact with the consumer through complaints. In this situation QA has many responsibilities and he asked if the role of consumers' representative should feature in the QA function as well as that of legal expert.

Mr. J. R. *Blanchfield* (Bush Boake Allen Ltd) asked if the consumer distinguished between variation and variability in a product. He suggested that consumers would use variation when referring to different types, possibly under the same brand name, of a particular kind of product, for example a stiff variety of peanut butter and a soft one. In contrast, they would use variability in perhaps a derogatory sense and apply it to a product which they expected to be consistent but which differed from time to time.

Mr. D. E. *Blenford* (Hildon Associates) asked whether, having accepted the definition of quality as something which met the consumers' expectations, we are in receipt of adequate details of those expectations. To use the expression 'value for money' begged the question because it was influenced by factors other than product quality. Packaging and advertising lead to consumer expectations, and hence greatly influence the perceived 'value for money'.

An important source of information, which reflects consumer satisfaction or otherwise, is complaints. However difficult it may be to design, effective research is necessary to establish what leads to consumer satisfaction and thereby enable products which will achieve it to be offered to the consumer.

Mr. R. L. *Stephens* (Marks & Spencer Ltd) said that it is important for food control to ensure a product of given quality meets the expectations of the consumer as defined in the paper. Questions relating to new products and market research concerning them are less important matters for food control. Consumers are becoming increasingly sensitive about the 'purity' and nutritional status of foods. This sensitivity is reflected in their attitudes towards additives of all kinds and to minor components of nutritional significance such as cholesterol and polyunsaturated fats.

Mr. P. O. *Dennis* (Brooke Bond Liebig) commended the definition of quality given by Dr. Slater and said that the definition given in Bell and O'Keefe's *Sale of food and drugs* was coloured by the attitude of enforcement authorities. For legal purposes, particularly those concerned with prosecution, quality has a fairly clear and narrow meaning; it is any existing legal standard or in its absence any standard an enforcement authority suggests and can persuade a court to accept. This kind of standard is not that of the market place, or that applied by consumers.

In his mind there is an absolute distinction between variation and variability. The usual practice in industry is to try to establish a brand image and develop brand loyalty. This is done by making a product which differs from that of the competition and is offered as a variation of it. The variation, however, is made to as consistent a quality as possible, that is with minimum variability so that the purchaser always gets what is expected. Variability is not under the control of the purchaser and is not usually wanted, whereas variation is under the purchaser's control and can be used to introduce change when it is wanted.

Mr. A. Turner (Cadbury Typhoo Ltd) distinguished between product safety in an ethical or legal sense and product safety as meant in the market place, where a general concern with additives and food composition is the usual consideration. It is for market research to determine the attitudes, expectations and requirements of the consumer towards these subjects. When market research has determined the market requirements, these should be written into the product specification and it is then up to the control function to produce a wholesome, safe product.

He asked what criteria could be used to judge the level of complaints that could be considered minimal.

Dr. C. A. Slater replied that the food controller must look after the interests of the company concerned, the consumer, and himself. If he does not the consequences are fairly obvious and he will soon cease to be a food controller.

He agreed that there has been a loss of variation in products. There are many causes for this, one being the pressure of legislation which requires an accurate description of the product together with a list of ingredients. His company makes two grades of peanut butter, a smooth one and a granular one, and there appears to be a small minority market for an oily form of the product. Some years ago his company produced an oily product but they had innumerable complaints about it.

The consumer is certainly influenced by packaging and advertising, but eventually only repeat purchases confirm that the product meets the quality requirements of the market.

Product development cannot be isolated from the control function because it is an essential part of the product development to include the control system necessary to achieve the specified product quality.

Some consumers and consumerists seem to believe food manufacturers to be irresponsible but, for obvious reasons, reputable manufacturers do their best to prevent injury to the health of their customers. This was his answer to consumerists. Food additives are only chemical substances and all food is nothing more than a mixture of chemicals, even as we ourselves are.

The only way of knowing that a level of complaint has reached a minimum is when there are none. By then the customer will have probably disappeared as well.

Mr. Turner suggested that the comparison of the numbers of complaints in various product areas might suggest an excessive number for one of them and point to faults in the production of a product.

Dr. Slater did not altogether agree. Complaints arise for a great variety of reasons and there is no way of determining the number of dissatisfied customers who do not complain. Sometimes a fault is already known, for example, grease derived from the machines making chocolate blocks is known occasionally to contaminate the base of the block and a consumer complaint tells one nothing that is not already known. Even if the production of one factory has more complaints of a particular nature than another, this may only be a reflection of the use of older machines, an already known fact. Great care is necessary in the interpretation of complaints, if they are to yield useful information.

6

Constraints of Cost

EDWARD DRUCE

Chief Chemist, RHM General Products Ltd

INTRODUCTION

Practitioners of quality control are not normally expected to be accountants. However, everybody involved in the manufacture of food readily appreciates that the manufacturer of food stays in business only as long as his product satisfies the customers, and, as customers, everyone appreciates that value for money is an essential part of the general satisfaction. Indeed, in defining the term 'product quality'—a vital definition in the context of this symposium—emphasis is always put on the fact that quality does not have the popular meaning of best in any absolute sense, but should be regarded, more aptly, as 'best for certain customer conditions'.

These conditions embrace two concepts, the first being the way the product is to be used; that is the way in which most purchasers regard quality, including those external parameters which have been referred to in other papers in this Section under the general heading of constraints, such as the requirements of the legislation in terms of composition and wholesomeness and tradition. The second concept in the quality definition is the selling price of the product. Product quality cannot be thought of apart from cost, and the development of any form of product or process is thus normally some form of compromise between conflicting requirements.

It is not intended to develop this theme further here, but it must be emphasised, however, as those who are engaged in product development know only too well, that their first and most important task in this respect is to set the level of design and the level of worth of the innovation to be achieved with a particular product that is being developed. Ultimately the total system for the production of the product and its distribution from the factory to the consumer has to be set out, and in any development programme from ideas to production and distribution it is important to define not only the desirable attributes of the product, but also its overall quality. The quality will in turn affect the value of the product to the customer and it will generally be necessary to evaluate several quality aspects to give an understanding of the range of value. At the same time, it is of importance to analyse the costs involved of added quality.

It is an inescapable fact that the production and distribution of foods requires an extensive knowledge by those engaged in the control of the quality of foods. Food science and technology, food law, analytical and microbiological techniques, and statistical methods and their application are basic to those who are responsible for ensuring that quality is designed into and maintained in products and their production. However, from what has already been said, it is clear that the control of quality also necessitates an understanding of the economic significance of quality activities, and even further be presented as a necessary activity to profit increase.

Publications in this field, however, appear to be largely written by specialists for other specialists, and so tend to deal with refinements in techniques. The object of this paper, is, therefore, to review the costs of quality in general terms.

THE WORTH OF A PRODUCT TO THE CUSTOMER AND THE COST OF ITS QUALITY

The problem that has to be considered can be stated in the following way. What quality of a particular product must be achieved to reach a certain value at a certain cost, or, alternatively, what quality can be improved to increase the value of the product at a profitable minimum cost increase?

The minimum quality standards for food products are usually easily defined. They require consideration of such matters as statutory compositional requirements, if they exist, product performance requirements including safety in manufacture, packaging protection, and so on. Thereafter the definition of quality standards becomes more difficult and diffuse, taking into consideration the complexity of all other market characteristics such as brand image, the potential advertising to be given to the product, and the means of meeting any claims about the product imposed thereby. To be able to resolve the problem, it therefore has to be possible to estimate both the value of quality, i.e. the price the customer will be prepared to pay for such quality, and the cost of producing it.

In Fig. 6.1 the relationships of worth and cost against quality are given. We may consider as an example the selection and slicing of vegetables to be used, say, in a canned soup. Particular constraints could be applied to the condition of the vegetables. The degree of precision that each piece could be cut to could be specified, with differing tolerances; as an illustration, 3 ± 1 cm, 3 ± 0.1 cm, or 3 ± 0.01 cm, and so on could be selected. It is obvious that these tolerances represent a range of both high- and low-quality standards. If a low standard is chosen, then it will cost a

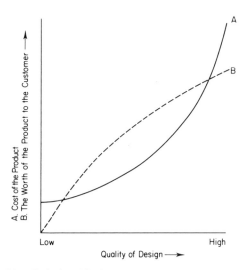

Fig. 6.1.   Relationship between cost and quality of design.

certain amount to produce, because vegetables will have to be bought and the fixed costs of running the factory still have to be met; hence any quality costs something. To increase the standard of quality costs little at first. More attention can be given to supervising the activity of the operators, and the slicing machine can be adjusted to cut the vegetables more accurately and so on. However, if the standard is to be raised further, a limit is reached beyond which neither the capability of the slicer nor the skill of the operators can be increased. Once this occurs the only recourse is to reject the product, and as the standard of quality increases so the costs escalate due to the increased amount of rejection. This is shown in curve A in Fig. 6.1.

We now have to determine what the improvement in quality means to the customer, because this will influence what he is prepared to pay for it and, therefore, its contribution to the selling price. When the standard of quality is very low, it has no value for the customer. In our example of sliced vegetables, irregular appearance and variation in the eating texture would be the outcome of having too low a standard. As the quality rises, the product becomes more acceptable and the price the customer is prepared to pay rises. However, there comes a point where the customer is satisfied with the product and would not be prepared to pay more for any improvement which he cannot appreciate in the vegetable soup (although he could have entirely different requirements and attitudes towards his perception of quality in the case of, say, canned vegetables in brine). This is shown in curve B in Fig. 6.1.

Thus, as the interaction of curves A and B show, there is always an optimum to quality. Above this optimum, the increased cost of achieving a higher quality more than offsets the greater market value of the finished product. Below this optimum, any reduction in the cost of manufacture is more than offset by a still greater reduction in value of the product. Relationships such as that considered here show very clearly that the selection of quality standards, and particularly the choice of tolerances, is an economic decision of the greatest importance since these greatly influence the manufacturing process which is to be used. Optimisation of value to the consumer and the cost of production results in maximum profitability, i.e. the choice of quality standards for which the difference between curves B and A are greatest.

ESTIMATING VALUE TO THE CUSTOMER—SETTING QUALITY STANDARDS

The estimation of value to the customer is not easy, and is perhaps more subjective and speculative because the value may depend very much on what market there is for the product, and clearly market research is a valuable tool in such an evaluation. It is not appropriate to give the detail of how such evaluations can be made, but it is emphasised that once the basic need to ensure that the product will meet its legal requirements has been satisfied, there has to be a close awareness both by marketing and production functions of the factors which can affect worth of quality to the customer, such as change in the consumer's demand, competitor activity, and changes in the economy and the environment. These are influential in setting the quality specification in the design of the product and its production.

ESTIMATING THE COST OF QUALITY CONFORMANCE

The quality specification must clearly be capable of being met by the plant and the operators responsible for producing and processing. This is referred to as the 'quality of conformance' and it relates to the fidelity with which the finished product conforms to the quality specification, its parameters, and tolerances.

There is no precise definition of what is meant by the term 'quality costs', and as almost everything done in the factory has something to do with quality, all costs could be considered as quality costs. However, in order to

TABLE 6.1
Failure costs

Activity	Function involved
Internal failure—	
Scrap	Production
Product giveaway	Inspection
	Material control
Rectification	Production
	Re-inspection
	Material control
Downtime (quality reasons)	Production
	Engineering
Warehouses—inspection	Stores
of finished products in	Inspection
stock	
External failure—	
Complaints	Administration
Return of goods	Administration
Investigation and	Production
analysis	Engineering
	Quality control
Replacement	Quality control and
	assurance
	Administration
Customer liaison	Sales
and compensation	
Warranty	Buying
	Administration

clarify quality costs, it is usual to put them into three main categories, as follows:

1.   *Failure costs* (Table 6.1).
     In this category, we can distinguish between failure found inside the factory, leaving us with consequences for product to be scrapped, or to be recovered and reworked, and their effect on productivity, and external failure where the faulty item has been distributed and reached the customer.
         We can never really tell exactly what the customer displeasure costs us, but clearly it can be considerable. There will be the immediate costs such as time spent in visits, letter writing, and the cost of replacement and reimbursement. In addition, there will be longer term costs such as loss of trade because that customer tells other potential customers how inefficient we are. The loss of goodwill can take years to live down.

2.   *Appraisal costs* (Table 6.2).
     Under appraisal are included all costs incurred in checking during the process of manufacture, and those costs that comprise a final

TABLE 6.2
Appraisal costs

Activity	Function involved
Process appraisal—	
Receiving—raw materials,	Quality control
bought-in finished items	Stores
Line inspection at stages	Quality control
of the process	Production
Inspection equipment	Instrument engineers
maintenance	Quality control
Final appraisal—	
Finished product inspection	Quality control
	Production
	Laboratory
Certification	
Tests—destructive	
Tests—non-destructive	Laboratories
Life/reliability	Consultants, etc.
Environmental	
Inspection equipment	Instrument engineers
maintenance	Quality control

TABLE 6.3
Prevention costs

Activity	Function involved
Quality planning—	
Quality investigation within the design specification in respect of:	Quality control and assurance Production/engineers
Raw materials Methods of manufacture Product characteristics	
Proving, sampling, or other pre-production trials and tests of prototype and processes	Production Quality control R&D technologists
Process control—	
Supplier approval	Quality control Buying
Planning of inspection routines and testing procedures and methods during production processing	Quality control Production Laboratory
Design and approval of inspection	Quality control Laboratory Instrument design
Training of inspectors	Quality control Courses
Specifying storage and handling—special conditions	Production Quality control Stores Transport

check on the finished product. Firstly, process appraisal may be considered. These costs comprise those of implementing and maintaining the system of controlling quality throughout the manufacture, i.e. the processing of the product to the standards set out in the quality specification. Secondly, there are the costs incurred in the acceptance of the product against conformance to the specification. Additionally, in this group of costs are included any concerned with product certification, identification, trials, etc., called for in any planned quality control procedure.

3. *Prevention costs* (Table 6.3).
    These are the costs incurred in planning, setting up and maintaining

a system to ensure conformation to an economic standard of quality.

Costs here may also be considered under two headings. Firstly, there is the planning stage, which normally takes place at the time when product and process development are put into a product specification. Such planning should have four major aspects. The first is to establish production conformance with the development specification, the second is to minimise production problems, the third is to reduce the cost of production, and the fourth is to set economic standards of quality.

Thus, as an example, the evaluation of the role of the raw materials that are to be used is notably an important aspect of quality planning, and value analysis techniques can often point the way to very significant economies, say, in purchasing raw materials.

The second heading under which prevention costs should be considered arise in connection with planning of the system of control to maintain quality conformance throughout the manufacturing and processing of the product as distinct from the appraisal costs incurred in operating the system.

In Tables 6.1–6.3 an attempt has been made to provide checklists indicating the major sources of the costs that arise from failure, appraisal, and prevention. Clearly, every company must determine the significant items in this figure which it will include in its quality costs and develop the quality cost structure best suited to its particular needs.

THE PRINCIPLE OF MINIMUM OVERALL QUALITY COSTS

Having considered the various sources of costs involved in producing products to a predetermined quality standard, we may now consider their evaluation. The definition of quality embraces the concept of production at an 'economic cost', and this phrase is of considerable significance of planning quality control in the factory. The overall objective is to achieve the required quality standard as cheaply as possible. We therefore turn our attention to the interaction of failure, appraisal and prevention costs on the quality |of| production. This relationship is shown in Fig. 6.2.

The abscissa shows the quality of production expressed as the percentage of work produced in accordance with the quality specification. Thus, 'no defectives' means that everything was produced 'right first time'. On the

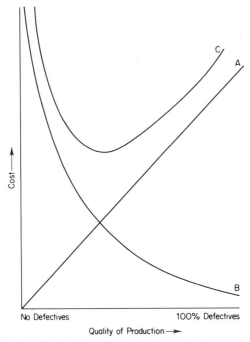

No Defectives   100% Defectives

Quality of Production ⟶

Fig. 6.2.   Costs of maintaining the production specification.

right-hand side is the other extreme, where everything that is produced has failed to conform to the standards that have been set for it. The ordinate represents the cost incurred in quality control activities.

Line A represents the failure and appraisal costs, and is approximately a straight line; it is difficult to pull these costs down once they have started to rise. The reasons for this are fairly obvious. The more defective products that are produced, the higher are the failure costs. The traditional method of meeting higher failure is more inspection. This, of course, results in a higher appraisal cost. This greater degree of inspection does not really have much effect in eliminating the defects. Defective product will still leave the factory and arrive in the hands of complaining customers. Appraisal costs thus remain high as long as failure costs remain high and continue to increase unless there is any successful preventive action.

Let us now consider the costs of preventive activity (curve B). As has already been shown, where there are high failure and appraisal costs, little is being spent on prevention, and the curve is very near the abscissa. Therefore, when prevention costs are increased, to pay for the right kind of quality planning, process control, etc., a marked reduction in the number of products which are defective occurs. Obviously, much greater effort is required to reduce the defectives further, with an appropriate increase in cost. In the extreme case, to require that a factory would never produce any product that did not conform to the specification in every respect, would demand an enormous expenditure. Thus, raw materials would have to be selected to very tight standards; machines would have to be purchased with infinitely better capabilities than those in use; selection, training, and operating standards of possibly the total workforce would need review; all to save a very small percentage of defectives. Thus, applied to curve B, the cost of attaining 'zero defective work' even by preventive means escalates steeply.

It follows that the quality of production obtained should be determined by the minimum overall cost of all control activities, and the addition of the curves for failure and appraisal to that for prevention gives curve C which shows the minimum cost. In such a system, when prevention costs are increased a reduction in the number of defective products occurs. This, in turn, leads to a substantial reduction in failure costs.

A similar sequence of events takes place with appraisal costs. Reduction of defective work in its turn has a beneficial effect on appraisal costs, since defect reduction means a reduced need for routine inspection and other testing.

Finally, when there is an improvement in quality planning, process control, and the performance of personnel (e.g. by better training), an additional reduction in appraisal costs results. The overall result is both a substantial reduction in the total cost of quality activities and an increase in the level of quality. It should, however, be remembered that even within the events that have been described there is a 'minimum cost' of defective work below which it is unprofitable to go. This point is taken up again by David Matthews in his paper (see page 180).

APPLICATION OF QUALITY COSTS

It is, of course, necessary to group the costs obtained into a quality cost report. Some of the data are readily obtainable from the normal accounting system. Others will have to be estimated, but it should be borne in mind that extreme accuracy is usually less important than identifying the principal quality cost sources.

The costs must be analysed if they are to be used as a basis for action. The process consists in examining each cost element in relation to other costs elements and the total. In this way, a number of cost sources which constitute the vital few can be identified and it is these which merit the highest priority of quality control effort to develop a system which eliminates or reduces the effect of these causes by good prevention activities. As has already been shown in Fig. 6.2, a minimum exists for total operating quality costs when the quality cost elements are in optimum balance, and an assessment of costs on a continuing basis is directed at demonstrating the reduction of failure and appraisal costs without a corresponding rise in prevention costs.

It is clear that the analysis of costs that has been made shows that if the principle of *minimum* overall cost is applied, some defective product will always be produced. Nonetheless, there is always a risk that when management becomes over-preoccupied with quantity of production—yield and output—and relatively insensitive to the quantity of defective products produced, it needs some basic motivation to assist the attainment of minimum overall cost. As will probably emerge from other papers in this symposium, the philosophies of 'right first time' or 'zero defects' do serve to achieve this objective.

DISCUSSION

Dr. J. Scholey (Brooke Bond Liebig) emphasised the costly nature of some defects which resulted from faulty distribution or storage of finished goods, particularly if they only become evident after sale of the goods. By the time the goods are finished a considerable part of their value results from the manufacturing and packaging operations. This value will be lost together with part or possibly all of the cost of the raw materials. When the failure is after sale a further cost of replacement is incurred together with almost certain damage to the manufacturer's reputation and sales, which leads to a cost in the form of lost profit making. A significant item in the cost of the control operation is the training of operators. However expert new staff may be, they always need some amount of training in a company's methods of control.

Mr. R. L. Stephens (Marks & Spencer Ltd) agreed with Dr. Scholey and said that although control activities cost money there must be a settled policy and not endless compromises between the controls instituted and the cost of their application. There must be an absolute minimum level below which the degree of control should never fall and always an optimum of control balanced against cost depending upon the quality level aimed at.

Mr. M. Sanderson-Walker (Birds Eye Foods Ltd) asked if it were possible to put a value upon complaints as opposed to their direct costs and to evaluate the consequential losses caused by complaints.

Mr. E. Druce replied that he drew no distinction in his paper between production and distribution cost aspects of control, and agreed with the comments on the cost of failure to control properly at all stages of the food operation. He believed that certain control costs were open to compromise but that others were not, such as those which were necessary to ensure compliance with legislation.

It must also be kept in mind that complaints received were usually only a small fraction of incidents of a similar type which were not reported. This made an evaluation of the consequential costs virtually impossible. Nevertheless, analysis of complaints had a value. The occurrence of foreign bodies was often simply explained and gave an immediate indication of an effective line of investigation, thereby reducing the costs associated with trouble shooting. The 'not quite right' complaint was more difficult to track to its origin but could also yield valuable information such as that the product was not as fresh as one thought or hoped when it reached the consumer.

7

Constraints of Legislation

PETER O. DENNIS

Chief Chemist, Brooke Bond Liebig

INTRODUCTION

The classical reason for climbing a mountain is simply because it is there, but for some of us there is still an element of choice in the matter. Why, then, should a food technologist become involved with legislation?— because with the mountain of legislation on food, there is no choice. We do not even have to go to it, it will surely come to us, and indeed compel us to climb its multiplicity of twisting slopes and pick a way through the tangle.

In recent years a new type of climber, the industrial technico-legal guide and mentor, has developed in response to the need for scientific and technical knowledge and experience to pick a way through the tangle. The legislators know the objectives of the laws they construct, the lawyers know how to construct them and the courts will interpret them and state the final result, but usually none of these bodies knows much about the effects the legislation may have on the control operation in the food industry.

This makes the industrial technico-legal function an onerous and even powerful one, because in conjunction with the legislators it:

1. Helps to create law by offering expert knowledge and experience of the composition, manufacture, and market demands of the products which the law seeks to control.
2. Gives expert opinion on standards and their enforcement.

On the industrial side:

1. It must be able to interpret already enacted laws and regulations which it may have helped to formulate.

2. It must be able to identify any form of risk a manufacturer may be taking and devise control systems to minimise or eliminate it.
3. In the last resort of the risk which has been accepted proving to be a bad one, its expertise may be the only defence between the accused and the consequences of conviction.

We are concerned with the industrial aspects of the legislative constraints upon the food operation, but it must not be forgotten that the contributions to the law process come from other sources, such as the enforcement authorities, legislators, and consumers, although they are not part of our present subject.

It is perhaps worth mentioning briefly, and without going into the full procedures, some of the ways by which food law is formulated and the involvement in this of the food technologist.

National law in Western Europe is drawn up by the appropriate Government Department, usually after consultation with its own scientists and technologists, industry, the enforcement authorities, consumers, and Government-appointed independent expert committees. In the UK there exist professional bodies of food technologists and analysts such as the Institute of Food Science and Technology and the Association of Public Analysts. These organisations are consulted during the course of drafting legislation.

For example, in the UK the industrial representations may be made by individual companies and their food technologists, but more usually by a trade association representing a sector or sectors of the food industry. The food technologist is certain to play an important part in shaping the views presented by the trade association. The representations can be made directly to the Government, but more usually one of the independent committees of experts which advise the Government seeks the industry's opinions before making its recommendations to the Government. Further industrial opinion is expressed after any reports are issued, and before and after draft legislation is published.

The formulation of EEC food law follows a similar pattern, although it differs in some details. As a result, the food industry has two methods of approach to the Commission of the EEC. It can express its opinions via European trade associations to the Food and Agriculture Industrial Committee of the Community (CIAA) and thereby to the Commission, or follow the customary procedure employed within its own country to make its views known to its national government whose representatives participate directly in discussions with the Commission and in the EEC

Council Working Parties. The Commission drafts its proposals for legislation after considering the official views of the governments of Member States, the general views of the European industry and those of the European consumers, but the final formulation of proposals is the work of a committee of government representatives, chaired by the country holding the Presidency of the Council of Ministers. As a consequence, the chair rotates once every 6 months.

For practical purposes there is no international food legislation. There is, however, an international organisation, the Codex Alimentarius Commission, whose work is aimed at drawing up international standards and codes of practice which it recommends to governments for adoption into legislation. It will be obvious that much of the work of this Commission is highly technical, and although its committees are composed of official government representatives, they are invariably accompanied by technical advisers from the food industry.

We shall look at the broad picture of food production which legislation colours, pick out the coloured areas, and see the constraint that legislation puts on the control systems used in those areas. Before doing so, however, it is worth looking at the reasons for the legislation because, if these are understood, they give clear pointers to the areas of the picture in which the control systems are likely to be affected.

Putting to one side any political and economic (some would say devious) reasons, the simple explanation is the now popular battle-cry of '*the protection of the consumer*'. Its universal popularity and adoption as a reason for action is a relatively new phenomenon, but as a philosophy and in its fundamental principles it is as old as trading itself, notwithstanding the principle of *caveat emptor*. A secondary, but important, effect of food law when properly enforced is the protection of the honest manufacturer and trader against unfair and dishonest competition. The phrase 'protection of the consumer' covers a wide field and we must define it more clearly for the purpose of food control.

I make no apologies for quoting Sections 1(1) and 2(1) of the UK Food and Drugs Act 1955, not only because I think they may be considered the foundation stones on which UK food law is built, but I think also they represent the most concise and best legislative statement anywhere in the world of the basic principles and philosophy which should motivate legislation concerning food. With the exception of a reference to quantity, the framework of these two Sections is, I contend, sufficient to cover all aspects of safety and fraud as applied to the manufacture and sale of food.

UK FOOD AND DRUGS ACT 1955

Section 1(1)

'No person shall add any substance to food, use any substance as an ingredient in the preparation of food, abstract any constituent from food, or subject food to any other process or treatment, so as (in any such case) to render the food injurious to health, with intent that the food shall be sold for human consumption in that state'.

Section 2(1)

'If a person sells to the prejudice of the purchaser any food or drug which is not of the nature, or not of the substance, or not of the quality, of the food or drug demanded by the purchaser, he shall, subject to the provisions of the next following section, be guilty of an offence'.

After a moment's thought, I think it can be accepted that even any advertising connected with a foodstuff is at least partially controlled within the phraseology 'not of the nature, or not of the substance, or not of the quality of the food ... demanded by the purchaser'. We may assume, therefore, that legislation is designed primarily to ensure that food is safe and not sold fraudulently. This leads us to consider, firstly, the whole process of food manufacture from beginning to end, and secondly, the marketing and sale of the finished product.

Any division we make of a food manufacturing process is bound to be arbitrary because the whole operation must be the integrated result of a team effort, and contraints in one sector will spill over and affect the work in the others. For convenience, we shall consider the operation starting with the raw materials and the manufacturing sequences leading to the finished product offered for sale on the shop shelf. Inevitably, we shall have to deal with considerations in one area which may appear more properly to be the concern of another.

RAW MATERIALS AND INGREDIENTS

The beginning of any food manufacturing operation is to be found in a field or in water from which either crops are harvested or animals culled. Whatever the environment, legislation of concern to the food controller begins there. Both crops and animals can be improved by special feeding and protection from pests and disease. Special feeding may involve additions to the soil or foodstuffs, and protection by the use of pesticides and therapeutic substances. Here, then, is the food controller's first point of constraint and it includes the environment itself because both soil and water are susceptible to contamination.

Whether a company grows its own raw materials, or has them grown under contract, the crop is under the control of the using company which, if it is wise, should specify the agricultural and therapeutic chemicals to be used. However, the majority of manufacturers buy most of their raw materials on the open market and know little of their origins. The use of chemicals such as fertilisers, pesticides, and feeding supplements is controlled by law in most countries and, significantly for the food controller, residues of these chemicals in the crops or animals are also subjected to legal limitations.

The problem is not as simple as knowing what is permitted in qualitative and quantitative terms. For example, DDT was once a permitted and very widely used pesticide but is now restricted on a world-wide scale. However, owing to its great stability—and hence persistence—DDT is still to be found in some crops and the fat of some grazing animals.

For raw materials, therefore, the food controller must make himself aware of the agricultural chemicals he may use or encounter, and take steps to institute control over them. This may range from in-house control of the types and quantities used in company warehouses and on company estates, through specifications laid down in contracts for supplies of raw materials, to the ultimate method of analysing all materials before use for such things as pesticide residues, hormones in animal fat, and antibiotics in poultry or milk. However, the examination of raw materials for legal compliance does not end here as, together with all purchased ingredients, they will be subject to the general legal requirements concerning the presence of various contaminants, and additives.

Thus the amount of lead, arsenic, or mercury occurring as adventitious contaminants, and of antioxidants and preservatives, etc., deliberately added but permitted in a food or an ingredient, will be limited. We shall return to these types of contaminants and additives when we consider the product and its composition, but it is as well to remember that the earlier control is introduced into the food manufacturing operation, the easier it is to maintain control during the later stages of the process, and the more effective the result on the ultimate product.

We have dealt with certain aspects of the cultivation of raw materials and then jumped to the harvested products ready to use. There is, however, a time between harvesting and the issue of the materials from the ingredients store. For vegetables and some fruit (certainly apples, pears, and oranges) the crop may be surface-treated with materials to prevent deterioration in storage or protracted transport. Treatment agents such as the antioxidant ethoxyquin, or scald inhibitors (for example, diphenylamine) and wax and colour for oranges, are all subject to legislative control. Animals present a very much more complicated situation than vegetable crops. Whereas the circumstances and conditions in which fruit and vegetable harvesting may take place are not a legislative worry to the food controller, animal slaughter is. Animals for human consumption must not die, they must be killed. The potential dangers associated with animal foods were recognised so early in man's history that measures to combat them became folklore and religious ritual long before organised legislative control was introduced. The official ante- and post-mortem inspections, together with the method of slaughter of an animal, are all subject to legislation. Every country has legislation covering some, if not most, aspects of meat production from the live animal. These may be animal and carcase inspection, the construction of slaughter houses and abattoirs, storage temperatures of meat, treatment of offal, and disposal of waste products. The list is too long to pursue in detail; suffice it to say that because the manufacture of food from animals of all kinds could result in products injurious to the health of the consumer, it is a highly coloured area in our picture of food production. The food controller is indeed constrained, that is to say compelled, to set up a very detailed control system when dealing with flesh foods, particularly if he starts with a live animal. The constraints do not finish when the meat reaches a cold store. The meat has to be handled and processed before it becomes a meat product, and the legislation ensures, again by controlling the conditions and circumstances of the handling and processing operations, that microbiological hazards and general contamination resulting from poor hygiene and plant construction do not put initially sound meat at risk, or lead to potentially dangerous products.

Exactly the same considerations must be applied to every food ingredient. A great deal of food legislation is general in its scope and covers all foodstuffs, so-called horizontal legislation; other legislation controls specific products and their derivatives, so-called vertical legislation. Horizontal legislation covers raw materials and ingredients, and the food controller must be aware of the regulations concerning such things as preservatives, emulsifiers and stabilisers, antioxidants, colours, and other additives, together with legislation covering contaminants such as arsenic, lead, pesticides, and other residues, and legislation dealing with hygiene and microbiological standards.

Depending upon the types of raw materials and ingredients used in the manufacturing operation, the next point at which legislation may place a constraint upon the control operation may be the office of the architect and engineer designing an abattoir and meat-handling facilities. If a company buys in all its raw materials and ingredients from independent suppliers, the first point at which the practical effects of legislative constraint will operate will be in the buying office. The specifications supplied to the buying office could simply require that materials purchased comply with all legal requirements. This solution, that is purchase under warranty, might be adopted in the absence of knowledge of the legislation, but would then, of course, be no better than demanding that all cats in the kingdom of the blind shall be ginger. The food controller must be able, with the legislation in view, to set his specifications to conform to it, and set up some form of system by which he can verify that the raw materials and ingredients comply.

We accepted at the beginning that our division of the food operation was arbitrary and to deal with packaging and plant purchase outside the manufacturing and packaging operations may seem out of context. However, on the principle that the sooner things are done correctly the less trouble and fewer problems there will be further along the line, we shall ensure that before packaging taint or excessive contamination occur in our product, we shall purchase suitable packaging and easily cleaned plant.

The food we are producing will almost certainly be packaged. Few packaging materials are totally inert and those usually used in the food industry, such as plastics, lacquers, tin-plated steel cans, paper, and board, are certainly not. It is hardly surprising, therefore, to find legislation covering the possibility of contamination of food by its packaging. Apart from the horizontal legislation previously referred to, which will put a constraint on, for example, the migration of lead into food from a can seam, or perhaps sulphite from paper or board, there is both legislation and proposed legislation specifically covering materials and articles in contact with food. Polyvinyl plastics, for example, are controlled in many countries such that they may not contain more than $1 \cdot 0 \, \text{mg} \, \text{kg}^{-1}$ of vinyl chloride monomer, and this may not contaminate a foodstuff to an extent greater than $0 \cdot 01 \, \text{mg} \, \text{kg}^{-1}$ of the foodstuff. It must also be remembered that even 'inert' materials will contaminate if they are breakable, such as glass. Lines involving the filling of glass containers must incorporate special precautions to prevent glass chips getting into the product and contaminating it with 'foreign bodies'.

A historic example of contact contamination is the high lead content in beer made from soft water which has passed through lead pipes. This brings us to the plant and machinery. In this area legislation abounds and is so diverse that it is arguable as to who should or might be responsible for compliance with it, but at the end of the day the food operation as a whole will have to comply with it and management must make sure the responsibilities are allocated. Whoever receives them, the food controller must be aware of the problems and know the solutions.

There are four broad classes of legislative requirements which must be borne in mind when plant and machinery are being purchased and installed:

1. There is specific food legislation controlling the limits of contaminants in food, and this will put a constraint on the materials of construction of the plant and machinery and the lubricants used in them. The mineral oil content of foods is controlled in most countries.

2. Hygiene requirements may specify, in a general way, plant design, temperatures of hot water supplies, or air temperatures in rooms where special operations are carried out, for example, meat-cutting rooms and refrigeration temperatures.

3. Factory and building legislation is frequently very broad in its requirements, but sometimes contains specific details in the case of food factories. There is often specific legislation relating to food premises in general and, of course, to abattoir and animal (including fish) processing plant in particular. Such items as materials of building construction, floor and wall surfaces, drainage, effluent disposal, and washing facilities are usually dealt with in this kind of legislation.

4. Health and safety regulations, continually increasing in extent and stringency, could put such a restraint on a machine as to make it unusable. The use of many substances such as tenderising enzymes in powder form or insecticide aerosol sprays can constitute a hazard. Similarly, solvents may enter into a process and lead either to a fire risk or to a toxic hazard.

It must now be obvious that it is simply not possible to compile an ideal model of planned allocation of responsibilities to deal with all the legislative requirements. This is a very serious constraint which the corpus of legislation, simply by its existence, puts on the whole food operation and demands that management takes specific steps to integrate its control systems into the management structure.

The raw material buyers, packaging buyers, and engineering buyers could, of course, be given rigid specifications, be told to buy against them and refer all queries back to someone else, but think of the time involved and the work and problems this would cause. I will pursue this theme no further because later papers, particularly those in Session III ('The Interfaces'), will deal with this kind of problem, which is one of general management.

RESEARCH AND DEVELOPMENT

As with packaging and plant purchasing, to deal now with R&D after the raw materials and ingredients may seem out of sequence, but it is difficult to do anything until there are materials with which to work. With the exception of the development of new materials such as novel proteins, the activities of R&D are concerned with known raw materials and ingredients. During the first practical creative steps taken by the R&D Department to formulate and make a prototype product, it should be assumed that the materials used and any process devised (if it is to be operated on existing plant) comply with the legal requirements. Many legal constraints do not apply to R&D activities as such but will do so ultimately should the products be offered to the consumer by sale or otherwise (e.g. free samples for market research purposes). The legal requirements must therefore be borne in mind throughout the development process and applied to R&D activities as appropriate, not forgetting that the marketing platform, from which a product is to be launched, must meet such legal constraints as those controlling vitamin, mineral, and nutritional claims. It would be pointless to develop a product which relied for its shelf stability upon more than the legally permitted amount of a particular additive, or did not comply with some compositional standard. Therefore, legislation puts a constraint on R&D work and is another factor which must be built into the control of research and development.

THE PRODUCT

All the vertical and horizontal legislation will apply to the product. Vertical legislation concerning a particular product will probably be a compositional standard requiring perhaps a minimum quantity of meat in a meat product or butterfat content in a dairy product, etc., but may include process requirements, such as times and temperatures of heat treatment. It may also control reserved names, labelling requirements, and so on for the product.

A consideration for companies which export their products will be the formulation if possible of internationally acceptable products. However, even within the limited sphere of the EEC it is only after long negotiations and with great difficulty that the product long known and sold as 'Chocolate' in the UK was permitted by national derogation in Denmark, Eire and the UK. This is because, even though UK chocolate complies with the EEC legislation with regard to the cocoa content, it also normally contains up to 5% of vegetable fat.

The legislation in a number of countries is coloured by religious considerations; obvious examples are Israel, India, and Mohammedan countries. It may, therefore, be extremely difficult, if not impossible, to formulate a universally acceptable product.

Having classified the product and consulted the relevant legislation, the controller can determine the appropriate designation, or reserved denomination, which may be allowed to be applied to the product. If such a product title or description is applied, the product must surely be made to comply with the appropriate compositional standards. It is an interesting question as to whether or not the reverse is true, namely that if a product happens to comply with a compositional standard, it must be described as, or given the appropriate designation or reserved denomination of, a product associated with that standard. Without doubt, increasing attempts will be made to ensure that this is so by definitions requiring particular designations. I do not believe that this is effectively so at present. I know of no European or American case law on this point.

An extension of these two positions is that of a product which resembles another for which a compositional standard exists but does not itself meet the standard and then is sold under a name or description which is not a reserved designation or denomination. I believe that under UK law at least, a manufacturer may make any product he chooses and sell it; providing he describes it correctly and does not market it in a misleading way.

Two UK examples are the 'minceburger', which does not comply with the standard for meat and cereal product commonly known as beefburger or hamburger, and the product Outline, which is sold as a 'low-fat spread' and has all the appearances of margarine but does not meet the compositional standard for it. I am told, however, that it is illegal to make and sell some products (e.g. low-fat ice-cream) regardless of the name given to the product. I find this extremely difficult to accept.

The point to be emphasised is that, apart from general horizontal requirements applicable to all foods, the vertical legislation may put very considerable restraints on the title which can be given to certain products in relation to their composition. Because of the present trend to produce compositional standards for a wide variety of foodstuffs, this is an area in which the food controller needs to be fully aware of new and impending legislation. There is obviously a feedback point here to the R&D activities in product formulations.

THE PLANT AND PROCESSING

We have to some extent already covered the constraints applied by legislation to the plant and processing used in the manufacture of foodstuffs. But to recapitulate and extend that cover we have a further look at the effects on the control system of both the horizontal and vertical legislation. Contamination of foods by adventitious additions is the subject of much horizontal legislation. Heavy metals are well known, obvious, and dangerous contaminants. Nevertheless, I once saw a vacuum band dryer being used in the manufacture of a food product and the travelling band was made of phosphor-bronze. There were problems of oxidative rancidity of fat in the product! Any part of the processing machinery may be a source of contamination, either of the type just referred to, or of such gross contamination as nuts, springs, etc., which break off during the manufacturing process. Plant and machinery must be cleaned and the detergents/sterilising agents employed may be controlled by specific legislation or covered by the general consideration of being possibly injurious to health if residues of them enter food.

Vertical legislation may well cover processing details such as heat treatment for canned products or other products which are generally accepted as either shelf-stable or semi-preserved. Regulations may also lay down specific methods of observing or recording a parameter such as demanding a mercury-in-glass thermometer on an autoclave or a processing time recorder, even though a recording thermocouple is also installed. There will almost certainly be legislation controlling the quality of water used, both for addition to the product and that used purely as processing water for washing plant and cooling cans.

Finally, there is the general horizontal legislation previously mentioned such as Health, Hygiene, and Safety Regulations and legislation concerning the environment, all of which apply to the manufacture and handling of food in the processing plant. This type of legislation puts a constraint upon food manufacturing plant and machinery and necessitates that both their design and operation be controlled. Most food manufacturing plants generate effluent in solid, liquid, or gaseous form. We need go no further than a meat-processing plant associated with its own abattoir to appreciate the problems that waste and its disposal create with regard to the requirements to control the biological oxygen demand of effluent and the requirements of the Clean Air Act and similar legislation. Pickle and acid-hydrolysed protein manufacturers have obvious effluent problems concerning the pH of discharged liquids and vented gases.

PACKAGING

All the constraints we have considered for processing can be carried forward to the packaging operation. A further complication lies in the packaging materials and we have already drawn attention to these in the raw materials section. Packaging produces units of the product and this immediately takes us into the area of weights and measures.

The earliest historical records relating to trade chronicle the punishment meted out to merchants who gave short quantity. Modern trading also is very much dominated by quantity, and quantity is very much dominated by legislation. In some countries national legislation may require approved and stamped machines to be used in the manufacturing and packaging operations. It is more usual, though, for the law to require stamped apparatus to be used in the market place to determine weighed-out quantities of product offered for retail sale to the ultimate purchaser. We will return to this point later under two basic systems of weights and measures enforcement.

The controller must ensure that the amount of his product in a packaged unit complies with the quantity declared on the packet. This quantity may itself be controlled by legislation; thus tea, coffee, bread, flour, honey, sugar, etc., may be sold only in prescribed quantities in very many countries, whereas pre-packed sausages, cheese, canned foods, etc., are allowed to be sold in any quantity convenient to the packer. In the interests of consumerism, however, there is much activity to extend the application of prescribed quantities to the standardisation of containers such as jars, bottles, and cans.

The controller's problems are not over when he has determined the quantity he may pack and his method of measurement. Accuracy must comply with one of two systems. The older minimum weight system still applies in a few countries, including the UK for some products. This requires that at the point of sale the quantity offered shall not be less than the declared or prescribed quantity, with certain sampling provisions arising from actual wording of the Weights and Measures Act. The more universal average system was adopted by the UK in 1980. The main difference between the two systems is the method of enforcement. Under the average system the actual quantity sold must on average be the prescribed or declared quantity. Limits of deviation of the actual weight from the declared weight are laid down. The number of permitted underweight, or indeed overweight, packs is limited and the limit of deviation beyond which a pack becomes illegal is also prescribed. Because of the statistical nature of the enforcement procedure, the control and enforcement must be carried out at the packing station and not at the point of sale. Within the average weight system it is imperative for the manufacturer's own protection to have approved and stamped equipment available to the packing operation, even if only for use as a reference standard and to set his check weighers which may not be acceptable for approval as legal weighing machines and stamping. In some areas the food controller has various fairly effective methods of exercising control such as warranties, official inspection and approval, and analyses carried out by consultants, but for weight he has no option other than to carry out the control and keep the control records in his own plant.

Packaging involves labelling and, as we shall see later, this is heavily controlled by legislation. Labelling legislation requires packaging to be designed so that at least certain information on the label of the foodstuff is visible at the time of purchase. A popular form of packaging is shrink-wrapping over a shallow tray. Although the shrink-wrapping is transparent the edge of the tray may obscure information on the packs within it. Should the shrink-wrapped unit be sold through cash and carry, an offence would be committed if the information required by law were not visible at the time of purchase.

DISTRIBUTION AND STORAGE

The only legislation which consistently affects distribution and storage and is normally of consequence to the food controller concerns hygiene and date-marking. Hygiene regulations may apply, as for meat and open-pack meat products, also to the vehicles used for distribution. They must be kept clean and not used to transport other types of products simultaneously with meat. The temperature in a refrigerated van may be controlled by a hygiene regulation which has a general requirement that the temperature of a product never exceeds an upper limit. Direct contact by meat and some meat products with the floor and sides, etc., of a vehicle is prohibited in most countries. It is evident that in distribution and storage the food controller has another coloured area in his picture. If, however, his control system is guided by the general principles that his products are stored and distributed so that they cannot become injurious to health, he will have achieved most of the legislative requirements.

Indirectly other legislation affects the organisation of stores and distribution systems. In many countries it is a legal necessity to be able to identify any batch of production so that, if necessary, it can be isolated or recalled after distribution. This kind of legislation has been drawn up in the interests of health and safety but will, however, be advantageous under the average weight system. For example, if a batch is systematically 3% underweight, it may well be possible, within the statistical requirements of the system, to mix the batch with other suitable batches to achieve a satisfactory overall result, although in the long run the underweight will have to be made up so that the average is met. Another indirect but important effect of weight legislation upon distribution and especially storage is the requirement under the minimum weight system to allow for loss of weight caused by evaporation of volatiles, usually water, from a final product. This is not usually a great problem but has caused trouble with some products, particularly more or less open-packed ones, for example some meat products and bakery products. These difficulties disappear under the average weight system.

The minimum durability of a food product will depend on many factors including the conditions under which it is stored and distributed. As we shall see later, the label on a pre-packaged food will, in some circumstances have to carry a date indicating the minimum durability of the product. This period, defined as that during which the product will remain substantially unchanged with regard to its essential characteristics, has to be determined by the packer. Similarly, if the product requires any special conditions of storage or distribution these must also be determined and stated on the label by the packer.

There are at least four low temperature storage conditions in common use: the ordinary domestic refrigerator, which may have a deep-freeze compartment, the conventional deep-freeze cabinet and chilled display cabinet in the retail outlet. Temperatures between $+10\,°C$ and $-20\,°C$ may be encountered within these methods of storage and will affect the life of many products stored within them. Thus, a foodstuff may well carry two or more 'minimum durability' dates, depending upon the temperature of storage and any instructions relating to them.

The EEC Labelling Directive enables Member States to exempt from date-marking food products with a minimum durability of greater than 18 months. This period is obviously going to be a very critical one and manufacturers will, where possible, strive to achieve it for their products. Here, then, is a considerable constraint upon the food controller to ensure that his date-marking is realistic and that conditions of storage and distribution relating to and recommended for it are maintained.

ADVERTISING AND LABELLING

Should the food controller think that having carefully controlled his raw materials, building, plant, machinery, process, production, storage, and distribution systems, his problems are more or less over, he would be sadly mistaken. He has yet to label his product and enter what is probably the most intensely coloured area of his picture. Every country has special legislation concerning the labelling and advertising of foodstuffs. It is always comprehensive and usually extensive in its detail.

It is impossible to make any kind of statement on a label which is not the subject of a piece of legislation. Even the simple, and to my mind innocuous, 'does you good' slogan has been successfully challenged in the UK. Without going into world-wide labelling legislative detail, it is readily apparent that here is an area in which the food controller must have a thorough knowledge. Apart from labelling it concerns advertising and fair-trading legislation, such as the UK Trade Descriptions Acts and Sale of Goods Act. National legislation usually covers the sale, distribution, and labelling of all kinds of merchandise, and unless foodstuffs are specifically exempted the requirements apply to them and cause a real problem in the food labelling area. Legislation concerning trading statements apparently remote from foodstuffs and more applicable to consumer durable articles, for example, may in fact apply to food. Thus, legislation concerning product liability and guarantees may well affect foodstuffs and their labels.

The constraint put upon the control system by labelling legislation raises no principles or problems, in terms of the system itself different from that of other legislation. It is simply more extensive and creates the need for a much greater liaison system. This is readily exemplified by considering what I think is the most comprehensive single piece of labelling legislation yet enacted. It may not be the most detailed (for example, it does not mention actual type size, although this is about the only detail excluded) nor has it yet been incorporated into the legislation of the Member States, but it must become law by the end of 1982 probably in a form not very different from its existing pattern. This triumphal masterpiece of consumerism is the EEC Labelling Directive. If its requirements are considered in terms of the various parts of the manufacturing operations, it will be seen that no part—with the possible exception of some engineering activities—is unaffected. Some of the requirements of the Labelling Directive are as follows:

'*Article* 2
1. The labelling methods used must not
   a. be such as could mislead the purchaser, particularly
      i. as to the characteristics of the foodstuffs and, in particular, as to its nature, identity, properties, composition, quantity, durability, origin or provenance, method of manufacture or production;
      ii. by attributing to the foodstuff effects or properties which it does not have;
      iii. by suggesting that the foodstuff possesses special characteristics when in fact all similar foodstuffs possess such characteristics.
   b. Subject to the provisions applicable to foodstuffs for particular nutritional uses, attribute to any foodstuff the property of preventing, treating, or curing a human disease, or refer to such properties; Community provisions or, where there are none, national provisions may derogate from this rule in the case of natural mineral waters.
3. The prohibitions or restrictions referred to in Paragraphs 1 and 2 shall also apply to:
   a. the presentation of foodstuffs, in particular their shape, appearance or packaging, the packaging materials used, the way in which they are arranged and the setting in which they are displayed;
   b. advertising.'

'*Article* 3
1. In accordance with Articles 4–14 and subject to the exceptions contained therein, indication of the following particulars alone shall be compulsory on the labelling of foodstuffs:

1. The name under which the product is sold.
2. The list of ingredients.
3. In the case of pre-packaged foodstuffs, the net quantity.
4. The date of minimum durability.
5. Any special storage conditions or conditions of use.
6. The name or business name and address of the manufacturer or packager, or of a seller established within the Community.
7. Particulars of the place of origin or provenance in the cases where failure to give such particulars might mislead the consumer as to the true origin or provenance of the foodstuff.
8. Instructions for use when it would be impossible to make appropriate use of the foodstuff in the absence of such instruction.

2. Notwithstanding the previous paragraph, Member States may retain national provisions which require indication of the factory or packaging centre, in respect of home production.

3. The provisions of this Article shall be without prejudice to more precise or more extensive provisions regarding weights and measures.'

'*Article 5*
1. The name under which a foodstuff is sold shall be the name laid down by whatever laws, regulations, or administrative provisions apply to the foodstuff in question or, in the absence of any such name, the name customary in the Member State where the product is sold to the ultimate consumer, or a description of the foodstuff and, if necessary, of its use, that is sufficiently precise to inform the purchaser of its true nature and to enable it to be distinguished from products with which it could be confused.
2. A trade mark, brand name or fancy name may not be substituted for the name under which the product is sold.
3. The name under which the product is sold shall include or be accompanied by particulars as to the physical conditions of the foodstuff or the specific treatment which it has undergone (e.g. powdered, freeze-dried, deep-frozen, concentrated, smoked) in all cases where omission of such information could create confusion in the mind of the purchaser.'

'*Article 6*
3.a. Added water and volatile products shall be listed in order of their weight in the finished product; the amount of water added as an

ingredient in a foodstuff shall be calculated by deducting from the total amount of the finished product the total amount of other ingredients used. This amount need not be taken into consideration if it does not exceed 5% by weight of the finished product.'

'*Article* 7
1. Where the labelling of a foodstuff places emphasis on the presence or low content of one or more ingredients which are essential to the specific properties of the foodstuff, or where the description of the foodstuff has the same effect the minimum, or, as the case may be, maximum percentage used in the manufacture thereof shall be stated.

    This information shall appear either immediately next to the name under which the foodstuff is sold or in the list of ingredients in question.'

'*Article* 8
4. Where a solid foodstuff is presented in a liquid medium, the drained net weight of the foodstuff shall also be indicated on the labelling. For the purpose of this paragraph, "liquid medium" means the following products, possible in mixtures, provided that the liquid is merely an adjunct to the essential elements of that preparation and is thus not a decisive factor for the purchase: water, salt water, brine, vinegar, aqueous solutions of sugars and fruit or vegetable juices in the case of tinned fruit or vegetables. Methods of checking the drained net weight shall be determined in accordance with the procedure laid down in Article 15.'

Compliance with these requirements self-evidently will call for extensive liaison by the food controller with every part of the food operation, particularly as there are certain exemptions from some of the requirements while in others there is specific detail as to how requirements must be met. Therefore, a detailed knowledge of the product is required in order to know whether or not the exemptions or special requirements will apply to them.

I would refer back to the eight requirements listed under Article 3 taken particularly in conjunction with Article 5.2, and leave the reader to work out the implications behind them in the context of composition, marketing concepts, packaging requirements, product title, and processing. Consider also how they impinge on the parts and stages of the food operation and the liaison system which must be developed to ensure the final food is legally marketed and sold. For example, whereas OXO cubes may at present be sold simply under the UK 30-year rule, in future they may have to be given an appropriate designation because OXO is a trade mark.

The Labelling Directive will only acquire the force of law in the UK when its provisions have been reframed into new 'Labelling of Food Regulations' which will replace many of the provisions of the 1970 Regulations. Extensive discussion of the issues involved and of the area still open for UK regulations outside the terms of the directive, will be found in the Reports of the UK Food Standards Committee resulting from its review of food labelling.

CODES OF PRACTICE

Methods of quasi-legislative control by means of Codes of Practice, more or less voluntarily applied, have been used in the UK with considerable success for many years. They are somewhat peculiarly British and are not readily accepted outside the UK except by the Codex Alimentarius Commission, which can only issue recommendations in any event. Codes for the food industry are drawn up preferably as a result of agreement between manufacturers and enforcement authorities (not a government ministry); alternatively, they are drawn up unilaterally by industry if, as is all too often the case, enforcement authorities cannot agree amongst themselves on the constitution of the code.

They have the merit that they can be simply written using understandable phraseology with an agreed meaning and are not therefore necessarily subject to the courts' interpretation of the words. Not being law, they can be easily discussed by simply calling a meeting of the interested parties and subsequently amended very quickly. Any standards created in them can be taken as the 'nature, substance, and quality' demanded under Section 2 of the UK Food and Drugs Act. At first glance they appear to be a very attractive method of dealing with difficult and complex problems in a simple and understandable way, and up to a point this is true.

In addition to having advantages, codes also have two drawbacks, namely their enforcement and demonstration that they are being complied with. Where standards are laid down in them that can be checked by analysis, codes can be enforced under Section 2 of the Food and Drugs Act. When more intangible requirements are to be met, such as those involving hygiene or processing methods, compliance or otherwise can be demonstrated only by factory inspection and perhaps the keeping of records. However, it can be argued that if these kinds of requirements were enshrined in law, compulsory powers of factory inspection and the demanding of records to be kept would of necessity have to be granted to enforcement authorities. I think this argument is a powerful one and that control can more easily and just as effectively be exercised within a voluntary system of codes of inspection.

SUMMARY

This survey of the constraints started with the natural environment and has pursued a somewhat tortuous course leading to the display on the retail store shelf. In order to summarise the points, the areas and subjects upon which legislation puts its constraints are listed below:

1. Raw materials and ingredients, their composition and con-taminants, handling, and nomenclature.
2. The product, its development, composition and contaminants, process aids, nomenclature, and advertising.
3. The plant and processing, health and hygiene including handling, materials of construction, safety, and processing details.
4. Packaging, the composition of packaging materials, packaging design, and weight control.
5. Storage and distribution, health and hygiene aspects, and general conditions of storage, transport facilities and points of sale.
6. Labelling and advertising, statutory information required, control of voluntary information, label design including print size and pictures, conformity of product title with composition, claims for the product, and the marketing presentation.

The Legislation

We have dealt throughout with generalities and usually little attempt has been made to direct attention or make detailed reference to specific legislation. This is because there is simply too much of it. The following information is an attempt to fill at least in part the obvious gap that this approach has left.

The EEC

Official Journal—*Official Journal of the European Communities*, Series L, Promulgated Regulations and Directives.

This can be obtained from the Office for Official Publications of the

European Communities, Boite postale 1003, Luxembourg, or from H. M. Stationery Office, P.O. Box 569, London SE1 9NH.

The UK
There is no official journal but a Daily List of government publications is published. Copies of this list and published legislation are obtainable from H.M. Stationery Office at the above address.

General
In the UK the British Food Manufacturing Industries Research Association at Leatherhead, Surrey, runs an extremely comprehensive information service which covers most countries of the world and the Codex Alimentarius.

DISCUSSION

Mr. A. Turner (Cadbury Typhoo Ltd) said that sometimes the law is imprecise or may not cover specific aspects of control or quality. The primary objectives of consumer protection and the intention of the law must then be used as guiding principles. A useful point to remember is that in codified law, common in Europe, that which is not specifically allowed is usually illegal unless direct permission to use it is sought and granted.

Because of the construction of UK law, problems with Section 1 of the UK Food and Drugs Act can occur when a decision has to be made as to whether or not an ingredient or process may be injurious to health. The removal of vitamin C during the processing of potatoes might create a potential hazard to health. Many manufacturers have decided it could and take steps to restore the vitamin C level. The discovery of aflatoxin led to the recognition of other potentially dangerous mycotoxins and their possible widespread occurrence in foodstuff raw materials often resulting from bad storage conditions. Food controllers must now decide, in the absence of statutory limits or codes of practice, what forms of control must be introduced and at what level to pitch standards in order to produce safe foods.

Recommendations made by official bodies such as the Food Standards Committee or other government committees do not constitute law but cannot be ignored lightly. They are the result of careful investigation and thought and far more often than not are sensible requirements which if ignored might be a basis for action under the Food and Drugs Act.

A difficult, but important, area of food safety and control on which the law is not detailed, and rightly so, is that of microbiological standards. UK law accepts that prevention is better than cure, the control of an operation is more rewarding than the inspection of the products resulting from the operation. Regulations, sometimes fairly detailed, are aimed, therefore, at securing hygienic and safe conditions for processing, distribution, and sale of food, but no effort is made to impose quantitative microbiological standards on the final products. Such control would afford little protection to the public because of the heterogeneous distribution of organisms in inadequately processed food and hence the difficulty in sampling at significant points in the operation.

The possible exposure of food to infection during storage and sale beyond the control of the manufacturer adds a further difficulty to having microbiological standards for products as sold.

The food controller must therefore specify sanitation procedures, food handling practices, heat treatment, packaging and ensure the delivery of safe products as far as practical at least to the point of sale.

These examples serve to illustrate the practical problems and aspects of meeting the law and complying with its spirit. These may be met by good manufacturing practices and a very useful method of establishing these is a Code of Practice, which may be (and frequently is) agreed with the enforcement authorities. The development of Codes of Practice will inevitably bring food controllers and inspection authorities closer together. Experienced controllers have pre-empted this situation and already established their liaisons.

Professor A. G. Ward (University of Leeds) thought the speaker's references to consumers were less than generous. His own experience was that, in the UK at least, the submission of consumers' views on various aspects of food legislation had been sensible and not specifically directed against industry. Indeed, the articles on food in *Which*, although points were made which industry would not accept, were informative and helpful to consumers. It would be unwise for the food industry not to seek discussions with consumers' organisations, which can be very valuable. We are fortunate in the viewpoints that have been adopted in the UK—a situation by no means always true overseas.

Mr. E. Druce (Rank Hovis McDougall Ltd) asked what could be done to ensure that when a control system is being designed it will incorporate legal defences, such as being able to show that all precautions and due diligence have been taken to comply with the legislation.

Mr. P. O. Dennis agreed completely with Mr. Turner's comments and underlined the necessity to study official documents and opinions in order to gain some insight into the grey areas of legislation which, although involving well understood objectives, contained no detailed methods of achieving them or detailed standards relating to them. He also agreed with Professor Ward's opinion of the expression of the consumer view in the UK. The comments in his paper relate to consumerists and not to consumers or their responsible organisations. In the UK he, too, found consumer organisations perfectly reasonable, although he was not always able to agree with their arguments. On the other hand, some sections of the national press appear only too willing to allow professional consumerists to publicise their biased and usually unjustifiable views and accusations. He also had in mind the outbursts of consumerism in the USA, the subsequent Delaney clause in US food legislation, and the results that had produced.

A properly designed control system will automatically contain built-in defences relating to due care and diligence, because it will require records to be kept to prove that adequate safeguards had been taken. Just as the law is sometimes imprecise in its requirements, it is equally imprecise with regard to the defences the manufacturer might employ, hence his remarks in the paper concerning the expertise of the food controller being perhaps the last resort to save the manufacturer from the more dire results of conviction for an offence.

8

Constraints of the Organisation

JOHN B. M. COPPOCK

Consultant; formerly Director of Research and Scientific Services,
Spillers Ltd

INTRODUCTION

On entering the food industry in 1947, one of the areas which was to attract my attention particularly was its attitude to quality control, including hygiene, and the then novel concept of toxicological knowledge of the additives and treatments in use. The reason for my interest and concern was that having been in charge of technical development in the fine chemicals division of a large pharmaceutical company, I was aware of the very stringent control demanded for the quality of drugs, their freedom from microbiological contamination, the hygiene of their manufacture, and the nature of any toxicological risk associated with their use, e.g. orally, by injection, or by other routes.

PREVIOUS EXPERIENCE OF QUALITY CONTROL IN PHARMACEUTICALS

In the main, the quality of drugs used in human medicine was laid down in the British Pharmacopoeia (BP), the purity, level of contaminants being defined in considerable detail and the edict of the company was that its products had to be equal to or better than the BP specification. If the Chief Analyst found a product was not in all respects up to specification, it was rejected and no pressure by any production manager could be put on him to vary his decision as he was responsible only to the Chairman of the company. Veterinary medicines were prepared to the same high standards; for example, products for injection had to be pyrogen-free in the same way as insulin or other injectable products used in human treatment. A copy of all the complaints came into my hands so the Director of Fine Chemicals Manufacture, to whom my responsibility lay, was immediately made aware of significant problems, such as the slow loss of tricresol through the rubber caps of insulin phials when, during the Second World War, they were exposed to rapidly changing air temperature conditions when crated in aircraft standing on landing strips in the near and far eastern theatres of war, or stored in makeshift warehousing, etc. Management was constrained to find a cure and with the utmost rapidity.

The same attitude was displayed towards the raw materials of production and I recollect the case which had to be made to the Government Chemist to obtain his support for the fact that certain nitration grades of toluene were unsatisfactory for saccharin production, to ensure the Ministry of Supply would authorise purchase of toluene of appropriate specification. A second problem involved obtaining permission from the Customs and Excise to use undenatured alcohol when it was realised that in barbiturate production methylated contaminants reduced the quality below BP requirements which were based on pre-war German imports. One did not apply for a waiver, even in wartime, of the required standards. The main constraints were not managerial, but of suitable plant and equipment, glass-lined vessels were in their early days, pressure vessels equally so. A good chemical engineering department was a necessity and building one's own tailor-made plant was vital; mixing and drying produced many problems, product quality depended very much on success in ingenuity of construction and adaptation and bore many similarities to similar constraints to be found on entering the food industry, many of which still remain. There was, of course, a big difference; in wartime manufacturing was on a 'cost plus' basis, and economic considerations were totally different from peacetime. This introduction may help those who are unaware of conditions in the 1940s to appreciate better some of the comments to be made about the food industry, where in 1947 quality control seemed to a newcomer from the pharmaceutical industry to be backward.

FIRST IMPRESSIONS OF THE FOOD INDUSTRY 30 YEARS AGO

It was clear, however, that the food industry had not been given the priorities that the pharmaceutical industry had enjoyed. Perhaps my first impressions were of antiquated buildings and equipment. My second impression related to the imprecision of defining biological raw materials, in contrast to how one could specify chemical substances. These led to constraints on the organisation that were different from those which I had experienced hitherto, despite my deep commitment in penicillin production, which, of course, depended considerably on biological raw materials, e.g. corn steep liquor, and on the maintenance of pure and active strains of the *Penicillium* species then used first in bottle and later in deep (i.e. fermentation vessel) culture. There appeared, however, to be one big similarity in 1947; both industries seemed to be production oriented and the influence of the accountant and extensive budgetary constraints were only just beginning to be felt. Food rationing was still in existence and the problems of excess capacity were not then apparent. The large food company was the exception rather than the rule, the combines were only just being created, and competition was friendly—one just did not hit at competitors' products by name. Most companies made far more products than they could probably economically justify, but the public was avid for food and the long years of deprivation had produced a demand more for variety than for quality. Many companies relied on consultants and consulting analysts for their quality control and advice, or on the food research associations, who probably were among the first to recognise the new trends, apart from a few very large firms who had laboratories of their own. The consolidating Food and Drugs Act 1955 had not been enacted, there was a 'prohibited' list of food additives and the concept of 'permitted lists' had not spread from the USA to the UK.

Quality matters in food were little discussed in the Boardroom; they were largely left to the Production Manager and the difference from the pharmaceutical industry was both dramatic and disconcerting. Shelf-life requirements, however, were totally unlike those for pharmaceutical products and could vary for foods from a few hours for a cream-based product to many months for a biscuit or canned product. The more one considered these differences, the more it was realised that quality control was related in the food industry to the nature of the products manufactured. At that time only the application of the principles of hygiene appeared to be the common need for the two industries, with the pharmaceutical industry already far ahead in their application. The food hygiene regulations as we know them had not been made and the majority of food establishments had little or no concept of the economics of creating good conditions of hygiene. Opposition to many of the hygiene regulations made under the 1955 Act was vehement. It was the costs that caused the subject of hygiene to penetrate to the Boardroom!

Food laws began to be discussed too, and, when the USA introduced its 'filth test', the consultations among top executives, together with the trade and research associations, immediately stimulated a major need for better hygiene. Thus, one of the constraints, i.e. of under-spending money on hygiene precautions, began to be eroded and no organisation could afford to produce under poor conditions of hygiene without facing going out of business.

In the early 1950s, hygiene considerations and packaging became linked. It was during this period that a number of smaller firms became bankrupt owing to the inability of their Boards to realise the crippling cost of packing a multitude of lines. Rationalisation of production became a constraint on the variety of a company's products and the food industry became increasingly cost conscious. Competition and discounts to large retail organisations, which were increasing their share of the market, dictated a new constraint on the organisation.

FOOD CONTROL AT ABOUT THE TIME OF THE FOOD AND DRUGS ACT 1955

During the period up to the Food and Drugs Act 1955 the various Ministries concerned encouraged bodies such as the Royal Society of Health to set up working parties concerned with all aspects of food hygiene, ranging from abattoir practice to bakers' wares. A number of Codes of Practice were evolved and discussed with particular sectors of the food industry. It was during this period that one very large selling organisation, which did not itself manufacture, began selling food in its stores, and demanded of manufacturers the high standards of hygiene laid down in these Codes. The influence of this policy was enormous. Although there was some resistance in the Boardrooms initially, it soon became evident that those who were prepared to improve their buildings and equipment and install proper quality control, including facilities for microbiological inspection, were going to receive a great deal of trade which otherwise would be lost. If there were feelings of dissatisfaction by the retail chain concerned, the Chairman did not hesitate to contact the Chairman of the manufacturing concern, the technique being reminiscent of the lines of responsibility in the pharmaceutical industry. So quality control, including its hygiene aspects, became an increased concern to the Boards of food manufacturing companies, both the suppliers of raw materials and the manufacturer of the finished product, each of whom were involved in the determination of good quality, including flavour, which the large retail organisation regarded with particular concern. Egg as an ingredient was at that time often associated with off-flavour and one of the constraints placed on the manufacturers was that they had to use egg of a particular origin otherwise their products could be unacceptable. These activities produced a strong side-effect inasmuch as a degree of cost consciousness, which was not then universal, became increasingly applied in the choice of raw materials and the need for adequate specifications also became increasingly apparent. Again, those companies which did not move with the times found themselves selling to the lower end of the market and again, in certain instances, went out of business.

INFLUENCES STEMMING FROM THE CREATION OF FOOD COMBINES

One of the major problems which faced any large retail organisation, and it still remains a concern to anyone involved in product development, was the maintenance of the quality of any product the initial specification of which had been agreed between the two parties involved, i.e. the retailer and his manufacturer. It was in this area, again in the 1950s, that I first discerned that, with the fine margins often involved, pressure could be put by the Company Accountant and the Finance Director on the Production Department to improve margins by saving for example on raw material costs. Such moves nearly all led to a progressive fall in quality, which finally the large retailer realised. On some occasions when, as Director of the British Baking Industries Research Association, I was in the presence of both retailer and manufacturer's staff, I witnessed the sudden removal from the counter of a product whose quality had diminished. Sympathy could be felt in the circumstances for the chagrin of the Production Manager, for example, who received the opprobrium of both sides. Usually a frank discussion of the nature of the constraints or pressures involved resolved the difficulty, but in an organisation which sells products of its own manufacture and where there are no outside restraining influences product quality can suffer, much to the despair of those in the Development Department. This department rightly feels that following the original development, usually done on a pilot scale and in concert with the Marketing Department, such changes have been made that the consumer is no longer getting the product as developed. The influence on morale can be considerable and it can be months before the backlash from this is realised in the Boardroom. It is probably first detected there through personnel changes, although profitability loss is the initial indicator.

Thus, within an organisation quality may vary because of economic considerations, which can be dictated by raw material cost, by pressure on margins, by Boardroom considerations such as the allocation of overheads, by labour costs, labour availability and discipline, and by monetary pressure resulting from accountants' surveillance of total costs, extending from the extent of company cash flow to inflationary pressures. All or some of these may be reflected in the Purchasing Department policy, in product price fixing policies which can depend on market share, in the influence of competitors' practices ranging from discount patterns to 'special offers', and similar new problems, almost non-existent in the 1950s but fast developing in the 1960s. An example is the large retailer who wants to sell 'own-label' products supplied by a manufacturer, from whom is expected a negotiated discount on often identical products sold under the manufacturer's own name and for which he has paid the advertising costs!

Concurrently with these factors was developing the large industrial complex, the company diversifying into many aspects of food manufacture, and sometimes also making products other than foods. This sharpened the realisation that the problems of quality control and the constraints on those responsible for its supervision could differ within the food industry; the bread bakers and the meat-pie manufacturers had products of short shelf-life to consider, whereas the biscuit manufacturer and the canner of peas or beans or fruits had long shelf-life products, but the last of these had particular problems of raw material harvesting. The meat industry again had different quality problems dictated by, for example, slaughtering, chilling, or freezing techniques, stresses on animals in lairage pre-slaughter, etc. The flour miller, although in a much less labour-intensive sector, had unique problems in selecting wheats for milling to provide a reasonably consistent flour grist appropriate for the final baked product. The jam maker had problems affecting quality which began with the horticulturist and his breeding of fruit varieties. The cheese maker had new quality problems to think of when antibiotics were introduced into mastitis treatment and animal feeds and produced residue problems in his raw material, milk. Finally, one realised that related aspects could be part of the quality evaluation of all food products because of their biological origin and the protective measures taken during growing which create residue problems of many kinds. These changes all had to be conveyed to the Boards of companies, who in turn had to rely on the advice of their specialists about the type of constraints affecting their organisation which would confront them in the new circumstances. It was not always easy to realise that systems of food quality control would vary with the type of product manufactured. The central laboratory would become increasingly important for developing analytical and other methodology relevant to microbiological and environmental problems, including mycotoxins; in contrast, the quality control operation itself would frequently require to be decentralised.

Thus, a large organisation could find itself with a variety of quality controllers, e.g. for flour products, baked products, extruded products, canned products for human use or as pet foods, spices and flavours, catering products, and animal feeds, to mention but a few, and each of these would require coordinating in some manner so that conditions of service, holidays, and working conditions were covered just as much as those areas of overlapping methodology. Techniques would require to be defined and undertaken centrally to reduce waste effort and to keep cost to a minimum without limiting efficiency. As most Boards divide the employees, in their minds, simply into the 'spenders' and 'makers', it is clear that harsher constraints tend to be applied to the former. The 'spenders', in times of economic stringency, have to justify their demands with great aptitude, for quality control is always an 'on cost', whether or not it can be partially defrayed by creating a company image which enhances the trust that the consumer has in its products and so increases sales. Such effects, however, can never be uniquely quantified. Boards are also aware of the legislative constraints put on them from various directions, not only by food law. They think, sometimes rightly, that their scientific advisers do not always appreciate these other directions when asked to contribute to and formulate an overall company strategy.

CHANGING TECHNOLOGIES CREATE NEW PROBLEMS

It is not always easy to forecast quality changes which can occur through technological development, either of the product itself or through the effects of changed processing techniques brought about by plant development. A Board must always have in its collective mind, when faced with capital expenditure, whether new concepts or new equipment can render its existing products either obsolete or considerably changed in character. The latter certainly occurred with the introduction of mechanical dough development in dough making. The texture and softness of the resulting bread was materially different from the more open structure of the traditional loaf. The extruded biscuit dough has revolutionised the manufacture of the dog biscuit. When such changes are taking place, with extensive change in capital commitment, the quality controller may well feel, unless he is fully in the picture, that constraints put on him by his directors are militating against the consistency of his products. Again, this is not peculiar to the food industry. One of the technical developments in which my department was involved in the pharmaceutical industry was the production of an improved quality of heavy magnesium carbonate. It was very difficult to keep those operating the old plant from wanting further capital expenditure on it, which would have been an absurdity; that type of constraint, within an organisation, finally affecting quality, requires much managerial time and tact to maintain morale, which in itself is part of quality assurance.

Consistent quality assurance can be linked with the product in the public mind through advertising, particularly visual advertising on the media, but the quality of the product in the pack or in the tin is nearly always subject to one or more pressures of the kind mentioned above. It is these constraints which often leave the quality controller with little influence on the precise nature of the product because of the shifting areas which influence its nature and create difficulty in maintaining precise specifications. Despite this, flavour and texture must reasonably be maintained and legal constraints met. It is the skill of the production director, the manager or the supervisor in coping with all these constraints and the degree of understanding he creates with his quality controllers which finally determine the profitability (or otherwise) of the organisation. It is my own firm belief that in the food industry there can be no 'food pharmacopoeia' and that it is not unreasonable that a quality controller should be responsible to his production director. It is true that in certain areas there can be more precision in control than in others; strict conditions of heating and cooling appropriate to the can size can and must be laid down in the canning industry, equally strict can be the conditions of producing frozen foods, but the biological variations of the raw material at harvesting can have immense effects on the quality of the finished product. Here, as in many other instances, the constraint on quality is often set by the degree of flexibility, for instance the amount of premium that a Board is prepared to pay in the first instance for its raw materials. The quality controller has no option but to work within these limits. In the final analysis, only the consumer and the influence of consumer action groups affect a Board in its decision, and these voices may be far less persuasive than statements of the availability and amount of finance at the time of decision.

INFLUENCE OF CHANGING PATTERNS IN RAW MATERIAL AVAILABILITY

In recent times the demands of developing nations have led to shifts in raw material availability which have dictated constraints within a company's power to purchase the materials it desires and made it seek alternatives. This has been very clear in the manufacture of animal feeds, where consistency of a product is determined more by the ability of a computer, given its terms of reference, such as certain protein and energy constraints, maxima and minima of amino acids, vitamins, and drugs (when required), to select on the basis of the analytical data fed to it which set of current raw materials meet the necessary criteria economically. So, for a broiler food, the ability always to pellet, granule or cube a given set of raw materials may not at this stage be very important. The animal feed controller has had to adapt to these conditions, as indeed has also the Production Manager in his efforts to produce for the rearer or farmer a product of consistent feeding value and nutritional status. Hence, the emphasis made in this paper of the need for a high degree of confidence which must be maintained between the production staff and the quality controller within an organisation.

OTHER CONSTRAINTS, SOME LESS OBVIOUS THAN OTHERS

In broad terms, most large firms (and the author has been associated with one since 1957) set up their quality control systems under the type of constraints discussed, although the detail of the systems has many variations. The re-use of food waste—and in certain parts of the food industry the cost of its disposal—have recently become a focal point among the discussions of executives and management. So also have the cost of energy and the influence of the Health and Safety at Work Act. All of these introduce new constraints in an organisation by siphoning off some of the money available for the 'spenders', i.e. R&D, Quality Control, Market Research, Personnel, etc., Departments. Money spent on personnel is, however, wisely spent and yet organisations vary vastly in their attitude to one of the biggest constraints on quality maintenance (and hygiene), i.e. personnel training at all levels. Good quality starts with the aptitude of a company's employees and this is particularly true in our industry, as there often is some degree of craft still required in food production. From the factory floor upwards, training for the job is essential and the returns in improved productivity and quality are more than commensurate with the expenditure.

It is a little discussed constraint but, through the various committees involved in further education on which I have served, it is clear there is still a long way to go before many firms in the food industry will realise the constraint they impose on themselves (as measured by their profitability, and the effectiveness of their work force) by not encouraging their Personnel Department, and at least one of their directors, to maintain close interest in the educational requirements of their own company and the food industry generally. In a period of rapid technological progress it is foolhardy still to devote only a tiny amount of a company's resources to education and training. Those that do more than the minimum know the rewards of so doing. Certainly in the baking industry I have seen this factor operate to the benefit of quality in many small establishments, for the baking industry was the first to introduce a National Diploma. The City and Guilds of London Institute, in its own awards and the Joint Committees it administers for National and Higher National Diplomas, have demonstrated unequivocally the value of adequate training. The Food, Drink and Tobacco Industries Training Board, since its inception in more recent times, has done much to improve the attitude of employers to training and is now concentrating more on further education. The Technician Education Council, which in 1980 or 1981 is taking over the function of the Joint Committees, in its proposed awards in Food Technology recognises too that some business studies are essential to the technician and technologist of the future; absence of organisation and method creates a constraint on productivity and quality. In the event this must affect the value and effectiveness of the control function. Thus, there are hidden constraints within organisations as well as obvious ones. It is hoped this contribution will stimulate further exploration into this somewhat ambiguous area of managerial responsibility which it has sought to enunciate and clarify.

DISCUSSION

Mr. E. I. Williams said that in his experience the quality control/quality assurance functions had not been accepted, in many companies, to be a vital part of the organisation and, as a result, the status of personnel working in these areas had been rather lowly. He considered some reasons for this to be:

1.   The craft orientation of traditional food industries, coupled with only minimal demands arising from food legislation.
2.   Persons employed in food control not always having the approach

and personal characteristics needed to establish good communications across various interfaces and hence the ability to build up effective working relationships.

3. The product inspection 'pass or fail' system, traditionally prevalent in many industries, did not make one many friends.

Despite some recent improvements in attitude there was still much to be done. The introduction of new technologies into food processing and distribution, the ever increasing legal constraints, and the influence of marketing departments and retailing organisations demanded more and more technical and scientific inputs into almost every sector of a food business, including that of quality assurance. The availability of graduates of the kind produced by Colleges of Food Technology helps to fill this need. Raised status should finally be reflected at Board level by recognition of the contribution this function makes to food companies.

Mr. R. L. Stephens (Marks & Spencer Ltd) agreed with Professor Coppock that it was the overall policy which determines the standards of quality and not the nuts and bolts of food control systems, however essential they are. Where the Board itself wants to obtain higher standards of quality, this can be done. Otherwise it can be very difficult.

Mr. D. Hicks (Beecham Products Ltd) suggested that Professor Coppock had exaggerated in describing the pressures from the Boardroom on product quality in so far that buyers purchase material to specifications which are designed to protect product quality and that unsuitable raw materials or finished products are often scrapped.

However, he supported Professor Coppock regarding the need for more technological training in the food industry. Food technologists in an organisation have a clear responsibility to convince top management of the need to support recommendations based on technology.

Professor Coppock agreed with the comments relating to Board attitudes. Mr. Williams' last point was valid and perhaps the M.F.C. qualification could bring about a change of attitude.

From a number of decentralised plants the best that can usually be achieved is a similar product from each plant. Unless the same raw materials can be supplied to each factory and these are processed using essentially identical machinery and methods, differences between the products from each factory were inevitable. It is extremely rare that a company can afford to re-equip all its factories at the same time and so with any advance in technology the risk of change in the product from the new plant must be accepted.

SESSION III

The Interfaces

9

Interface with Product/Process Development

ROY SPENCER

Director of Research, J. Sainsbury Ltd

INTRODUCTION

Any organisation, no matter what its size or its purpose, be it a nation, a business, a club, or an individual, consists of several, possibly many, component parts which interact with one another in some way. Further, almost any organisation can itself be regarded as a component of a larger organisation and as interacting with other components of that larger organisation. The success of any organisation depends to a large extent on the effectiveness of these internal and external interactions.

What I have just said might seem irrelevant to this Symposium, or else to be so obvious as not to have been worth saying. Yet what we are considering in this Session of the Symposium are, in fact, certain interactions between some of the component parts of an organisation, communications of one sort or another across the interfaces between the quality control function and other functions in a business organisation, and indeed with other organisations. The reason we are considering this area is partly because of its importance to effective quality control and partly because of the problems it presents. I am confident that no one with any significant practical experience of the food control operation in a large business will dispute with me that the major and most difficult problems are not technical but are concerned with communications and organisational controls. Cybernetics is as relevant as the better known sciences to the food control operation.

PRODUCT DEVELOPMENT

Product development is the term generally used to include the development of radically new products and processes and also the improvement of

145

existing products and processes, areas that I prefer to refer to as product innovation. A food manufacturing company that does not innovate successfully is likely to see its competitive position progressively eroded and in due course to become a casualty in the battlefield of the market place. The ability to innovate successfully is not a guarantee of commercial success but it is an important contributory factor. I must emphasise the need to innovate *successfully*, for an unsuccessful innovation is a waste of scarce and expensive resources, a wound which makes the combatant less fit for battle, to continue the military analogy. Hence the vital importance of organising for successful product innovation, part of which is the effective integration of the eventual control procedures.

CONCEIVING A NEW PRODUCT OR THE FIRST STEP IN INNOVATION

Product innovation starts either by the perception of a *need* or by the perception of an *opportunity*. Whether it is need or opportunity, it could be related to changes in the market place, for example in consumer demands, in competition, or in availability of raw materials. It could be related to changes in science and technology, for example the development of ingredients such as starches or proteins with novel properties, of texturising processes, or of new packaging systems. It could also be related to legislative changes, for example restrictions on preservatives or changes in compositional regulations.

These various kinds of change should not, however, be considered in isolation for frequently they, too, interact with one another and recognition of this could provide an early indication that a need or opportunity might be arising, and timing is the first essential of successful innovation. For example, medical research on the aetiology of coronary heart disease might focus the consumer's attention on reducing calorie intake, which could lead to opportunities for low-calorie drinks, but toxicological research on conventional low-calorie sweeteners might lead to legislation limiting their use, or at least to consumer resistance to products containing them, with a need for alternative sweeteners.

By whatever means the idea for a new product might arise, it does arise as an idea, a *concept*, which is usually expressed in general terms, for example:

a vegetable fat 'cream'
a crispy savoury snack
a chewy chocolate bar

and a greater or lesser degree of research (as distinct from development) might be needed before the concept can be seen to be evolving into a product, research, for example into emulsification, or into texturising, or into rheology. It is necessary at this stage for careful consideration to be given to two matters, in what might be termed a feasibility study. Firstly, what is the likely cost to the company of developing and introducing the product, and secondly, what is the likely size of the market for the product when developed. Many a beautiful product idea has died almost at the moment of conception as a result of such a feasibility study.

If the results of the feasibility study are encouraging, then the necessary research might be undertaken and, in due course, which might follow closely after the establishment of the concept or might occur years later, there is seen to be a technically feasible product—a product perhaps, but still one in embryo since there is as yet no real idea of how the product should develop into what it is hoped will become a market leader. Identifying what the product should be so as to become a market leader is pre-eminently the role of the marketing function in the business organisation. The result of this process of identification should be a marketing brief.

THE GESTATION PERIOD OR THE DEVELOPMENT OF A NEW PRODUCT

The marketing brief for a new product identifies and specifies those attributes of the product which are likely to be important to its success in the market place. It will inevitably include a general description of the product as it will be perceived by the customer or consumer, its appearance (size, shape, colour, admixture), flavour (taste, texture, aroma), and presentation (packaging or display). It will also inevitably include a target price. It might compare or contrast the new product with similar products already on sale. It will assume that the new product is safe, that it conforms to the appropriate legislation, and that it will be consistent. Above all, the marketing brief will concern itself with *ends* and not *means*; means are the responsibility of other parts of the organisation. However, the marketing function should be aware at an early stage what is likely to be achievable with the means available. By 'means' I include the currently available production facilities and their costs, including production costs, or the cost of providing new facilities and operating them, the state of the scientific and technological art, current or anticipated legislation, the availability and cost of raw materials, and the feasibility and cost of whatever controls appear to be necessary. Thus, while the marketing function is responsible for the production of the marketing brief, it should be produced as a result of interactions between those parts of the organisation that are to be responsible for achieving it. The major parts are:

the innovators —research and development
the accountants—cost accountants, financial appraisers
the producers —purchasing, production, warehousing and
                 distribution

and last but not least,

the controllers —laboratory, line quality control, instruments

It is very desirable that there should have been some interactions even at the product concept stage, and in smaller organisations this is likely to occur spontaneously and informally. In larger organisations, for example with wide product interests and central research and development facilities, it is desirable to ensure a regular communication between the centralised innovators and the peripheral producers of the organisation by more formal procedures, perhaps mediated by nominated pairs of individuals in the central innovatory component and the peripheral production components. It is essential, however, that representatives of at least these four major functions come together with the marketing function on a formal basis at the very earliest stage of the development of a new product to form a *Project Team*, responsible so far as that new product development is concerned to a nominated *Project Manager*, who has overall responsibility for that project.

This is not the place to engage in a general discussion of project management. Suffice it so say that it is a well established technique designed to coordinate and control multi-disciplinary inter-related activities so that they can be brought to a speedy and satisfactory conclusion and that there are a variety of procedures available to the Project Manager to aid him in this.

The composition of the project team and the specific duties of the Project Manager are likely to vary from organisation to organisation and from project to project. It might be a large team or as small as three or four people and any individual might be engaged full or only part time on the project. The Project Manager might be responsible for this project alone or for several projects, or indeed he might also have other duties. What is imperative, however, is that the responsibilities of the Project Manager and thus of the Project Team as a whole shall be clearly defined, as shall the specific responsibilities of individual members of the team, and also that the resources to be applied to the project shall be specified. The defined responsibilities may or may not include establishing the marketing brief. They must include carrying the project to some clearly specified stage, which might be to a product launch or some earlier stage. They should also include communications to 'interested' parts of the organisation that are not directly represented on the project team. It is, or should be, self-evident that any member of the team is responsible for communications within his own 'line management' stream, up and down the 'line', but depending upon the composition of the team and the organisation of the Company, it might be necessary to ensure that regular communications are established with, for example, the following functions:

public relations or consumer affairs
personnel, employee relations, house journal
distribution, transport, warehousing
management and financial accounts
legal advisers
parts of the company concerned with 'competitive' products

The project team is likely to have one further responsibility, the elaboration of a series of specifications covering the raw materials which will be converted into the new product, the manufacturing processes used, including packaging and weighing the finished product, and the subsequent storage of the product. These various specifications are ideally brought together as one inclusive product specification, which should include all the bases on which the control function will operate to ensure the quality of the product.

THE RESPONSIBILITIES OF THE CONTROL FUNCTION

The control function has three main responsibilities in the development of a new product:

1. Generally to contribute to the elaboration of a product specification.
2. Specifically to design a system of quality assurance which will ensure that the product specification is met as far as it is practicable and economic so to do.

3. Finally to test, validate and where necessary modify, the designed quality assurance system in the light of experience as the new product is introduced, and to introduce quality control procedures. In this regard I favour an arrangement whereby a new product is particularly carefully monitored by the control function for a period after its introduction until it is clear that it is 'under control'.

It cannot be emphasised too strongly that product development is most likely to be successful when it is a team activity and the control function is an integral part of the team. To regard the control function as an appendage to product development, to be added almost as an afterthought 'to quality control' a finished product, is a waste of expensive resources from which the company can only suffer harm. There are always various ways in which a marketing brief can be converted into a product. There will always be a range of raw materials from which to choose and the choice need not be solely on price. Reliability is also likely to be important, not only in ensuring continuity of production but also in reducing the cost of excessive raw material inspection. It might be possible to introduce in-line production controls, for example, graders, sorters, or foreign body detection/rejection devices, that might widen the choice of raw materials or limit the extent and hence the cost of finished product inspection. There is likely to be a choice of processes which will lead to essentially the same product and individual processes might be controllable to a greater or lesser extent or might affect the choice of raw materials or the extent of quality control effort necessary. These and many other considerations are important during the development of a new product and it is an important part of the control function to ensure that due attention is paid to them.

THE PRODUCT SPECIFICATION

There are no doubt as many views on what should be contained in a product specification as there are food technologists who are responsible for producing them, and undoubtedly the circumstances of particular companies or indeed of particular production units will bear heavily on such views. At the very least, however, the product specification must contain a description of the product as it leaves the production unit, and this description must be one that has maximum *utility*. A statement that the product shall be red in colour probably has little utility, since redness is a very general concept. A statement that the product shall match in colour part of a colour chart in order to meet a marketing view that there is a consumer preference for such a colour has considerable utility. A statement that the product shall have certain reflectance spectral characteristics might have a greater scientific precision but might in practice be less useful, i.e. have less utility. Similarly, a statement that the product shall contain no food poisoning micro-organisms has no utility since this is not determinable, whereas a statement that a given number of units from each batch shall be sterile when subjected to a given test has considerable utility, not only in its own right but because it relates to the process used and perhaps to the raw materials, and also to the control process. This leads to the view that the product specification might usefully also include details of critical raw materials or production processes, for example that major ingredients shall contain not more than a given number of particular bacterial spores (as shown by a given test) and that the heat process shall be of a particular F value (as determined in a given manner). An extension of this view is that key controls over critical parameters should be included in the product specification as it is elaborated during the development of the product.

QUALITY ASSURANCE SYSTEM

I earlier used two terms, *a quality assurance system* and *quality control procedures*, and I believe it is important to distinguish between these two terms. A quality assurance system is a design, a plan, established in order to ensure that quality, as defined, is maintained within specified limits. However, it is more than a specific design or plan, it is a system. The parts interact with one another; there is feedback; it is, ideally, self-correcting. In a heating process if the temperature rises above that specified, the rise in temperature is not merely indicated on a thermometer, an alarm might sound to warn an operative to close a steam valve, or, better, the valve might be closed automatically, or, even better, the valve might be closed automatically and the time of the process might be reduced automatically so that over-processing does not occur. Such an arrangement would justifiably be part of a quality assurance system whereas the thermometer itself (as distinct from the temperature sensor) is more related to quality control procedures, a monitoring and recording of facts, often only of historical value.

It is not part of my remit to go into the intricacies and interactions of quality assurance and quality control, but one reason why I make the distinction is that it is an important responsibility of the control function in the development of a new product to determine what is an appropriate quality assurance system which will interact with the other considerations of the project team. The quality control procedures are much more parochial, which is not to say that they are unimportant, for in many food processes the quality assurance system is little more than a set of simple monitoring procedures leading to quality maintenance via human intermediaries. And this is where I would like to end this paper, in a sense where it started, for these human intermediaries are part of the business organisation. They must be communicated with and they in turn must communicate back and with others. There must be control over their activities and their activities must control the activities of others. Successful product development, successful in that it makes a profit for the company, in the last resort depends upon the product meeting the requirements of the customer and hence depends upon the quality control staff being effective in achieving their particular objectives.

DISCUSSION

Dr. R. B. Hughes (F. M. C. Ltd) said that while the control function's main role in new product development was to ensure that the product could be manufactured to a consistent quality from the available materials under safe and hygenic conditions, the product and process specifications must not be so rigid as to prevent continuous production of the food simply because every detail of the specifications could not be met.

In some circumstances the product team will have a role as a representative of own-label customers. This kind of purchaser frequently has considerable experience in the type of product required and will want to be closely involved in its development and manufacture.

Professor J. B. M. Coppock (Surrey University) said that product and process development included modifications to existing situations as well as completely new products and processes. There are many factors, particularly changes in legislation affecting labelling, composition, the use of additives etc., which can cause problems with recipes and processes. He agreed it was very important for specifications to be flexible enough to cover necessary changes but they must never be so loose as to lose their purpose.

Mr. R. L. Stephens (Marks and Spencer Ltd) said that with novel products and with processes which were truly new the control function had special responsibilities to ensure that both the processes and the resulting products were safe and wholesome.

Mr. I. V. Adams (M.A.F.F.) asked if special considerations or efforts were called for from the control function for products which were 'dying' in marketing terms and for which efforts to revive them might involve cutting product costs and a lowering of product quality.

Dr. R. Spencer in his reply agreed that specifications had to be suitable and it was a matter of defining 'suitable'. The criteria involved did of course change with the legislative and supply positions. By a careful appreciation of the essential characteristics and functions of an ingredient or a process it was often possible to write into the specifications a general requirement. For example, perhaps any fruit acid may be suitable in a given product or possibly any method of comminution could be made to produce a satisfactory product. If this latitude could be given it made substitution much easier.

He thought that the basic concepts and fundamental principles involved in new product and process development were not changed simply because the subject of the development was novel or revolutionary. For any product or process the key characteristics, whether familiar or not, had to be identified, preserved and controlled. Any differences between the approach to the development of existing products and processes and that for novel products and processes were of detail and should not be of principle. Eventually the final product had to be economically successful, safe and wholesome.

Products which were on the decline in a marketing sense were perhaps often not worth the attempt to save them. It is a matter for judgement by the marketing department as to the course of action to be taken. A number of options are available: perhaps a cheaper and lower quality product is called for; perhaps a more costly improved quality is required; or perhaps a product of modified characteristics is wanted. The action required depends upon the reasons for the decline.

10

Interface with Materials Purchasing

IAN R. REID

Manager—Technology, Campbell's Soups Ltd

INTRODUCTION

In the last paper we have seen how product/process development relates to the food control function. One outcome of this relationship is the provision of a specification for each ingredient used in the product, embodying the essential technical requirements established during development. In many cases this specification will not be a full purchasing specification required for the ingredient and, prior to submission to the Purchasing Department, it will be necessary for the Quality Control Department to add many other ancillary constraints.

RAW MATERIALS SPECIFICATIONS

As a good example of this, let us consider tomato purée. The Product Development Department will have set the technical specification for the material with reference to its particular use and will have covered the parameters which are necessary for this purpose, say colour, acidity, and flavour. Other technical characteristics, for instance the concentration ratio of the purée to the original tomatoes or the Howard mould count, are not vital from an R&D point of view and may be left as a matter of choice to other departments or may be dictated by legal requirements.

There will also be needed by the Purchasing Department further details concerning packaging options, for example cans, drums, or bulk. Whatever the container used, it must be specified with regard to such things as size, lacquer, base weight, and tin coating as appropriate, depending upon the usage rate of the material and possible storage life required in container,

155

purchase of long-term stocks against favourable prices, and other commercial and production considerations.

Finally, it is necessary to add the tolerances which can be accepted and it is vital to ensure that unattainable or only rarely attainable standards are not set. In many cases, particularly with unfamiliar or natural ingredients, it may be necessary to use the R&D Department to make a series of small-scale batches or single-plant batches to determine the tolerances that can be accepted as these require incorporation into the specification.

Having established a specification which is acceptable to the R&D, Quality Control, and Purchasing Departments, it remains only to be sure that it can be met in the market place. If any difficulties arise, it is obvious that modifications must immediately be made until this condition can be met.

Purchasing specifications, once properly drawn up, must never be regarded as sacred cows. Those concerned with purchasing and purchasing specifications must be sufficiently alert and flexible to react quickly to changes, sometimes very rapid ones, in the availability or characteristics or both of purchased materials. Crop failures and political decisions, for example, can cause fluctuations in availability and price. Changes in the technology involved in the production of ingredients and other materials may lead to changes in their characteristics. Those responsible for purchasing are, in my experience, a fruitful source of new or modified versions of familiar ingredients or materials. Frequently it is the Purchasing Department which introduces these versions to the R&D and Quality Control Departments. A company fails to listen at its peril; from ten ideas presented only one may be of value, but who can afford to miss that one?

As an aside, the product development function must always be aware of the availability of ingredients. I recall one memorable occasion when the development of a new product had virtually reached the production stage when it was discovered that the annual requirement of one particular spice oil exceeded the annual world-wide availability; needless to say, changes rapidly followed.

If we assume that all of the foregoing requirements have been successfully completed, we must now consider the development of a workable system which will as far as possible preclude the use of defective material in production. I would suggest that it is seldom, if ever, necessary to subject each and every delivery of every ingredient to the full gamut of all the tests suggested by the detail of the specification; if this has to be the case then I would recommend the replacement of purchasing personnel by others who will deal with reliable suppliers, a less expensive alternative!

A few comments on the selection of suppliers must be made at this point. The Purchasing Department is usually charged with obtaining adequate supplies of the materials required, *which meet the required quality standards*, at the lowest price. They must never be allowed to overlook the ultimate requirement of a satisfactory end-product. It is suggested that where possible the appropriate member of the Quality Control Department should visit the premises of suppliers together with a Purchasing Department representative, whether in the UK or abroad. This enables technical man to speak freely to technical man, more or less without commercial restraints, and to appreciate each other's problems. If a supplier knows that a hydrolysed protein with a solids content of less than a certain value will marginally affect a compounded product's flavour and, more significantly, will alter the water activity to a point where the product might spoil, there is little doubt that each consignment will be checked before despatch; the decisive information is that a low solids content found on receipt will automatically lead to rejection. There is no tolerance and no means of correction of sub-standard materials.

On such a visit the opportunity can be taken to review the supplier's hygiene and quality control practices. It can often have a salutary effect on a 'difficult' purchasing man to have his latest cheap source of an ingredient turned down because of unacceptable hygiene/quality control at his potential supplier's plants. It is also frequently of value to have technical staff from suppliers visit one's own plant. Usually only the larger firms at the present time employ staff of M.F.C. or potential M.F.C. standard, which requires a broad basic knowledge of food materials and their uses in food industry processes. Suppliers will know their own products but there can be considerable value in educating them in one's own particular uses of those products and hence particular requirements.

In the inquiry into the last incident of botulism in the UK, caused by canned salmon, the marketing firm involved had apparently not had technical people in the producing plant. Even if they had it would not have prevented the tragedy, but from a public relations aspect, if nothing else, such a visit could have been of considerable value.

An interesting legal point arises concerning plant inspection. A recent case in a Magistrates Court against a firm marketing a private label product manufactured for them outside the UK was dismissed because the marketing firm had taken steps to review the practices of the manufacturing plant. They had obtained a warranty on the goods supplied but had also taken the necessary precaution of checking that there was some substance behind the warranty and that it was not merely reassuring words.

The need to apply appropriate sensory tests to ingredients should be regarded as axiomatic.

Each ingredient has its own peculiar critical parameters and the main effort should be concentrated on these. Some examples are the free fatty acid content and peroxide values of edible oils, the thickening, stretching, and dough-forming properties of flours and starches, and the bacteriology (particularly the thermophilic spore count) of many ingredients to be used in canning.

Each supplier has to be positively advised that defective material will be returned, but equally he has to be assured that he has had a fair deal. There are many sampling plans available such as those issued by BSI, the US Department of Defense and the UK Ministry of Defence, but it should seldom be necessary to revert to their use in the food industry; such schemes are too complicated for routine use and should only require to be used when the proving of a point 'beyond reasonable doubt' is required. Sampling between five and ten boxes or bags of a lorry-load delivery should in general provide adequate protection, particularly when long-established suppliers are being used. An adverse result from such sampling can be tested by a similar composite sample from a further five to ten packs after which few suppliers will be able to resist rejection. A similar system can readily be followed with deliveries in bulk.

Further circumstances merit comment in this connection. Ingredients may be bought against a pre-shipment sample submitted by the supplier. This is a common practice, especially if the supplier is developing a material or its process of manufacture. In any instance, it is necessary to ensure that the bulk delivery is as the sample; delivered material not matching the sample can mean rejection. Alternatively, for routine materials the purchasing contract may contain an agreed quality acceptance level.

We must also consider the situation when a delivery of an ingredient is only marginally outside purchase specifications. Considerations here are firstly whether it is technically possible to use the ingredient at all and secondly whether, after a pretreatment or reconditioning process, it is practicable and economic to do so. In either case any change in the economics of using the material will have to be calculated. The initial steps in either event fall solely in the province of the technical man.

Obvious examples of the easily corrected situations are: (a) a delivery of burnt sugar with a lower than expected colour strength, a natural or synthetic flavour of low strength, or a tomato paste of low solids; all can be accepted provided increased usage can be tolerated; (b) the acceptance of a delivery of vegetable oil just exceeding specifications for free fatty acids or peroxide value where usage can be immediate with no prolonged storage period; (c) a marginally sub-standard delivery of flour to be used in the baking of biscuits may be directly usable; minor differences in either dough strength or stretch and flow properties can be corrected with similar minor changes in the fat, and liquid contents of the mix; (d) frozen vegetables may be fully acceptable except for an excess content of extraneous material which must be removed. Before such correction is agreed, the economic consequences of so doing must be taken into consideration, and where an increased cost is incurred by any preliminary treatment the Purchasing Department may well negotiate a compensatory price reduction for the material.

Most processing plants will have the ability to clean up ingredients but, of course, at a cost, and the decision on whether or not to do so probably depends on two factors: if rejected, can an immediate replacement be obtained, and if not, is the supplier willing to accept all or part of the reconditioning cost? The Purchasing Department must be supplied with all relevant details to enable proper economic negotiations to follow. It then becomes the responsibility of the Quality Control Department to ensure that whatever is agreed is carried out. In this case responsibility is accepted to ensure that both user and supplier receive a fair deal and that only the necessary reconditioning is carried out.

From the foregoing it might appear that I am happily prepared to accept sub-standard ingredients. I should emphasise that this is not so. However, many years ago I was asked a question by the then factory manager of the plant from which we obtained the majority of our cans, which for a cannery is probably its largest single 'ingredient' purchase. He asked 'How much quality can we all afford?'. The point he was making is that a can supplier could supply 100% perfect cans, we could insist on 100% perfect ingredients and in turn produce a product complying 100% with our quality standard. The product which would reach the consumer should be perfect (realising that there is no such thing as 100% inspection), but would certainly not be affordable by the consumer.

It is the function of the technologist to have sufficient knowledge of his own company's products and processes to help to decide how much the quality of an ingredient can be allowed to vary. As part of his economic thinking he must know precisely the costs of the tolerances set on the parameters for each ingredient, and perhaps even more important the cost of the risks involved if the rules are 'bent' to meet a particular situation, without sacrificing final product quality to any significant extent or altering composition so as to infringe regulations. One last thought on checking ingredients: I recall from my student days a lecturer whose favourite *bon mot* was 'Chemistry is the study of the innate perversity of matter'. If that was true of inorganic reactions, how much more is it true of a biological food material?

To return to purchasing specifications, we must understand and be able to apply the important distinctions between *necessary parameters*, defined as those which require relatively rigid control to avoid changing product quality, and *desirable parameters*, defined as those which indicate high-quality manufacture but which will not necessarily improve or detract from finished product quality.

An example can again be taken from tomato purée. The essential parameters are solids content, colour, and acidity, but the same material for quasi-legal purposes has to conform to a maximum mould count. It is questionable whether within the normal limits experienced a high or a low count contributes much of value to product quality. By the same token there are legal limits in the UK covering the maximum permissible lead content of the finished product and similarly maxima for individual ingredients. It is entirely possible that using all ingredients with lead contents at or near their respective limits that the final product can be unacceptable; this is particularly so in canning where lead is inevitably added to product from the 2/98 solder (2 parts tin, 98 parts lead) commonly used in can manufacture. Another example can be seen with wheat flour. The specification will certainly be written in terms of dough-making properties, as measured by various pieces of equipment such as the farinograph and/or the extensograph, or in terms of thickening properties, measured by the amylograph or otherwise. To these requirements the level of colour may need to be added, if the flour is used in products for which colour is important, for example certain types of biscuit. However, anyone who wishes to export baked products to the USA is well aware that the authorities enforce strict limits for rodent hairs and insect parts. Product quality as seen by the consumer is not affected by the presence or absence of these but it behoves manufacturers, whether engaged in export or not, to carry out filth tests as high results indicate poor practice at farm and mill, and can lead to costly rejections.

It should also be appreciated that the purchasing specification to produce substantially identical final products may not be identical for every company or every factory within a single company, as equipment inevitably varies from plant to plant, as do water supplies and other factors. The assessment of quality of peas for canning and freezing is generally made by the use of tenderometers. These instruments are often standardised across the country by use of samples supplied and certified by the Campden Research Association. I have found, however, that different UK companies have different views of the adequate time of blanching of peas to inactivate peroxidase prior to freezing.

Without going into the details of the test, except that time of colour development relates to time of blanching, we find in:

Factory A—
Satisfactory means no colour development after 3·5 min.
Factory B—
Satisfactory means no colour development after 1·5 min.
Factory C—
Colour development in 0–15 s means underblanched.
Colour development in 15–30 s means normal.
Colour development in 30–60 s means slightly overblanched.
Colour development in 60+ s means grossly overblanched.

Thus, peas with the same tenderometer reading going to the three factories will receive three different blanching treatments. Subsequent freezing of the peas will obviously provide the consumer with three different products. In order to bring the eating qualities together using the three different blanching procedures, it would be necessary to start with peas with different tenderometer readings. Similarly, if used for canning the hardness of the water employed in blanching and liquor preparation can have an effect as the calcium in the water has a firming effect. Water in the UK varies considerably from area to area, from soft in Scotland and the North to very hard in the South and West. The different results obtained in the tenderness of canned peas caused by varying water hardness are probably not significant if they relate to products from a company operating a single plant, but could be significant when products packed in various plants of the same company are compared.

In considering non-essential parameters we should also look at the end use for which the ingredient will be employed. Sugar or sugar solutions can be purchased which are identical in every respect except for differences in colour. Where these are to be used in products having a relatively dark colour, such as Christmas pudding mix, canned soup, canned baked beans or biscuits, colour in the sugar ingredient to the degree normally experienced is of no particular significance. Where the ingredient is used in the confectionery industry to produce clear boiled sweets or in the baking industry to produce a white filling, it becomes essential that a 'water-white' material be specified.

I would summarise this section by saying that a purchasing specification drawn up with a particular end use in view may need modification, tightening or loosening, by a realistic technological appraisal when the end use is changed.

Most of the foregoing assumes that supply lines are relatively short and therefore material is delivered to the purchaser in the condition in which it left the supplier's plant. Inevitably this is not always so; for example, Michigan pea beans have a 5000-mile journey between source and using plant, and similarly tomato purée for the UK may have originated from Portugal, Spain, Italy, Bulgaria, Greece, or Turkey. Some damage en route is almost inevitable, although in recent years this situation has vastly improved with the advent of shipping containers.

In the past, both mechanical damage and damage due to water seemed to be always with us. It therefore becomes necessary that contracts with suppliers should incorporate suitable clauses so that materials which arrive in less than satisfactory condition can be segregated and handled by the underwriters. In the absence of such a clause, it then behoves the purchaser to effect suitable insurance. When the vendor has negotiated the insurance it is vital that in the event of problems he be informed immediately so that he and/or his insurers can inspect to assess liability at the earliest opportunity.

Where material arrives in damaged condition this is probably one of the rare occasions when the best approach to ensuring quality is to employ one of the accepted published sampling schemes. Where negotiations have to be carried out, possibly at long range with vendor and insurers and where it may be necessary to resort to legal action, there is no doubt that a defect level which can be demonstrated to be over that indicated in such sampling plans will carry weight, whereas results obtained by a random check would not.

PACKAGING MATERIALS

So far we have looked at how we should draw up purchase specifications and carry through sampling and checking of ingredients. We should now consider the factors that apply to packaging material.

For canning, the most complicated issue is which construction of can is best for any particular product. A can, while apparently a simple piece of packaging, is far from being that; thickness and temper of the body, and external and internal thickness of the tin coating and the internal and/or external lacquer, all have to be specified and checked, and similar considerations apply to end plates.

We are fortunate in the UK in that, in my experience, the can manufacturers practise a very high level of quality assurance. It is therefore only necessary to agree how this should be augmented on receipt by the using plant, and for this purpose examination of a relatively small sample drawn as far as possible from every pack in the delivery is probably adequate; a standard statistical sampling programme should be used only if controversy arises.

In very recent times materials in contact with food, notably flexible packaging, have come under legal control. Thus, PVC is controlled with regard to its content of vinyl chloride monomer and its ability to diffuse and migrate into food. Warranties should be obtained from the supplier where the necessary analysis is beyond the capability of the purchaser. The food control function has the responsibility for assessing and setting the specification intended for each particular material, purchasing, arranging supplies and to the quality control function falls the responsibility for ensuring that quality standards are met.

Other packaging material, for example labels and cartons, which are not in contact with product require less stringent examination. Nevertheless, there may be important considerations regarding possible taint from printing inks, can corrosion problems from excess sulphite in board, and product protection during handling.

A most important point concerns the information printed on labels and any part of this which may have to comply with legislation.

Lawyers are rarely well versed in the intricacies of the various regulations which affect the details which should or should not appear on product labels, and as already mentioned in another paper, the technologist has a part to play in this.

It is generally the best method to provide the Purchasing Department with a full, detailed, written instruction on what is to appear on the label. Label design must inevitably fall within the province of the marketing personnel, but technical control staff must be able to exercise a veto if they step out of line. When design and copy have been put together by the printer, a proof should be checked prior to a full-scale print run. Typesetters and printers are far from infallible.

PACKAGING MATERIAL AND SHELF-LIFE

Another important consideration, in view of the EEC Labelling of Foods Directive, is the effect that the packaging material can have on the shelf-life of the product, now that there will, for many products, be a need to indicate a minimum durability date on the packaging. Products with a shelf-life of over 18 months will be exempt from compulsory open-date marking. While the majority of canned products will be exempt, many dehydrated and semi-preserved products will be included. It is the responsibility of each manufacturer to decide the effective shelf-life for his products, but as shelf-life can be affected both by changes in formulation and by changes in packaging it becomes apparent that the situation must be kept under constant review. Because of these factors the Purchasing Department may not simply buy an alternative material which is cheaper and apparently satisfactory. The determination of shelf-life is the function of the technologist familiar with the product and its possible environment. The technical information and suggestions given by suppliers about their products may or may not be useful or even relevant in assessing their effects on the shelf-life of a compounded food.

GENERAL MATERIALS AND MATERIALS OF CONSTRUCTION

Thus far we have considered ingredients only. The technical departments will also be involved in liaising with the Purchasing Department on specifications for many other materials used in a food plant.

Cleaning materials should be suitable for the surfaces and equipment for which they are used, for example a cleaning material for aluminium equipment should not be caustic in nature or rapid corrosion will result. Similarly, any material used as a surface steriliser must not taint the food with which it may come in contact.

There are a variety of anti-corrosion materials used in boiler plant and hydrostatic sterilisers to prevent corrosion in steam pipes and elsewhere. Such materials must not be capable of imparting flavour or odour to the product.

Generally, the material best suited for a food plant is stainless steel, but it should be realised that there are various grades of this material and we should be involved with suppliers to ensure that the most suitable one is used. Rubber and plastic used as gaskets, pistons, trays, etc., in contact with food materials must be inert to prevent taint. The correct specification for each application must be drawn up.

There will be many instances where materials less expensive than stainless steel will perform adequately, but there is no doubt that for equipment stands which will nightly be treated with cleaning materials of a corrosive nature and possibly subjected to chlorine solutions at the same time, there is really no substitute; painted iron, unless the painting is continuously renewed, will flake and rust in a short time.

In general, all fasteners in positions where corrosion can take place over exposed food should be made of stainless steel or plastic. The use of cadmium-plated nuts and bolts must be forbidden.

Unless otherwise specified, many instruments and recorders will be fitted with glass. It therefore becomes important that purchase orders shall specify that clear plastic material must be substituted.

Except for food finally packed in glass containers, there should be *no* glass in a food plant other than mercury thermometers for heat process control, which should have a protective plastic screen, and fluorescent lighting tubes, which can similarly be protected by plastic sleeves or diffusers.

It is of interest to point out that the sole reference to the construction of buildings for a food plant is to be found in The Food Hygiene (General) Regulations 1970 (S.I. 1970 No. 1172) in Section 26. This section reads:

26.—(1) The layout of food premises shall (a) be such as to provide adequate space, suitably sited, for the purpose of the removal of waste from food and the separation of unfit food in compliance with the requirements of regulation 9(b), and the storage of any such waste and unfit food prior to disposal.

Other sections of these regulations, however, impose constraints which must be observed but this entire regulation is written in terms so wide that interpretation becomes the vital factor.

In addition, there are certain more specific requirements in the following EEC Directives:

77/99/EEC   Meat Products
64/433/EEC ⎫
71/118/EEC ⎬ Red Meat and Poultry Meat
72/462/EEC ⎭

SUMMARY

Ingredient specifications: must be sufficiently restrictive in parameters critical to maintaining product quality within the agreed limits. The acceptance or rejection of sub-standard ingredients will depend upon their possible use by formula revision or pre-processing before use and the economic effect on the final product of such operations.

There is no substitute for dealing with honest, reliable vendors who operate a proper quality control system of their own. There is also no substitute for paying visits to vendors' plants and meeting the quality control people; technologist speaking to technologist breaks down communication barriers rapidly.

Each specification must be tailored to the use of the ingredient.

Packaging: must be entirely suitable for the particular product, which will certainly involve storage tests to ensure that flavour and odour transfer problems giving rise to taint do not arise. It must also comply with all the relevant legislation and must be approved prior to use. This applies particularly to printed packaging, which is best checked before final artwork and printing plates are completed.

The food control function has a responsibility for all aspects of a manufacturing plant, which extends far beyond the manufacturing of the product itself, and with regard particularly to the Purchasing Department must have a voice in deciding:

1.   Materials of construction of the building.
2.   The materials used to construct and install equipment.
3.   Instrumentation and control equipment.
4.   Cleaning materials, water and boiler treatments, lubricants.
5.   All the ingredients and packaging for the product.

In all of these we must remember that the function is to keep the company out of trouble with suppliers, with the enforcement authorities, with customers, and most important, with those on whom we most depend, the consumers.

DISCUSSION

Mr. D. Bolton (Rank Hovis McDougall Ltd) asked if crop failures were dealt with by prior investigation of alternatives that may never be required or by relying on market forecasts to indicate the possibility of crop failure, necessitating quick re-formulation.

He stressed the advisability of visiting suppliers' premises. Although the costs of visits in the UK are accepted, problems could arise with visits abroad due to constraints set by the Board. He noted that some company lawyers were of the opinion that visits over a minimum period of 12 months were necessary before being acceptable in Court as defensive evidence.

He commented that no mention was made of flavour as part of a specification and said that in his opinion it is desirable that it should be included when dealing with natural raw materials. The country of origin of the material can affect the flavour, particularly with spices. He asked if this was also true for tomatoes. The spice trade has its own panel of referees in London, to which any importer can appeal if not satisfied with the quality supplied against a contract. When an appeal is upheld a reduction in price is agreed.

With reference to the blanching of peas it is essential that methods independent of personal assessment should be stipulated wherever possible. This ensures that results between laboratories within the same company and between supplier and user are strictly comparable.

Mr. A. Turner (Cadbury Typhoo Ltd) said a flexible approach has to be adopted towards applying limits, since 'bending' limits is inevitable from time to time. Commonly, quality controllers do not have the resources to carry out sampling plans at the level required to give the desired degree of confidence. Consequently, a screening test approach may have to be adopted and, sooner or later, the judgement of the quality controller will determine acceptability or rejection.

A product specification should reflect its degree of vulnerability to each ingredient and the sensivity of the ingredients to each of the factors embraced by their specifications. Categorisation in this way enables alternatives to be appraised—where alternatives exist—so that when the inevitable happens, an orderly approach can be adopted to resolve the difficulty.

Mr. A. Dulin (Marks & Spencer Ltd) said that allowance for variations in natural raw materials are built into specifications by the use of tolerance limits but these must be restrictive only in parameters critical to maintaining essential product characteristics.

If sub-standard raw materials are to be used together with appropriate treatment or recipe modification, the final product quality must be maintained. This is the main aspect of reaching decisions in this matter rather than economic reasons. Who takes this final decision—quality controller, raw material purchasers, production or marketing personnel?

Professor J. B. M. Coppock (Surrey University) said that much can be done to get suitable ingredients by close collaboration with the grower. Varieties of strawberries and peas, for example, have been developed which are particularly suitable for canning and command a premium price. The same is true of barley for brewing. Process control or alteration by the supplier, sometimes instigated by the purchaser, can improve ingredients. Thus, dried fruit from Turkey has been greatly improved by process changes introduced by the technologist of a British buyer.

Sometimes a producer can, without warning and perhaps unknowingly, alter the chances of the successful use of an ingredient by the purchaser. The white to yolk ratio of eggs is important to the quality of some cakes. Changes in this ratio as a result of development in poultry breeding could be to the detriment of the baker who is then forced to find ways around the problem such as buying egg yolks and white separately.

Mr. I. R. Reid replied that no one can plan against the effects of crop failure because if this happens everyone competes for the same alternative materials which inevitably increase in price. When this happens serious consideration has to be given to ceasing production.

It was important to visit suppliers' plants, if only from the public relations aspect, to provide against anything adverse happening which was attributable to the product marketed by the buyer. The incident may not have been prevented even with the buyer's staff in full attendance, but at least all precautions would appear to have been taken by the buyer.

Some variations in raw materials are measurable by laboratory tests and limits can be set in specifications. Flavour is often characteristic of the process and type of plant used. With tomato purée, if its taste is reasonable you should use it, provided it satisfies the chemical and microbiological requirements.

Materials which do not meet specifications can be used only by the combined efforts of production, purchasing and quality control personnel, with the final decision resting with the control function. If the final product specification cannot be achieved, the marketing function becomes involved and decides to accept or reject whatever product can be made. It is accepted that different test methods give different results but, provided the results can be correlated with what the consumer wants, any method may be used.

11

Quality Assurance/Production/Productivity Interface

DAVID MATTHEWS

Quality Assurance Manager, Kellogg Company of Great Britain Ltd

INTRODUCTION

Let us walk out of our luxuriously appointed office and go into the factory, to take a random view of a moment in the life of a process operator. He is standing there by his equipment and he really is in a bad mood. Someone, either round the corner, or three floors away in the warehouse, will not accept the food that he is making. He cannot find the Inspector, and cannot understand how people expect him to make the right sort of food when these Inspectors set the standard, and no one in Processing Department is clear what it is. His equipment is running satisfactorily, it is only 5 °C over the limit, and anyway with the raw material that he is given these days, how can he expect anything but problems? The process has never worked properly since he had the Australian raw material in 1953, and what is more, he cannot even find the maintenance man to put the temperature control on his equipment right. He is also upset by the scruffy environment and machinery, and can never find anyone from the hygiene gang to clear it up for him. All in all, our process operator is having a bad day, and what makes it worse is that it is no different from most other days.

WHY HAVE AN INTERFACE?

Let us look very briefly at the background of the Production/Quality Assurance Department interface—a short history lesson.

Prior to mass production, products were made by craftsmen who operated self-inspection of their product. The craftsmen made all or most of the item themselves and, because of the small scale of the operation, the quality audit was done by the master or owner of the business.

169

The craftsman knew exactly what he was making—in all probability he also knew exactly what the customer did and did not like about his product. The whole of the production process in the old days was controlled by very few people, and virtually everything to do with the product was within their own control.

The complexion of industry changed with the advent of mass production —typified by the early production of automobiles. The significant change for our purposes was that the process lines were often operated by illiterate ex-farm hands, who had no clear idea of what they were doing, and they certainly did not understand the product. Further, they were very remote from the consumer.

In the old-style print shop, beloved of Western movies, one man has total control of the complete manufacturing operation. Any mistakes made are (a) his own, (b) quickly correctable, and (c) not too expensive. However, as the scope of the operation increases, so too do the variety and cost of defects.

Initially, far too many faults were found in the finished product, so the mass-production chiefs of the time came up with the idea of having finished product inspectors. These inspectors knew a lot more about the product than the line operators, and they could be trusted to make sure that nothing faulty got out into the market.

Unfortunately, this was and is a very expensive way of doing things— rejecting a product at the end of a long and complicated production line— so gradually the inspection system extended back down the line until it came to its ultimate destination, with the input of raw materials into the factory. This production system demonstrates the concept of inspector-controlled quality.

The problem with this system—exaggerated somewhat in the opening scenario—is that the operators generally absolve themselves of any responsibility for the quality (and hygiene) of their output. Problems are always someone else's fault, and very rapidly the quality of hygiene standard develops into not 'what the customer needs', but 'what you can get past the inspection'. This situation is exacerbated in many companies by having inexperienced low-status inspectors pronouncing on the output of experienced, high-status operators.

So now we have a new approach—operator-controlled quality—trying to restore the craftsman ethic to modern production. The inspection of a product is left to the operator, and quality assurance moves into an audit role.

Of course, in a food factory, we are interested in sanitation as well as the 'quality' of the product—and by sanitation I mean all aspects of hygiene, building construction, housekeeping, equipment standards, etc. The concept of operator-controlled quality is equally applicable to operator-controlled cleanliness—and quality and sanitation may generally be considered to be synonymous in this paper.

BASIS OF THE PRODUCTION/QUALITY ASSURANCE RELATIONSHIP IN THE COMPANY

This relationship depends on many factors, which can be broadly split into main categories—the overall company effect, and the 'domestic' Production/Quality Department interface. Many of the company inputs are dealt with in other papers, but let me itemise a few of them here:

1. Overall marketing and pricing policy—what class of product do we manufacture?
2. Cash flow and investment programmes.
3. The overall industrial relations climate.
4. The difference in status, pay, etc., afforded to members of the Quality Assurance Department, as opposed to the Production Department.
5. The amount of authority delegated to the Quality Assurance Department—often depends on the size of the company.
6. Attitudes to legislation and Environmental Health Authorities— trying to dodge or stay ahead of legislation.
7. Training policy.

The 'domestic' Production/Quality Assurance Department relationship can be affected by:

1. Ratio of number of inspectors to number of operators.
2. Shift systems.
3. Mix of male and female staff.
4. Union activities—and disposition of shop stewards.
5. Personal relationships at all levels between the two departments.
6. Badly written and confused quality instructions for use on shop floor, with no guidelines or action levels.

Now, can we set up a system that gives some chance of a harmonious relationship between the Quality Assurance and Production Departments? There is certainly no simple answer, and many of the problems lie in the area of industrial management rather than the technical aspects of food control. However, the following sections attempt to suggest some areas worthy of attention.

Product Approval and Quality Plan

Do not let the R&D Department inflict a product on the factory without involvement with the Production and Quality Assurance Departments at least. People get very frustrated mixing 7.532 91 kg of ingredient A with approximately 50 tons of B, to get product C. Attitudes suffer even more if the inspector will then only pass a finished product containing $6.2973 \pm 0.01 \%$ moisture. Make sure the production details are rational, with tolerances fitting the product, equipment, and measuring instruments.

Raw Materials Assurance

It is vital that the Production Department knows that the Company has a system, and that the Quality Assurance Department does its best to obtain satisfactory raw materials for processing. It is worth spending time here, as this is one of the areas where we can get away from the traditionally negative image of quality control.

Provide as Much Operator Control as is Feasible

Whenever possible, set processes up so that the operator feels he can control his destiny. Make sure the operators train in quality standards and hygiene conditions for their product, as well as the production method. Try and train inspectors, if you must have them, at the same time as operators, and maintenance men. The more these people can participate in jointly constructive discussions, the more your bad relationship problems are likely to melt away.

Provide as Much Objective, Quantitative Measurement as Technology will Allow

One of the food industry 'minefields' is subjective measurement. Face up to the following facts:

1. Industrial status or job function is irrelevant to one's ability to make subjective judgements on food quality.
2. When it comes to subjective judgement, everyone, from the Managing Director to the brushhand thinks differently—and no one person can be right.
3. The consumer is less discriminating than you think.

Thus, the more that objective measurement can be used on such aspects as colour, taste, and texture of foods, then the less room there is for argument. Any objective measurement must be related back to the original market research and statistically based consumer tests, which are the only reliable guides to market preference.

Where technology is not advanced sufficiently, and subjective judgement is essential, then the following should be considered:

1. Provide the best practicable conditions for the inspection, e.g. standard lighting, quiet room.
2. Try and provide 'standard samples'. The human being is very poor at absolute measurement but very good at comparison. Where possible, try and make the standard samples at ·the limits of acceptability.
3. Get the different people who make subjective judgements (e.g. Production, Quality Assurance, Marketing Departments) together on a routine basis—particularly in a shift-working factory.
4. Examine modern techniques, such as the 'repertory grid' for aligning people's subjective judgement.

Provide Clearly Defined Action Levels for Various Product Defects

We may as well accept that things will go wrong—the question is, how do we deal with the faults that are discovered? In general, food faults can be divided into three separate degrees of severity, with corresponding action levels (see Table 11.1 for an example).

The Production Department must be made aware of rules such as those in Table 11.1 so that they can understand why certain action is taken when a product is faulty.

The quality Control Department has an obligation to present quality information in such a way that most conceivable product faults have an associated action level. Non-routine faults would have to be referred to Quality Assurance Department supervision, or a Shift Supervisor during the 'silent hours'. (See Table 11.2 for an example of well presented 'faults and action levels'.) Note that information presented in this way can be used in either an inspector-controlled or operator-controlled situation.

Act Rapidly but Responsibly when a Process Breaks Down

If a product is held, or a process stopped, then there is a particular obligation on the Quality Assurance Department to provide rapid

TABLE 11.1
Defects and action[a]

Action Level on Defects—
   In general there will be three levels of action: Critical, coded $\otimes$; Major, coded $\ominus$; Minor, coded $\odot$. The action level defines the type of corrective action required when a defect is discovered

1.   *Critical Action* $\otimes$:
     This level of action is taken when a fault is discovered that would seriously affect customer acceptance. At this level, the offending packing line is shut down until the fault is corrected, and all product held back to the last good check.
2.   *Major Action* $\ominus$:
     This action is used when a serious fault is discovered, but it would be either illogical or impractical to hold cases back to the last good check (e.g. missing line codes on cases). In this instance the offending packing line must be shut down until the fault is corrected, and the line itself cleared of product.
        Note: failure to shut a line down for major action will result in critical action being taken on product produced after the fault is discovered.
3.   *Minor Action* $\odot$:
     This applies to action taken on a fault which is mildly objectionable, but should not harm customer acceptance too seriously. Every effort should be made to correct the defect found as soon as possible, but it is not normally necessary to either shut the line down immediately or hold cases in the warehouse.

Communication of Defects and Action—
   It is essential that on finding a defect, or taking action, the Inspector notifies the line operator of the fault and the action to be taken as soon as possible. The Q.A. Foreman should be notified of 'holds' as soon as possible—after communication with the warehouse and completion of the special report.
   Note—It is important that Inspectors and operators realise the difference between 'defect category' and 'action level'. Defect category defines the seriousness of a product hazard or machine fault—action level defines the action taken when the fault is discovered, either by machine operator, mechanic or Line Inspector.

The tables in parts III and IV of this Manual relate defect category and action level for you. You will see that, in general, category 1 defects require critical action $\otimes$ (e.g. metal detectors not seeing stainless steel), but category 4 defects can also demand critical action $\otimes$ (e.g. inner sealing). Further, not all category 1 defects demand critical action (e.g. metal detector not seeing 3 mm lead).

[a] Taken from *Quality Assurance Packing Line Manual*, 2nd ed., 1978. Manchester: Kellogg. p. 4.

TABLE 11.2
Line safeties—family size[a]

Factor	Defect category	Standard	Tolerance	Action level	Comments
Photobell	4	See p. 12/13 of Manual	See p. 13 of Manual	⊙	
Top sealers	1	i. Should have no loose or trailing parts that can fall in sack	None	⊕	
	1	ii. Should be no anti-freeze leaks on straight line sealers	None	⊗	
	1 or 4	iii. Should not adversely mark sack or carton	Provided seals not burning or excess glue build-up	⊙	Check with A.C.I. for action on serious faults affecting food
Top sealer warning lights	4	Should work	Production Dept. discretion	⊙	
Sacker paper safeties	4	Must work	None	⊕	
Wax deflector plates	1	Must be present and effective at sacker exit	None	⊗	
Sacker tucker fingers	1	Must be free of wax	Any adherent wax would not fall in a sack	⊕	If build-up is so bad that wax may have gone in packets see A.C.I.
Filler product hazards	1	No foreign or loose material that could fall in food, either on or in filler	None	⊕	Check with A.C.I. if foreign material present
Fast scale safety	3	Should work	Use range chart	⊕	Use rules from statistical net weight control chart
Statistical weight control chart	3	Check on 4 packets from one head—should be consistent with filler operator data	Allow for normal variation in food density and head performance (see pp. 15–19 of Manual)	⊕	Any problems—consult with A.C.I.

[a] Taken from Quality Assurance Packing Line Manual, 2nd ed., 1978. Manchester: Kellogg. p. 8.

information; otherwise there could be an unnecessarily large quantity of unusable part-processed food.

It is difficult to adjudicate on paper for the most harmonious method of immediate trouble-shooting when a product or process goes wrong—in any case, harmony is often the last priority in such circumstances. The best advice seems to be to rely on previous experience—but in general one should look for a blend of technical competence and extensive process experience to solve the problem. These two factors are rarely manifest in one person, and so the decision maker will have to balance advice from several sources.

In a production crisis, one always finds the fastest way to get back on stream. This may be to 'bag off' the process materials—or deliberately pack bad food to be 'held' and reclaimed later. This attitude is acceptable, as the Production Department will bear the cost of any action taken, and the Quality Assurance Department can keep back any suspect material from the consumer.

Once all the fuss has died down, then suspect food can be sampled and analysed to obtain data for a more leisurely disposition decision. Where food has to be blended back into a process stream, this should be done with some degree of quality supervision, to prevent over-enthusiastic reclaim adversely affecting the main stream.

Make Good Use of Continuously Generated Process Information

Apart from static information contained in Manuals, the Quality Assurance Department will continuously be generating data on existing production. Where applicable, this should be relayed to both Quality Assurance and Production Department personnel as quickly as possible. Amongst ways of doing this are:

1. A continuously updated information board in some strategic position (such as by the coffee machine).
2. Use of a radio network.
3. Recording the last set of plant results as you collect the next samples, on the plant itself.

Any major production bottlenecks or wastage points should be studied to try and find the cause, and prevent a re-occurrence. This type of exercise can often usefully be done by a 'task force' containing representatives of say Production, Quality Assurance, Maintenance, Process Development, and Engineering Departments. Some analysis of quality costs can be useful at this stage, to judge the scale of answer to the problem that would make economic sense.

These data can also be used as input for statistical analysis of plant behaviour. Statistical analysis is really a separate subject in its own right—deserving of a separate paper. However, some useful applications for statistical analysis are as follows:

1. Determining if a process is capable of being 'operator controlled'.
2. Showing with what confidence different sampling systems can be used.
3. Determining ingredient 'overages' to ensure meeting product claims.
4. Setting packet fillers to ensure meeting weight claims.
5. Analysing methods of waste reduction.

Another value of statistical disciplines, often unappreciated by laboratory chemists, is to highlight the inadequacies and dangers of 'one-shot' testing.

Differentiate Between 'Specification' and 'Fitness for Use'

We should consider the difference between 'fitness for use' and 'conformance to specification' when making decisions on disposition. Conformance to specification means whether or not the product you are making fits the written-down specification. However, we all know that in the food industry it is extremely difficult to write comprehensive specifications, and we cannot possibly anticipate all conceivable permutations of quality parameters. Thus, even though a product may not conform to the written specification, it may be fit for use.

The 'fitness for use' decision should always be taken by the Quality Assurance Department, even when we are in an operator controlled situation. This decision will often be made by the Quality Assurance Department in conjunction with the Marketing Department where the fault relates to consumer acceptance.

Differentiate Between Control and Audit, and Act Accordingly

In the modern, high-speed, high-output factory, the Quality Assurance Department should be controlling as little as possible. By controlling, I mean actually holding output until it has been inspected, analysed, and passed by the Quality Assurance Department.

There are some instances where this is necessary, e.g. a protein claim in a slimming biscuit needs to be checked before release; some dairy products need microbiological clearance before release—but, in general, the function of the Quality Assurance Department should be to audit production.

Audit involves measuring parameters of food output and reporting back to the Production Department—but for information and management control of the process. (Of course, if an audit uncovers something horrific, it can be used as a very expensive version of control.)

Whenever possible, these audits should be made quantitatively, and should be given in a form that is easy to understand. This theme is developed later in the paper.

Examples of audits are ' % acceptable (to experts) food quality', ' % acceptability of warehouse', ' % cleanliness of the food process', 'consumer complaints per million packs of food' (an audit forced on us in an imperfect world).

Audits are best used for information and target setting, and fit well into a management by objectives system.

Install Control and Audit Systems that 'Won't Go Away'

The experienced production operator knows that any new quality assurance system, particularly related to hygiene or clean-up is only the result of the last symposium attended by the Quality Assurance Manager. There is no doubt that by making token gestures towards the new imposition, the whole thing will be forgotten in 2 weeks. The canny shift operator is even more convinced that the moment the day staff go home, he can return to his well established routine.

How do we get inside the life of our happy friend, when we judge that changes or improvements are needed? Here are some possible guidelines:

1. Make sure you can justify the change 'to the hilt'.
2. Get senior management backing as an essential pre-requisite.
3. Communicate to everyone affected by the change, before making it. Modify the change in the light of reasonable, responsible suggestions from other quarters, if you still retain the original objective.
4. Install a system that is harder to stop than keep going.
5. Monitor the effect of the change, communicate results, and modify further if necessary, in the light of experience.
6. If there are any further modifications, make sure the operative knows the benefits to himself of the change.

Attention to the above guidelines should move you away from the 'seven-day wonder' situation to a controlled and stable one. If operators feel it is harder to 'buck' the system than follow it, they will eventually follow it.

Communicate—And Do it Effectively

There will always be information, even in an operator-controlled situation, that the Production Department will require from the Quality Assurance Department, e.g. finished food audit analysis results. It is important to present this information in a way that can be rapidly understood and assimilated by the recipients. As a general rule, try and report by graphs (normal or Cusum) to the shop floor, and only by data summaries to management. Information presented in a messy, stodgy, or confusing way will generally be ignored.

Further, do not fall into the trap that the Quality Assurance and/or R&D Departments have some 'secret' information—this will often lead to operators leaving product judgement up to the Quality Assurance Department, with consequent loss of product quality and efficiency, and a deterioration of relationships.

COSTS

Within the previous 11 sections, I have made passing reference to costs. However, money deserves much better than a passing reference, and the next three sections cover specific aspects of the cost/productivity factor, related to product quality. The first point is a particularly emotional one as it hits people where it hurts—in the pay packet.

Effect of Bonus Schemes on the Quality Assurance/Production Interface

It has been suggested that the modern food factory has to pay equal regard to output, quality, sanitation, cost, and safety. Thus, any bonus schemes that ostensibly relate just to output can only be satisfactory if the organisation has internal checks that prevent irresponsible output, at the expense of the other factors. Alternatively, it is possible to report all the above factors quantitatively and combine all five, straight or weighted, into a scoring system which relates to a bonus scheme. However, this latter system can be difficult to implement because of shop-floor mistrust of a complex system, especially when this relates to wages.

The problem with bonus schemes is that short-term benefits are soon realised (next week's pay), but a decline in product quality takes longer (next month's consumer complaints and next year's sales) to produce an

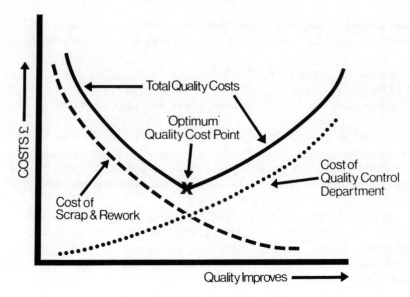

Fig. 11.1.   The cost myth.

effect. It is worth spending some time explaining the effect of 'shoddy' output on next year's bonus.

Effect of Productivity/Method Study on Quality Systems

Most modern factories have agreements which allow for the use of work study in setting up new operations. It is important that the work study relates to quality parameters. Otherwise, we could have a change in working methods which inadvertently affects the quality of the product, without anybody realising it, during the early stages.

This problem generally comes under the heading of communications, but it has to be borne in mind. It is often very difficult to change once a new method of working has finally been implemented, and it could be at this stage that the wider effects of a change in quality would be noticed.

Myth of the 'Optimum Quality Costs' Graph

Students of textbooks on quality assurance will be familiar with the graph in Fig. 11.1, which is supposedly used to determine optimum quality costs. The graph implies that the more you spend on quality staff, then the lower becomes the cost of scrap and re-work.

I would suggest that the second graph (Fig. 11.2) is a more accurate

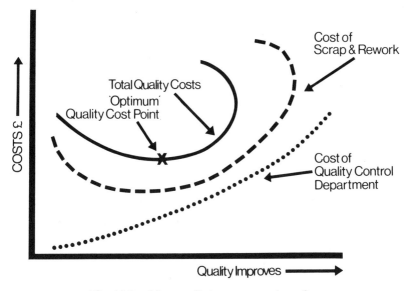

Fig. 11.2. More realistic representation of costs.

representation of the true situation, and helps put quality assurance/production/cost relationship more into perspective. The reason for the shape of Fig. 11.2 is that, over a certain point, the more quality staff you have the more they will generate (a) quality rejects for insignificant faults; (b) communications problems; and (c) a climate where operators abandon any responsibility for quality and sanitation. In other words, work is undertaken which does not in fact improve the quality of the product.

SUMMARY

To summarise the points discussed in this paper, I suggest the following are worthy of consideration in establishing the framework of a good Quality Assurance/Production Department relationship. Hopefully this framework will be consistent with obtaining the maximum benefit from the quality/cost ratio. It should be said that these points are in no particular order, and I make no claim for complete coverage:

1. Admit that the Quality Assurance Department provides a service to the Production and Sales Departments—not a haven for technologists.

2. Get the Production Department to realise that a food company cannot survive today without due regard to the quality and hygiene of its goods.

3. Pay a lot of attention to the planning of new products/systems and ensure that adequate training is given in relevant departments.

4. Provide a sensible, easily assimilated information flow to the Production Department. Make as much quality/hygiene information as possible
    a. objective;
    b. quantitative.

5. Let the Production Department make as many of their own decisions as possible, e.g. in-process standards, conformance to specification.

6. Talk to the Production Department in their own language, e.g. cases per hour, money, yields. The Quality Assurance Department needs to get inside the psychology of the Production Department to make an effective and telling contribution.

7. Set up inspection and audit areas so that the Production and Maintenance Departments feel welcome. Provide easy access to product information and performance against targets.

8. Remember where everyone's wages come from—sales.

9. Avoid bonus schemes based on production only, unless your communications and audits are good enough to keep things in control.

10. When you have a major confrontation with the Production Department—make sure in advance that you are going to win something!

The Quality Assurance/Production Department interface can be a difficult area—but technical competence, cost awareness, and common sense should ensure that you create a basically positive reputation for your Quality Assurance Department—and that is probably the secret of a harmonious co-existence with the rest of the factory.

BIBLIOGRAPHY

1. Juran, J. M. (1962) *Quality control handbook*. New York: McGraw-Hill. This is the definitive work on all aspects of quality assurance. Chapter 11 is particularly relevant to this paper.

2. Groocock, J. M. (1974) *The cost of quality*. Times Management Library. A very good, concise treatment of quality management, by the European Quality Director of I.T.T.
3. Thomas, L. (1978) *Quality Assurance*, Journal of the Institute of Quality Assurance 4(4). pp. 116–120.

DISCUSSION

Mr. D. E. Blenford (Hildon Associates) said that a major problem is the reconciliation of the objectives of Production, one of which is to achieve maximum output, and the Quality Control demand that the quality standard is consistently met. It is necessary therefore that the Quality Function is credible. Factors which help to establish credibility are a self-evident competence of the Quality Function staff, a clearly laid down division of responsibilities and carefully explained reasons for the division.

Quality Control and Quality Assurance must be differentiated. Quality Control has to work side by side with Production as an integral part of the management of the production team. But the Quality Control sections have a functional responsibility to the Quality Assurance Department to see that product and process specifications are met.

Mr. Blenford asked for an explanation of operator controlled quality and asked how successful it was.

Dr. R. B. Hughes (F. M. C. Ltd) asked for amplification of the statement that the Quality Assurance Department should be divorced from the Production Department. This sounded contrary to the opinion generally expressed on the relationship between the two departments.

Mr. S. G. Elliston (Wander Ltd) said that if Production made something incorrectly it may be their responsibility, but not necessarily their fault. It was part of the responsibility of Quality Control to pick up mistakes and to warn Production that they were occurring. Because of this activity he did not agree that Quality Assurance made nothing—it produced information upon which Production based its output.

Professor A. G. Ward (Leeds University) related the suggestion that it would be useful if 'The Management' in a company could be examined for competence, especially in its ability to communicate, to the attitude of candidates in the M. F. C. examination. In his long experience as an examiner he had found that on many occasions it was crystal clear that a candidate had no thought for the person who had to read and understand the written answers which he was submitting. Subsequent oral examination, if it was applicable, was important and could clarify much but it may then be too late for the candidate to understand the need to communicate. The parallel of the M. F. C. candidate and the manager—a position to which the candidate should aspire—in respect of communication seems very apt.

Mr. D. W. Matthews agreed in his reply that the credibility of the Control function is vital. It must adopt a positive attitude and so must not simply keep rejecting faults and ideas. Whatever action Quality Assurance takes it must be able to justify its decision.

He said that he did not mean to imply any isolation of Quality Assurance from Production but the responsibilities of each department must be clearly defined and allocated. They could often overlap, as with consumer complaints.

He agreed that Quality Assurance did make something and in fact sold it, namely information for which management had to pay.

12

Interface with Distribution and the Consumer

R. BRYAN HUGHES

Director, Food Science & Technology, F.M.C. Ltd

INTRODUCTION

At an earlier IFST Symposium dealing with Food Storage and
Distribution, Miss Daphne Grose of the Consumers Association and a
member of the MAFF Steering Group on Food Freshness, recalled how
pleasurably surprised she was at the flavour of freshly gathered and cooked
vegetables, and equally with the flavour of a biscuit taken off the end of a
production line. She went on to say, 'The vegetables and biscuits had one
thing in common—they were in the peak of condition. Have too many
traders and consumers ignored, forgotten, or never known that all foods,
whether fresh or processed, begin to deteriorate from the moment they are
harvested or manufactured? Even those whose flavour improves as a result
of the changes have optimum storage times'.

The key phrase in this statement is 'peak of condition'. In hard
commercial practice, it might be more realistic to refer not to a 'peak' but to
a 'plateau' of acceptability where the plateau relates to the period after
manufacture during which a product is acceptable, both organoleptically
and in terms of safety, to the consumer. This plateau, therefore, relates to
the 'life' of a product, this will be considered in more detail later.

Perhaps consumerists and others make too much of the alleged abuse of
food and hanker after those halcyon days when food was freshly available
to all those with the strength to turn a sod or draw a bow. But we all know,
whether we like it or not, that during the past 200 years, with the
development of the industrial society, the migration of people into large
conurbations has made essential the need for a lengthy distribution chain
between the manufacturer and the consumer. It is the duty of the

manufacturer and of the retailer to ensure that the food which passes along this chain arrives at its ultimate destination—the consumer—in an acceptable form.

Whatever the type of food, the objective is to hold it in an acceptable condition for as long a period as possible, in other words, to achieve a plateau of acceptability which is as broad as possible. In this way sufficient time is permitted for the movement of the food along the chain of distribution.

The purpose of this paper is to consider the role of the food control function in maximising the life of a food. Much of it will relate to the operations at the production end, but the paper also considers in some detail the problems encountered during distribution and how these can be overcome. No matter how much care is taken in making food in the factory, all will be wasted if it is subsequently abused by the manufacturer, the retailer, or the consumer.

All foods have a 'life' or a period of 'minimum durability'. Various definitions have been offered for these terms by a number of expert committees, but for our purpose we need consider only the broad requirement, that a food once made and packaged must remain in a satisfactory condition during its subsequent distribution, including storage up to the point where it is used. The EEC Labelling Directive defines minimum durability as 'the period during which the food will retain its specific properties when properly stored'. The object of the Directive is the introduction of open-date marking on all pre-packed foods, and this will be achieved within 4 years or so.

Although making considerable demands on those who make and distribute foods, open-date marking will help in achieving the desired control. It will apply to foods having an expected life of 18 months or less, but all foods have a finite durability or life beyond which they become unacceptable. The problems of minimum durability are most acute in highly perishable very-short-life and short-life foods and I shall largely illustrate my discussion by reference to foods in these categories, especially those containing meat, with which I am most familiar. How well equipped are we to meet this challenge and how can we ensure that the foods we make have the maximum possible life and consistently achieve this? It should not be overlooked that the problems relating to the distribution of highly perishable foods have been with us for many years, and are not a result of the probable introduction of open-date marking, and therefore it can be assumed that the manufacturer, distributor, and retailer already exercise satisfactory control in most cases, otherwise our industry would not exist.

I shall now discuss the relevant controls which have to be exercised at all stages in the chain.

THE MANUFACTURER

The manufacturer has the greatest influence on the life and quality of the foods he makes. Selection of raw materials of the right quality is essential. All raw materials entering a manufacturer's premises must comply with specification in relation both to composition, and bacteriological and chemical quality, and the food control function must ensure that this is so by undertaking the necessary sampling and testing. Raw materials must be adequately protected by good packaging, and be free of filth and other foreign matter, insects, and vermin.

The selection of ingredients having the right bacteriological standards is vital to the acceptability and durability of foods made from them. In the case of commodities such as meat, fish, and milk, and of uncooked foods such as sausages and burgers, the initial bacterial load has a highly significant effect. Preservatives such as sulphur dioxide and sorbic acid are permitted in a range of foods in order to inhibit or slow down degradative changes due to microbiological action, but these have only limited value at the levels of addition permitted and become less effective with increasing bacterial load.

The same comments apply to the bacteriostatic effect of salt, nitrate, and nitrite used in the manufacture of cured meat products. Other processes such as chilling, freezing, pasteurisation, cooking, and drying all assume a certain bacterial load on the food above which the process becomes increasingly less effective and indeed may ultimately fail. In many foods, durability is limited by the development of rancid flavours. Frequently these are promoted by bacterial action, and the scale of the latter may render ineffective the use of permitted antioxidants.

As well as affecting quality and durability, the bacteriological condition of ingredients may also affect the safety of a food made from them. Certain meats, especially poultry, are frequent carriers of salmonellae. Heavy infections may not be controllable by a given process, and therefore continual monitoring of certain raw materials, even where retrospective, is necessary to ensure that the infection on the material is within an acceptable level. Highly heat-resistant micro-organisms such as *B. stearothermophilus* may be present in raw materials of vegetable origin, often used in canned foods, and if present have to be recognised when arriving at a safe heat process.

These examples amply demonstrate the need for strict enforcement of bacteriological standards for food ingredients. These standards will have been established through experience for any raw material and will be determined to a large measure by the type of food to be made from it, and the durability expected of it. Thus, standards may vary for a given ingredient. Meat to be used in fresh sausages will require a higher standard than meat which is canned. Hence the application of 'universal' bacteriological standards for certain raw materials, currently being recommended in certain quarters, is neither logical nor desirable.

Much of the bacteriological work on raw ingredients has to be retrospective in nature, i.e. the ingredient is used and the food often eaten before laboratory results become available. Nevertheless, work of this type is of considerable value in determining reliable sources of supply of raw materials.

I have dwelt at considerable length on the importance of bacteriological monitoring of raw materials. Many other aspects of quality also must be considered in this context: the condition of fats in relation to incipient rancidity, and their composition as indicated by simple measurements such as the slip point; the physical properties of flours should be monitored; prepared meats to be used in foods should have the correct ratio of lean to fat and be free of excessive collagenous material. Colour and flavour intensity should be checked where relevant. The aim of the manufacturer is to make foods of a consistent quality. This can only be achieved by using raw materials and ingredients of known composition and performance.

Foods must be manufactured in premises which are hygienically acceptable. Controls must be exercised which ensure that the fabrics of the buildings, floors, ceilings, walls, etc., in all areas are properly maintained and cleaning schedules applied to these and to all equipment to ensure that they are clean and hygienic. Standards of cleanliness must be monitored at regular intervals using the relevant microbiological technique. All staff must be trained in the reasons for good personal hygiene and how to achieve this. The manufacturer must ensure that staff are provided with all the requirements for good hygiene, such as adequate toilet and washing facilities, and the regular supply of clean protective clothing, including headgear. The wearing of jewellery should not be permitted. Good hygiene discipline, as well as minimising bacterial contamination, also encourages good housekeeping. It reduces the risk of contaminating products with foreign matter such as hair, dirt, and metal objects. Persons who are suffering from certain illnesses or exhibit certain symptoms must not work on production lines until they have been medically examined and passed as fit to do so. The latter precautions apply particularly to persons who handle foods, such as certain dairy products and cooked meats which are not to receive further heat treatment after manufacture.

Despite all care, foreign matter may from time to time contaminate foods during manufacture. Unfortunately, much of this will pass undetected, but metallic bodies, and especially those containing iron, can be detected by the correct use of metal detectors. These should be used on all products after the manufacturing process.

I shall now discuss the role of the food control function in the manufacturing process itself. Foods must be made against a full specification which lays down all formulation, fabrication, and processing details. It is the responsibility of the food control function to ensure that this is adhered to. In this respect, responsibility falls on all concerned: production management and staff, quality assurance personnel, and service functions such as engineering.

All weighing and measuring must be carried out on equipment whose accuracy is checked regularly. Special care must be paid to controlling those stages of a manufacturing process which determine safety as well as quality of a product. These include chilling, freezing, thawing (of frozen ingredients), drying, curing, smoking, and heat processes such as pasteurisation, cooking, baking, and canning. Foods which have been heated must be cooled rapidly through the 50–10 °C zone to avoid growth of spoilage and pathogenic micro-organisms, and maintained at an acceptably low temperature. The food control function will ensure that prescribed centre temperatures are achieved during cooking or canning, and will monitor can-seaming and other vital operations. Wherever possible, control checks should be carried out on the production line, so that faults can be rapidly corrected, resulting in minimal loss of production.

Foods after manufacture must be packaged as rapidly as possible. Where packaging makes a special contribution to the nature and quality of the product, e.g. in the vacuum packaging of cured meats, the efficiency of the vacuum sealing operation must be closely controlled.

Wherever possible, each individual item of food should carry a manufacturer's code, which tells him where and when that particular item was made, so that in the event of any subsequent complaint or doubt regarding the food prompt and relevant action can be taken.

Foods after final preparation must be stored under the best conditions of temperature and humidity. Very-short-life and short-life foods must be despatched from the factory as soon as possible in order to maximise their life during distribution and retailing. This requires effective liaison between the Production and Sales Department and an efficient stock control system. The application of a manufacturer's code or open-date is an aid to the correct control and rotation of stocks.

All foods should be sampled before they leave the factory. Regular tasting sessions should be carried out, and these should involve not only quality control staff, but also production management. Laboratory sampling should be carried out to monitor the safety of products. This applies to canned and possibly frozen foods prior to despatch, but must be retrospective in relation to short-life foods.

Before leaving the area of the manufacturer's responsibility, a few words should be said about the importance of correct packaging. Packaging makes a significant contribution to the durability of a product. In its simplest form, packaging protects a product against physical damage, and accidental contamination during distribution and storage. The materials used must be strong enough to achieve this, and the control function must ensure that correct selection is made. Many companies do not have equipment to test packaging materials objectively, but they can readily be evaluated under actual conditions of handling, and this should always be done before a change is made.

As well as offering protection, packaging frequently serves other specific functions. Materials may be selected for their high impermeability to water, i.e. they prevent drying-out of foods, e.g. bacon, or prevent ingress of water into foods, or for their high permeability to water which allows movement of moisture from product to atmosphere as is desirable with baked pies. Cured meats and frozen foods require films with a high oxygen barrier to discourage discoloration or rancidity. Fresh meat is packaged in film having low-oxygen barrier properties in order to preserve colour. All packaging materials in contact with food must be inert, should not contain undesirable trace materials which may be leached out into the food and should not impart off-flavours to the food. Packaging technology becomes increasingly complex. Many manufacturers are neither competent nor equipped to monitor the quality of the packaging they use, but should closely heed the advice given to them by packaging manufacturers and other sources of information. They must be aware that a change in packaging may affect the durability of the food concerned. It may affect its safety also, so that casual changes in packaging must not be made. It is the duty of the food control function to ensure that such changes are not made, and that the packaging used is the most suitable available for safeguarding the life and safety of the food.

Packaging is useful also as a carrier of information. The need to mark products with the manufacturer's information has already been mentioned. It may carry a sell-by date. Instructions on handling and preparing the food can be printed on the packaging and it is part of the control function to ensure that such information is adequate and correct.

Thus the many contributions which the control function in the factory can make towards ensuring maximum durability and safety of a food may be summarised as follows:

1. Monitoring selection of raw materials and other ingredients and packaging of the specified quality.
2. Ensuring that the manufacturing plant and equipment are maintained at a high level of cleanliness.
3. Educating staff in the need for good personal hygiene and good factory hygiene, and monitoring their performance.
4. Ensuring that foods are made according to specification, with special regard to those operations which influence the durability and safety of the food.
5. Ensuring that foods are properly coded and that full production records are maintained in case of problems arising.
6. Ensuring by organoleptic, compositional, and bacteriological examination that all foods comply with the required quality standard.
7. Monitoring the movement of products along that part of the distribution chain under the control of the manufacturer.
8. Dealing with problems arising from consumer dissatisfaction, and ensuring that wherever possible, the source of the complaint is removed.

THE DISTRIBUTOR

Distribution of foods between manufacturer and retailer usually follows one of two routes:

1. Direct delivery into store by the manufacturer. This relates to smaller individual retailers and chains which do not have their own delivery systems. For a manufacturer who distributes over a wide area, this will normally involve shipment to an outlying depot or trans-shipment point in a large 'trunker' vehicle followed by direct delivery into stores by a fleet of out-based sales vans. Vehicles may be uninsulated, insulated, or ideally, insulated and refrigerated.

TABLE 12.1
Delivery vehicles
A. Vehicle types

Type	No.	Percentage
Uninsulated	23	28
Insulated	34	41·5
Refrigerated	25	30·5
Total	82	100

B. Foods delivered by different types of vehicle

Foods delivered	Vehicle type			
	Uninsulated	Insulated	Refrigerated	Total
Fish	—	1	—	1
Meat/meat products	11 (30·6%)	21 (58·3%)	4 (11·1%)	36
Meat and dairy products and/or cakes	6 (37·5%)	8 (50%)	2 (12·5%)	16
Dairy products/fats	—	4 (21·1%)	15 (78·9%)	19
Cakes	6 (85·7%)	—	1 (14·3%)	7
No food specified	—	—	3	3

Trunker vehicles are increasingly of the latter type and, provided the operator loads his vehicles correctly and realises that the refrigeration capacity is sufficient only to maintain products at a given temperature and is not sufficient to reduce products to required temperature, then adequate temperature control is achieved. In the case of meat products, 5–7 °C is considered adequate. When properly controlled, these large direct-delivery vehicles should not present a weakness in the distribution chain.

For sales or delivery vehicles, the temperature picture is not so satisfactory, even when these are insulated and refrigerated. The problem arises from the need for the vehicle to make frequent stops involving opening and shutting doors, which allows entry of air at ambient temperature, and exposes products to undesirably high temperatures over a period of several hours. Adequate insulation and refrigeration, however, do avoid the extremely high temperatures which are otherwise achieved in hot sunny weather.

Furthermore, the operation of out-based vans often necessitates the carrying over of a certain quantity of stock from one day to the next. In these circumstances refrigerated vans are plugged-in at their base and used as refrigerators, or stock is transferred into the depot's refrigerators. Nevertheless undesirable fluctuations in temperature may occur.

Tables 12.1 and 12.2 are taken from the MAFF Steering Group on Food Freshness's Final Report (1976) and are derived from figures obtained early in 1974. Table 12.1 indicates that at the time only about one third of the vehicles were insulated and a quarter refrigerated, and only 11·1 % of those vehicles delivering meat and meat products were refrigerated. This situation has improved considerably since then and will continue to do so, but a large number of unrefrigerated sales vans still operate. Table 12.2 shows data collected by the Meat Research Institute, and demonstrates the advantages of refrigeration on vans.

2. The second most commonly used method of delivery applies to large multiples or groups of independent retailers. Here the manufacturer delivers bulk loads of products into central depots and the retailer or his agent then incorporates these into composite loads for delivery into individual stores. In this way off-loading is much less frequent than with manufacturers' sales vehicles, the vehicles are larger, and temperature problems are reduced.

In relation to temperature control, the Achilles heel in the distribution chain between manufacturer and retailer is the sales van with its frequent delivery stops. It is also an extremely expensive form of delivery owing to the rapid escalation in fuel and vehicle costs. Nevertheless, it is difficult to envisage a satisfactory alternative so long as the small individual retailer exists.

Growth in cash and carry operations will go some way towards relieving this problem. The likely advent of date-marking will increase the rate of movement towards fully refrigerated sales fleets, and will also encourage the move towards distributing in frozen form those fresh products whose quality is not adversely affected.

Before considering the retail outlet, I shall refer briefly to the problem of stock rotation associated with a trunker/sales van operation. This is vital at both depots and on vans themselves. Some years ago the Sausage and Meat Pie Manufacturers Association—as it was then called—introduced a delivery coding system for sausages and pies which is still in use. This involves

TABLE 12.2

Temperature of meat products in transport

Extract from a survey by the Meat Research Institute, Summer 1971. Thirteen vehicles carrying meat products, chiefly sausages and some brawn, from a few factories in the Midlands were investigated at random using thermistor probe thermometers attached to battery-operated miniature electric recorders. Although the results are too limited to allow generally applicable conclusions, they nevertheless present a sample of current practices.

Vehicle	Loading period	Loading temperature (°C)	Delay before starting journey (h)	Temperature at start (°C)	Length of journey (h)	Temperature at finish (°C)
Mechanically refrigerated (pre-cooled, refrigeration continuous)						
1	p.m.	8–9	$\frac{1}{2}$	8–9	2	6–7
Insulated, unrefrigerated						
2	a.m.	5–6	1	8	$5\frac{1}{2}$	14
3	p.m.	10–11	3	19–20	12	14
4	p.m.	10	3	14–15	12	13–14
5	p.m.	5–7	3	14–16	12	14–15
6	p.m.	8	3	16–18	12	12–13
7	p.m.	8–9	3	11	12	12–13
Uninsulated						
8	a.m.	3–4	$\frac{1}{2}$	3–4	7	23–28
9	a.m.	4–6	1	4–6	$6\frac{1}{2}$	21–23
10	a.m.	1–2	$\frac{1}{2}$	2–3	7	16–18
11	a.m.	0–1	$1\frac{1}{2}$	1	$6\frac{1}{2}$	15–16
12	a.m.	7[a]	—	—	8	31
13	a.m.	7[a]	—	—	8	28–33

[a] Estimated.

marking the wrapper and outer container with a digit which represents the last day on which the product can be delivered into store. It prevents the salesman from holding stock for too long on his vehicle and aids the retailer in stock rotation. Open-date marking will further help the distributor in this respect. The food control function is furthered by manufacturers issuing clear instructions to their van salesmen regarding the handling of foods in their care, especially those which are highly perishable. Whilst the responsibility for proper stock rotation in shops must remain with the retailer, the manufacturer's representative should ensure that the products are being properly handled, and advise accordingly.

THE RETAILER

We now turn to the important role of the retailer. His task is to sell very-short-life and short-life foods in the correct sequence, according to their age, as rapidly as possible, and, whilst in his store, to hold them under optimal temperature conditions. Looking, as I do, at the situation from the manufacturer's viewpoint, it would be wrong for me to be too critical. Most retailers do an excellent job. Often they are faced with a confusing array of manufacturers' codes which are largely meaningless to them. However, there are those who make no effort to handle stocks correctly, and will tend to over-order and then expect the salesman who is delivering to remove and replace out-of-date stock.

A responsible retailer will do his best to order only sufficient quantities of products to cover his needs until the next delivery is made, even at the risk of empty shelves near the end of the trading day. This is especially important at weekends, when surplus products may be carried over until the following Monday. Most manufacturers issue handling instructions to retailers on how they should handle products when in their care. As well as suggesting correct temperatures, advice is given on how products should be handled, especially those which are removed from their protective covering. In the case of cooked products which are to be consumed without further heating, such as ham, good standards of hygiene are important in relation both to equipment and to the operative.

Correct temperature control is of great importance in the retail outlet. The Final Report of the Steering Group on Food Freshness includes a survey carried out by local authorities early in 1974 on chilling facilities and covered about 8 % of all premises within England and Wales. These were the salient findings:

1. Only 3·2 % of premises lacked any form of chilled display unit or storage facilities.
2. 12·5 % of all display cabinets were classed as inadequate for a variety of reasons, which included overloading, poor maintenance, inadequate temperature control, and poor convection.
3. In 17·1 % of the cabinets tested, the average food surface temperature was greater than 10 °C.
4. Only 32·1 % of the cabinets were fitted with temperature-indicating devices, and 81 % of these were not accurate.
5. The surface temperature of meat products (excluding pies) should not exceed 4 °C. In practice, it was found that over 78 % exceeded this figure, and 10 % exceeded 10 °C.

In general the picture, as with delivery vehicles, was not satisfactory and indicated the need for considerable improvement. This was emphasised in the Report of the JCO Food Science and Technology Board's Working Group on Food Refrigeration (1976), which called for Codes of Practice for the handling of perishable products and for research into more efficient display units and methods for controlling temperature.

As with the manufacturer, the advent of date marking will place great responsibility on the retailer. In one respect it should help him because he will be able clearly to identify the age of the products delivered to him. He will be concerned at the possibility of purchasers 'rummaging' through stocks in order to obtain the freshest product which is on display, resulting in older stock, even if perfectly acceptable, being rejected. That this can happen was shown by the experience of the bread manufacturers when they introduced the Happy Monday, Tuesday, etc., method of identification, and which had to be discontinued because of sharply increased rejection rates. Only the retailer can resolve this dilemma by closer supervision of stock rotation and adequate refrigerated out-of-store storage so that the latest delivered products will only be displayed when those previously delivered have been sold. Nevertheless, increased wastage will occur in some cases and this extra cost must in the long term be borne by the purchaser.

Before moving to the final link in the distribution chain, the consumer, I shall consider briefly the dilemma caused by the cash and carry operations. As stated earlier, one potential benefit deriving from these is that they ease the problem of the van selling operator by enabling him to make one 'drop' of products which covers several of his potential customers.

However, a cash and carry operation represents yet another link in the distribution chain, and will take up to 24 h or more away from the life of the product, leaving correspondingly less of the life for the retailer and consumer. There is no doubt that such operations perform a useful service especially to smaller retailers, but inevitably they will be amongst the first to feel the strain when date-marking is introduced. The need for vigilance as described for the retailer will apply with even greater force in this area. Similar concern, but to a lesser degree, relates also to freezer centres, which also extend the period between manufacture and consumption. Frozen products generally have a generous life, but degradative chemical changes do occur, especially where fat is associated with the food.

THE CONSUMER

Having (hopefully) survived the trials and tribulations of distribution and retailing, the product has now found its way into the housewife's basket. What will now happen to it is probably the least predictable of all the links in the chain. How long will she hold it before consumption, and under what conditions?

Here it is essential that every possible advice be given in the way of detailed handling instructions on the wrapper. The EEC Labelling Directive requires, as well as minimum life data, information relating to the best storage conditions for use. One can only hope that the purchaser will take the trouble to read the information which is provided, but it is incumbent on all manufacturers and retailers to provide this.

What will happen to foods which are not packaged by the manufacturer? How can these be date-marked? The simple answer is that they cannot, and this is a very serious situation because it could encourage an undesirable move towards the increased sale of unwrapped products, a move which in some instances has already started for economic reasons.

The Steering Group on Food Freshness in its Interim Report has made suggestions about overcoming this problem by requiring retailers to display notices such as 'unwrapped, very-short-life foods are displayed on these premises under refrigeration' when the products are held under refrigeration, or 'unwrapped very-short-life foods are sold within 24 h of production, display, or of initial removal from refrigerated store', when they are not.

The Group recommends that the display of such notices should be mandatory or, if enforcement is not considered feasible, should be backed by an agreed Code of Practice. Whatever the outcome, it seems to me that disciplines which are proposed for pre-packed foods cannot be applied to non-pre-packed foods, and this presents a serious weakness in the effectiveness of date-marking. Caterers in particular use large quantities of non-pre-packed, very-short-life foods, and surely this is an area above all where product freshness is of paramount importance, if only because of the potential scale of any food poisoning outbreak should anything go wrong. I feel that this whole question of controlling non-pre-packed foods has been largely overlooked and requires further serious consideration.

Increasing quantities of prepared foods and meats are presented to the consumer through channels other than the conventional retail outlet. Of these, catering establishments are the most important. The 1970 Food Hygiene Regulations stated that foods in such premises should be held at temperatures below 10 °C or above 63 °C, thus avoiding the temperature range which encourages microbial proliferation. Catering establishments often contain vending equipment which dispenses heated products, such as meat pies. Unless temperatures are maintained at a sufficiently high level during the holding period, such equipment can present a serious hazard to the consumer.

I have not mentioned the need for cleanliness and food hygiene practice along the distribution chain, because this is obvious. All distribution vehicles, depots, retail outlets, display cabinets, catering establishments, vending equipment, etc., must be kept scrupulously clean. This applies equally to containers such as plastic trays which are used to transfer products.

Despite all the care taken by those concerned in making and distributing foods, complaints will arise from retailer or consumers. Few consumers complain without reason, indeed many do not when there is just cause to do so, and we should all realise that the number of complaints received represents only a proportion of the defective foods sold. Consumer complaints generally fall into two categories: those due to the presence of foreign matter on or in the food, and those due to the food being out of condition when purchased or eaten.

Where the fault lies with the manufacturer he should take immediate action to investigate thoroughly the true nature of the complaint. Where a foreign body is involved, full information must be fed back to the production unit. An investigation must be mounted to discover the possible source of the complaint and corrective action taken. All staff likely to be involved in producing the defective food should be informed. In the case of foods which are still in circulation and where the nature of the complaint is sufficiently serious, e.g. causing illness, every effort should be made to withdraw stocks carrying the same code, especially where a batch process could be the cause of the defect. If infection by a member of the manufacturer's staff is the possible cause of the complaint, production in the relevant area must be stopped until plant and personnel have been examined and cleared.

Where a complaint has been lodged with a local authority, full cooperation must be given by the manufacturer in attempting to reduce the problem. Where the fault lies with the retailer, the manufacturer must cooperate in any investigation aimed at preventing a recurrence.

In most companies responsibility for dealing with customers and consumers in these circumstances falls to the Quality Control staff. It is a vital function in helping to preserve good relations between the customer and the manufacturer and ultimately the customer and the industry.

CONCLUSION

In this paper I have attempted to cover the role which the food control function plays in helping to ensure that foods reach the consumer in the best possible condition. Most of that role is played out in the factory where the food is made and in the distribution between manufacturer and retailer. It should ensure that foods are made under controlled conditions in clean factories and, once made, are moved rapidly along the distribution chain through depots and sales vans. It is in the interest of all of us to ensure that the customer is satisfied with what he or she eats. This can only be achieved by good will, cooperation, and a recognition of each other's problems on the part of the manufacturer and the retailer.

Finally, I would refer back to the quotation from Miss Grose cited in the Introduction. I am sure that the consumer has not forgotten that foods deteriorate from their birth. I am also equally sure that so long as the consumer retains his discriminating powers, then we who labour in the field of producing and retailing will not be allowed to forget either.

DISCUSSION

Dr. R. Spencer (Sainsbury Ltd) advocated greater liaison between manufacturers and distributors, including wholesalers, multiple chains and single retailers. This would help to solve some of the problems which existed.

The conditions of distribution and sale were very important because they could affect the shelf-life of a product, particularly those with short shelf-lives, and this in turn affected the profitability of a product. Products of short shelf-life need to be speedily, and sometimes expensively, distributed. They had to be sold quickly, sometimes involving price reductions in order to clear the stock. They also had a great potential as sources of complaints.

It is possible, although not necessarily convenient or easy, for the manufacturer to date-mark unpackaged foods, but it is probably more convenient for such food to be marked at the retail outlet. However, it is not unreasonable to expect the manufacturer to provide any information necessary to the retailer and also to supply instructions for the consumer.

Mr. A. Turner (Cadbury Typhoo Ltd) said that the manufacturer could not be present at the interface with the consumer except by means of the labels on his products. The star system of chilled storage was a well known example of an attempt to instruct the consumer. Another method of contact was the guarantee of satisfaction offer frequently printed on the label and he asked if it was thought it served any useful purpose.

Professor J. B. M. Coppock (Surrey University) drew attention to the necessity to have product recall systems available for immediate use when faulty products were discovered after distribution.

Mr. M. Sanderson-Walker (Birds Eye Foods Ltd) agreed with Professor Coppock and drew attention to '*Guidelines for Product Recall*' published by the American Grocery Institute. He said that an overall view of the distribution chain must be taken and if possible, information given to those concerned with every part of the chain. The star marking system used for chilled and frozen foods was a very good example of this blanket-type information.

Mr. J. R. Blanchfield (Bush Boake Allen Ltd) asked what the manufacturer could do to monitor the conditions throughout the distribution chain.

Dr. R. B. Hughes in his reply agreed that close liaison between all parties concerned with distribution was desirable. It was not too difficult to establish this between manufacturer and the first customer in the chain. After delivery to that customer it was a matter of judgement as to how much further to go. This related to the steps the manufacturer can take to monitor the conditions of distribution. Having taken all the precautions he can within his own control, such as rotating stocks properly, monitoring the temperatures and condition of his own vans and instructing his own salesman to withdraw out of date stocks, the manufacturer can only advise and offer to help the distributor. The value of a guarantee panel on the label depends on the nature of the product. Short shelf-life products are either satisfactory or, usually self-evidently, not and if the latter the consumer does not buy or eat them. The accidental purchase of an unsatisfactory short-life product usually leads to a very rapid complaint. A guarantee panel might encourage consumer complaints and if the manufacturer can derive any useful information from them a valuable purpose has been served.

Certainly product recall systems must be established but they must also be used carefully. Very-short-life products which should be used within hours or a day of purchase will probably have been eaten or thrown away before a fault is discovered either by the manufacturer or by a consumer. This applies particularly to instances of food poisoning especially if it is caused by microbiological infection. If the control system is satisfactory, any fault in the product will be a random one or even a unique example because systematic faults will be picked up by the controls. By the time a random defect is picked up by the consumer it is almost certainly too late to instigate a recall which will have any effect, except to cause unnecessary alarm to other consumers who have eaten the product. However, each incident must be judged according to the circumstances, the risks involved and the ability to take effective action.

SESSION IV

Practical Applications

13

Canning a Mixed Range of Products

EDGAR T. MOSS

Manager, Quality Assurance, The Nestlé Company Ltd

INTRODUCTION

The responsibilities of a factory Quality Control Manager will be determined by the size of the company and the method of operation. With a large organisation, especially when there are several manufacturing centres, it is convenient to have a central Quality Assurance Department which will be responsible for some or all of the following:

1. Ingredient specifications.
2. Packaging specifications.
3. Manufacturing specifications.
4. Finished product standards.
5. Analytical method standards.

These items have been covered in earlier papers in this Symposium, and it will be assumed that the canning factory under consideration has all of this information provided. It must be stressed, however, that this is the basis of a good control function within the factory and its importance must not be overlooked. In a smaller company it will often be part of the job of the Quality Control Manager to set up much of this information in addition to the functions detailed in this paper.

FACTORY ORGANISATION

There can only be one manager at a factory and that is the Factory Manager —all staff at the factory must report to him. It is usual, therefore, to have an organisation such as:

Factory Manager

Production | Quality | Engineering | Accountants | Personnel

205

The Quality Control Manager works alongside the others shown above as a management team under the direction of the Factory Manager. The point can be made that the Factory Manager is responsible for both the quantity and quality of his production so that there may be occasions when quality is disregarded in order that quantity targets are met. Such a situation is a poor reflection on the quality of the Factory Manager, but it is usual, to safeguard the company, for the Quality Control Manager at the factory to have a functional responsibility to the Quality Assurance Manager at Head Office to whom reference can be made on such occasions.

QUALITY CONTROL MANAGER

This Manager is usually in charge of the factory laboratory and is sometimes known as the Factory Chemist. His job function can be summarised as follows:

To plan and co-ordinate all those functions, including the factory laboratory, necessary to ensure that the quality of all raw and packing materials entering and finished products leaving the factory conform to Company standards of quality and hygiene.

The remainder of this paper details the various ways in which this objective can be achieved.

TOOLS FOR THE JOB

In a canning factory, the Quality Control Manager will normally have qualified assistants looking after various parts of the process. These are detailed in the next section, but the point is made here that, apart from technical qualifications necessary to carry out the work, it is important that all quality control staff are conscientious in their approach to the work. This may be an obvious platitude but it is important when engaging staff to have this in mind. Quality control by its very nature is an endeavour to maintain the same standards day after day; it therefore has a high degree of monotony which can lead to carelessness if left to certain individuals.

The methods for measuring the important parameters will be available to the laboratory staff, but the Quality Control Manager will need to provide training and ensure that the methods are being correctly applied.

It is wise to run checks from time to time which will show that the method remains satisfactory and that the operator is carrying out the work without error. This may be done by feeding the sample a second time (blind) to the same operator, and by having another operator evaluate the sample. Sometimes a piece of laboratory equipment may deteriorate or a standard solution may go off-standard without the operator being aware; checks must therefore be built in to the system to show up such defects.

THE CANNING PROCESS

There is no intention of including a complete account of the factory process in this paper, but it is useful to give a brief summary because the quality control function can then be related to it. The point should also be made that the Quality Control Manager must be conversant with the whole technical operation of the factory in order to perform his job; he should not spend more than half his time in the laboratory, he should be using his skills in the factory.

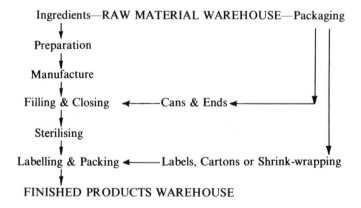

Ingredients—RAW MATERIAL WAREHOUSE—Packaging
↓
Preparation
↓
Manufacture
↓
Filling & Closing ◄——Cans & Ends ◄———
↓
Sterilising
↓
Labelling & Packing ◄——Labels, Cartons or Shrink-wrapping
↓
FINISHED PRODUCTS WAREHOUSE

QUALITY CONTROL ORGANISATION

A typical organigram is as follows:

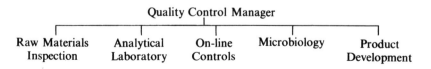

		Quality Control Manager		
Raw Materials Inspection	Analytical Laboratory	On-line Controls	Microbiology	Product Development

Depending upon the size of the factory, some of these functions may be joined or even carried out by the same person, but the need for each type of work remains. The way in which this organisation fits into the factory operation is fairly clear on comparing the organigram with the factory process. The following section deals in some detail with the various operations.

QUALITY CONTROL OPERATION

Raw Materials

The Quality Control Department must be involved with the receipt of all raw materials (ingredients, packaging, and other miscellaneous items such as chemicals for cleaning). It is usual to employ a system whereby the laboratory is notified of the arrival of any such material so that samples can be taken for examination. The storekeeper will normally check that the quantity delivered corresponds to the delivery note; he may also be the one who takes the sample on behalf of the Quality Control Department. Time taken in educating the storekeeper in quality control methods can be very rewarding; he can give an 'early warning' of possible trouble. When operating a 'positive release' system—which is certainly of great assistance in controlling factory quality—it is necessary for the Quality Control Department to give approval to any delivery of any raw material before it can be issued by the storekeeper.

At this point it is worth emphasising that a major effort by the Quality Control Department should be in this area. If only approved materials are used in the factory then the opportunity for manufacturing poor products is reduced by a very large factor. Put another way, many of the quality problems arising in a factory are related to a quality defect in some raw material.

Sampling is obviously of great importance. Books have been written on this subject and it is impossible in this paper to do more than suggest how one should approach this aspect of quality control. A complete list of all raw materials should be prepared and each item considered individually. There may be reasons other than quality control which can determine the degree of sampling; for example, the price of vegetables may depend upon size and quality so that a good sample is required—this would not be necessary for controlling the eventual product quality if all the rejects were to be taken out during the sorting operation. Confidence in certain suppliers can be built up over successive good deliveries and this can lead to a reduction in sampling—but never to a zero level. When materials arrive in bags on pallets it is usual to make a composite sample by taking a little from several bags on each pallet; it is important that the sample hole is effectively sealed when this is done. Further confidence in suppliers can be built up as a result of direct contact, especially when visits can be made to their premises.

Ingredients

Every ingredient received at the factory should have been purchased to a specification and it is the quality control function to ensure that the sample conforms to it. The importance of a good specification is obvious; the factory Quality Control Department picks out the vital parameters and carries out tests on these.

When microbiological problems can arise then the samples must be tested and rejected if found above set limits for total count, coliforms, or salmonella. Some materials (e.g. flour, starch, sugar) should be checked for the presence of heat-resistant spores which could survive the can processing temperature. Other materials may contain moulds which could have produced toxins that could survive processing.

It is evident that the final canned product will be commercially sterile and there may be no health hazard, but product quality demands the use of good raw materials and poor ones cannot be up-graded by sterilising in a can.

Packaging

It is sometimes simpler to get the supplier to take a representative sample rather than do this on arrival at the factory. This is true of labels, where the printer can take samples during the run. It is also possible to get a supplier to control statistically the quality of a consignment before it leaves his factory; if the Quality Control Department of the canning factory is fully conversant with such a system, for example operated by the can supplier, this will save a repetition at considerable cost being carried out on delivery.

A few years ago it was not considered particularly important for the Quality Control Department to take much interest in packaging materials. With the increasing costs associated with packaging this view has changed; in addition, the quality control of these materials adds considerably to the smooth operation of the factory. For example, high-speed labelling machines will operate efficiently only when the labels are of consistent quality (grain and type of paper, lacquer surface, etc.)

On-line Control

Although not a necessity, it is usual to have a laboratory situated on the production floor in addition to the analytical laboratory, which may be some distance away. This laboratory is in the front line and performs several functions, most of which demand quick decisions that have a direct bearing on the production lines. There must be a good understanding between quality control personnel and production supervision because often the responsibilities overlap. For example, it is clear that production staff are responsible for weighing the ingredients into a batch but it is equally the quality control function to check that this is being done correctly. There is obviously a patrol function of quality control whereby someone checks various important facets of the manufacturing operation. Again, the point should be made that an alert operator can give an early warning of many problems.

Samples will normally be taken from each prepared batch and laboratory checks made to give approval prior to filling. These checks must, of course, be as quick as possible because production will be held up until release is given. The acidity (pH) is an important parameter which is easily measured, but often it must be admitted that main checks are sensory. Such testing will usually reveal an error, if one has occurred, in the batching of ingredients.

Net weight controls are usually the direct responsibility of someone from the Quality Control Department, although it is possible for production personnel to do this with a check being made on a less frequent basis by the Quality Control Department. Samples should be taken for weight checks so that filling machine adjustments can be made if required. With high line speeds of several hundred cans per minute it is necessary to check every 15 min because, if a fault is discovered, several thousand cans (since the previous check) become suspect. Automatic check weighers can reduce this work but still require the Quality Control Department to check their operation. It is the responsibility of the Quality Control Department to check all the net weight control sheets (especially when these are prepared by production personnel) and to keep them for at least 1 year for presentation to the local Trading Standards Inspector as may be required.

Apart from the normal reasons for net weight control, there are specific reasons associated with cans which require mention. The processing of a can of most products relies upon the head-space to permit convection heating of the contents. This is particularly true of agitated retorting. It is therefore important to control the head-space because an over-filled can leads, in many cases, to under-processing as well as to 'peaking' (i.e. ends being distorted during processing).

It is not possible to include in this paper a detailed system for net weight control. The importance of the subject is clear both from a legal viewpoint and from the financial implications of not filling accurately. The Quality Control Manager must be fully conversant with all aspects of net weight controls.

The can code is embossed on the end just prior to it being seamed on to the can. Checking this is a further example of the patrol function of the Quality Control Department. Not only should the accuracy of the code be checked, but also the alignment of the letters—the end of the can must not be punctured at this stage!

The temperature of the product at filling is usually important, and can be very important, owing to its influence on can sterilisation. A recording thermometer is often fitted at this point; it is the duty of the Quality Control Department to check that all is in order. Normally someone from the laboratory will include such a duty as part of a patrol function—there are many similar checks which must be made, each taking only a few minutes, to ensure smooth operation of the factory.

The control of the can seaming operation completes the 'on-line' checks prior to processing. It is a fitter's job to adjust the seaming machine so that good seams are made. Because of this it is sometimes considered that the fitter should perform the checks that must be made on the closed cans to ensure that they are in order. In other situations it will be left to the Quality Control Department to take the samples and strip the cans down for measurements to be recorded. It is of little consequence who carries out this work so long as it is performed conscientiously and the results are checked periodically by the Quality Control Manager.

The method of inspection of can seams cannot be fully explained in this paper. The importance of this operation cannot be over-emphasised. One can from each seaming head (or station) should be taken as soon as possible after start-up and then every 1 h or 2 h, depending upon the performance (or the need). Several books describe in detail the method of can seam examination; for example, that issued by the Metal Box Company[1] is extremely clear and easy to follow. The courses run by that company, both for fitters and Quality Control Inspectors, are also recommended.

The results of the seam controls should be recorded so that trends can easily be seen. Wear takes place, especially on the seaming rolls, so that there can be a very gradual deterioration which can be corrected if this is shown by the records.

Sterilisation

Often known as 'processing', the sterilisation process is the heart of a canning factory. Either batch or continuous sterilisers of many varieties are in use but all have the same purpose and require similar controls to be made. Excellent books are available (e.g. that by Hersom and Hulland[2]) giving both the theory and practice of can processing; it is not intended to summarise even the important points here, but the duties of the Quality Control Department at the factory are detailed.

Taking into consideration the product in the can, the can size, and the filling temperature, a set of conditions will be determined for the steriliser so that an agreed F_0 value is attained in processing. This F_0 (or 'process value') is the equivalent number of minutes at which the can is held at a temperature of 250 °F (121 °C). This use of the term 'equivalent number' refers to the lethal effect which the process has on *Clostridium botulinum*, and it can be best explained by an example. A process with $F_0 = 10$ is one in which the product is held for 10 min at 250 °F (assuming instantaneous heating and cooling) or for the equivalent time at any other temperature to give the same effect on *C. botulinum*. With an F_0 value of 3 (the minimum for low-acid foods) the chance of survival of *C. botulinum* spores is less than one spore in 10^{12} containers. If the pH of the product is below 4·5 then a heat process for *C. botulinum* is not required. However, some spore-forming organisms may grow, although these are much less heat resistant, so that a process with $F_0 = 0·7$ is sufficient. Products with a pH below 4·0 are usually hot-filled without further processing.

Mention has been made of the checks on filling temperature; in addition, the retort temperatures and pressures as well as the retort cycles (i.e. the length of time at the sterilisation temperature) must be carefully checked. The recording charts for the retort operation should be checked by a senior quality control person the next day prior to filing for record purposes and keeping at least 2 years. At least once per week the thermometers on all retorts should be checked against pressure gauges and recording charts, and at monthly or 3-monthly intervals against standard reference thermometers.

Whenever a 'new' product is first processed, checks must be made to ensure that the sterilisation temperature and time give the approved lethal value. Because of the considerable changes in heat transfer to the centre of the can which can occur with changes in viscosity or solids/liquid ratio, it must be remembered that a 'new' product for processing can result from a minor change in recipe. With static retorts such checks are made by temperature measurements in cans at various places within the retort (considerable differences can occur from one position to another in a retort). The resulting time/temperature graph is used to calculate the lethal value; instruments are available which do this automatically whilst the process is in action. With continuous retorts more devious methods must be used to obtain this information. Radio-telemetry can be employed, but this necessitates an expensive rig which should be installed preferably when the retort is first purchased. Micro-temperature recorders can be placed in cans which pass through the retort so that the information can then be obtained; difficulties are still experienced in obtaining reliable instruments.

The use of very small glass bulbs containing selected organisms is an alternative approach which has been used very successfully; it does require a degree of microbiological skill which is sometimes not available within a factory. A spore suspension of *Bacillus stearothermophilus* is prepared so that the spores have a D value of 4 min (i.e. at 121 °C it takes 4 min to destroy 90 % of the spores present). A known number (of the order of 10 million) of spores are introduced by a microsyringe into the bulb, which has a volume of 0·05–0·1 ml. The bulb is sealed and positioned in the can prior to it being processed. After processing the bulb is retrieved and the number of remaining viable spores are counted after plating out and incubating at 60 °C for 24 h. The F_0 value can then be determined from

$$F_0 = D(\log A - \log B)$$

where A and B are the spore numbers before and after processing, respectively.

While it is very desirable for any factory to have sufficient expertise to be able to determine its process requirements, mention should be made of the assistance which can be obtained in checking lethal values from both of our Research Associations—at Leatherhead and at Chipping Campden; this help is of great value to the small factory which does not have sufficient back-up expertise within the company.

A further point which should be mentioned is the need to ensure that all cans are processed before passing to the labelling and packing section of the factory. With batch retorts it is vital that no cage is permitted to by-pass the retort and go direct to labelling; this is done by good documentation and can be further secured by the use of some form of chemical paint (on a ticket put with the retort cage or on individual cans) which changes colour at the processing temperature. With continuous retorts the same danger is not present but care must be taken to avoid the possibility of a can being picked up from a conveyor leading into the retort and placed back on a conveyor leaving the retort.

Can Cooling

Before leaving the retort, or immediately after processing, the cans are cooled. It is important that the temperature is brought down to 50 °C or thereabouts as quickly as possible to prevent over-cooking of the product. In order to assist the drying of the cans prior to labelling some residual heat is beneficial—hence the reference to 50 °C and not to room temperature. Checks should be made on the water used for cooling to ensure that the microbiological standard is maintained (at less than 100/ml total count). When cooling water is recirculated, as is usual, the addition of chlorine must be controlled to give a residual level of at least some free chlorine; a level of 5 ppm of chlorine after use is recommended.

Incubation

In certain special cases there may be a need to incubate the whole production for a period of 1 or 2 weeks at 30–32 °C. This could apply when persistent trouble is experienced with a seaming machine so that many 'suspect' cans are produced. Normally, however, sample cans are taken for incubation and the production will be 'held' until the results are available. In order to check for leaker spoilage (i.e. due to poor seaming or poor cans) at least 1000 cans should be taken during a day from one line. From batch retorts it is usual to take six (or other suitable number to ensure the 1000 per day) cans from each cage; from continuous retorts the samples can be taken at the end of the production line—one case per pallet being an acceptable system. These cans will be incubated in a 'hot room' held at 30–32 °C and will be individually inspected after 5–7 days. Cans which show no sign of 'blowing' are normally returned, after inspection, to the warehouse with the production, which is then released for sale. If blown cans are found then the cause must be determined and the corresponding production examined for this fault.

Further samples will be taken for other incubation tests relevant to the product and, in part, to its destination. For example, six cans per line may be taken at some time during the day for incubation at 40 °C for 3 weeks. These cans, after incubation, will all be opened and tested for possible pH change as well as for 'blowing'. A drop in pH and evidence of flat sour spoilage indicate that an increase in processing time may be necessary to overcome problems with some ingredient; alternatively, the ingredient may need particular attention to reduce its thermophilic load. If the product is to be exported to a hot climate this is much more important than for the home trade. Samples may also be incubated at 55 °C for 3 weeks to obtain information on residual spores although, under normal storage conditions, no problems are likely to arise from spores which grow at 55 °C but do not grow at 40 °C.

Labelling and Packing

Little attention on the part of the Quality Control Department should be necessary at this end of the production line. Checks will obviously be made from time to time on the correct labelling of the cans and the formation of the cartons or shrink-wrap packs. The code on this final pack should also be checked for both accuracy and clarity—it is surprising how easily such simple operations become faulty.

Finished Product Testing

Apart from the incubation samples which have already been discussed, it is obviously necessary to examine samples from each batch or on a short time basis to check that all is well. Generally the pH of these samples will be recorded after incubation. It may be that some legal requirement (e.g. the meat or the fat content) indicates that an appropriate number of samples per day should be analysed for these components. The solids to liquids ratio or drained weight of a product can be another important factor, especially when using a two-stage fill, as for beans in tomato sauce.

Samples should be taken for examination after storage for a long period —usually 1 year. It is suggested that at least two cans per line each day should be stored for this purpose. These samples also serve for reference if, during the year, some query arises concerned with production on that day.

Warehousing

The movement of stock from the factory warehouse to depots or to customers is not the direct responsibility of the Quality Control Department but it is a duty to ensure that no 'Held' production is despatched. This is done by fixing clear notices on each pallet which must not move, with wording such as 'HELD BY Q.C.'. After investigation of this held stock, the Quality Control Department may decide it is up to standard so that the notice can be removed or, sometimes more easily, covered with another one saying 'RELEASED BY Q.C.'. If the stock is to be used for some other purpose or even to be destroyed, this can be written on the 'HOLD' notice so that the warehouse staff can deal with it. Only the Quality Control Department staff should be permitted to affix the 'HOLD' or 'RELEASE' notices.

As indicated under 'Incubation', all of the production of canned goods must be held for at least 5 days so that checks for leaker spoilage can be made. There is no need to label every pallet with a 'HOLD' notice for this purpose; it must be a fundamental instruction that no stock is moved within this period of time. If the incubation samples reveal faults then the corresponding pallets in the warehouse will have 'HOLD' notices placed on them. Sometimes production will be held before it leaves the production line. For example, when a closing machine is giving trouble and is being adjusted the production must be held. Again, a batch product may not be up to standard but it may be more economical to fill it and sell to staff rather than try to correct it or, alternatively, put it down the drain.

Plant Hygiene

The Quality Control Manager may have a hygiene specialist on his staff to give full attention to this important function, but he must still take an active interest himself. Hygiene is, to a large extent, an attitude of mind which must be apparent in the factory management if the importance is to be understood by all employees. It is a Quality Control Department duty to ensure that plant is effectively cleaned at the end of the day or shift. This implies that the Quality Control Department becomes involved when new plant and equipment are under consideration; the ability to clean is a point which can be easily overlooked in the desire to obtain increased output. The correct chemicals to be used for plant cleaning and the methods to be used will be specified by the Quality Control Department and checks must be made to ensure that these instructions are being followed. The importance of can runways being cleaned must be emphasised, as this can be the cause of leaker spoilage. Immediately after processing a can is in danger of being infected by micro-organisms entering under wet conditions. All runways carrying these cans must be regularly disinfected, preferably by an automatic method, and then cleaned every day. The Quality Control Department microbiologist should check that this is effective by taking swabs at least on a weekly basis. A contract with some firm for control of rodents and other pests will usually be accepted practice; but the Quality Control Manager must ensure that the baits are kept in good order, that warehouse stacking leaves a gap around the periphery of the warehouse, and that instructions left by the service firm are being carried out.

EMERGENCY PROCEDURES

An emergency to one person can be something which is normal to another. In a canning factory the Quality Control Department must be able to handle situations which can arise so that the product safety is maintained with minimum financial loss to the company. In conjunction with the Production Manager, the Quality Control Manager will decide whether, and how, a sub-standard batch can be rectified (for example, by blending with another purpose-made batch) or whether it must be put to waste. Experience is obviously a great advantage in making such decisions; it is useful, however, if such action is recorded for future assistance to someone else in another 'emergency'.

Plant breakdowns often create emergency situations and the Quality Control Department must act quickly to deal with the product. This is particularly true if the trouble is concerned with the can processing. Any cans which are under-processed due to some plant failure must be held and either re-processed (if the product will not deteriorate badly by the additional cooking) or 'cut open' to re-use the ingredients, or put to waste after puncturing the cans (to prevent them 'blowing'). The Quality Control Manager should be prepared for this type of emergency, which may occur only very infrequently.

Power failures can have disastrous consequences and plans must be made for dealing with the product at various places throughout the factory if such a failure occurs. Again, the major problems arise with cans which have been filled and not processed.

The major emergency which every company hopes to avoid is a full-scale 'product recall'. However, the system at the factory must be such that the necessary information can be quickly found. Whilst it will be the job of the warehouse manager or transport system to locate the suspect production, it is the Quality Control Department's responsibility to have all the records relating to that production. The authorisation of the raw materials used, the analytical data from production batches, the processing charts, and the incubation results must all be on file for reference.

TRAINING OF FACTORY STAFF

This is not meant to suggest that it is the function of the Quality Control Department to act as a training section, but there is a real need for interest to be taken in specific areas of the factory. The emphasis on hygiene within the factory has already been mentioned and it is obvious that the Quality Control Department must set the example and be ready to give the reasons when necessary. The instruction of retort operators is most important and the Quality Control Department can help in this.

Mention should be made of a series of audio-visual aids which are available from the American Food Processors Institute under such titles as 'Can Handling', 'Evaluation of Can Double Seams', 'Planned Sanitation', and 'For the Retort Operator'. In addition, the more recently produced aid 'Retort Operations' (from Campden Food Preservation R.A.) is an excellent means of instruction for both process operators and junior quality control staff.

Quality control within a factory is only possible with the active participation of all on the production floor. Seen in this light, the time spent in training can be very rewarding.

FACTORY MANAGEMENT CONTROLS

To prevent too much paperwork, it is normal to report by exception. In other words, if all is satisfactory nothing is reported. Unfortunately, in this imperfect world, the Quality Control Manager usually has something to report. A document system for rejecting unsuitable ingredients will enable the Purchasing Department to take action. Records of all production 'held' for any reason must be seen by the Production Manager, and usually by the Factory Manager. Whilst it may appear to indicate that the Quality Control Department is doing a very useful job, a large number of held pallets can also be construed in just the opposite way. A good quality control system should prevent the production of sub-standard goods.

Although the laboratory should not make reports when production is going well, it is important that records should be kept in good order. For certain controls, such as net weights and retort charts, there is a legal obligation to preserve records for 1 year and it is part of the quality control organisation to do this. Consumer complaints, especially those relating to foreign matter, are of direct interest to the Quality Control Department. Each one must be examined and the circumstances evaluated. Those thought to be due to a fault in the factory must be regarded as a serious indictment of the quality control operation. Of course, quality control cannot be directly responsible for every accident which leads to a consumer complaint, but it must be responsible for trying to ensure that a similar fault does not or, better, cannot occur in the future.

QUALITY ASSURANCE

As was observed at the beginning of this paper, a central Quality Assurance Department in a multi-factory company will be responsible for getting the specifications and standards applied by each factory Quality Control

Department. In addition, this department will carry out audits from time to time within the factory to ensure that all the controls are operating satisfactorily. The type of question asked on such a visit is indicated on the copy of a Factory Check List, an example of which is given in Appendix I. The complete quality control system at a factory can be detailed on separate sheets, one set dealing with raw materials, another with packaging materials, and so on. Examples of this are given in Appendix II; it must be understood that the details are compiled by the factory Quality Control Department with assistance, if necessary, from the central Quality Assurance Department. These documents are extremely useful to the Quality Assurance Department but the more important use is to the factory Quality Control Department at the time they are prepared. Every test carried out by the Quality Control Department is critically considered and it is often found that a test is no longer of any importance and can be dropped whereas, perhaps, some other test needs to be done more frequently in order to be sure that it is effective.

PRODUCT DEVELOPMENT

A brief mention should be made of this very important part of the activities of most companies. It is obvious that this is not strictly quality control, but it is equally true that the Quality Control Manager must have some involvement because he will be responsible for controlling the new product when manufacture commences. In practice, as indicated in the organigram in the section on Quality Control Organisation, it is usual to find at a factory a section of the Quality Control Department which undertakes all the work associated with the trials made on new products. The information obtained is then a major contribution to the central function of preparing the specifications referred to in the Introduction to this paper. With a small company it would be normal for the Quality Control Manager to be directly responsible for all of this work.

REFERENCES

1. *Double seam manual.* London: Metal Box Co.
2. Hersom, A. C. and Hulland, E. D. (1969) *Canned foods—an introduction to their microbiology,* 6th edn.

APPENDIX I

Example of Factory Check List

Factory.....................
Date ....

FACTORY VISIT CHECK LIST B

1. *Laboratory Organisation*
   Job Structure
   —Have job descriptions been issued for all jobs?
   Methods
   —Are L.I.s in the custody of the factory chemist?
   —Methods in use differing from L.I.s—are they listed, with details of authorisation and/or reasons why used? (List to be kept with L.I.s).
   —Are working instructions issued to lab. assistants?
   Norms & Specifications
   —Are N's (norm sheets) in the custody of the Factory Chemist?
   —Norms in use differing from N's—are they listed, with details of authorisation and/or reasons why used? (List to be kept with N's, if any held.)
   Communications
   —Are there any obstacles to easy communication between the Factory Chemist and other members of the factory management team on matters concerning quality?
   —Is the Factory Chemist sufficiently well informed about complaints?
   —Is he informed promptly about deliveries of raw/packaging materials?
   —Is he informed about age of materials in store?
   —Is he notified in advance of production programme?
   —Are requirements for submission of samples of new products understood and complied with?
   —Finished products—is release system positive and effective?
   —Are there any obstacles to communication with Quality Assurance Department?
   —Organoleptic examinations—are they carried out under suitable conditions?
       Are standard type samples used?

Is freedom of expression assured?
Is frequency of expression correct?
Is method of panel selection right?
Are records kept for each day's examination?

2. *Quality Assurance System*
Structure of the System
—Are product fact books available for each product/group of products?
—Has the Q.C. system been examined critically, test by test, as to efficiency and cost/benefit ratio?
Raw Materials & Packaging Materials
—Are the requirements of LI-03.000 (Raw Materials Sampling and Examination) known, understood and applied?
—Are consignments of Raw Materials identifiable?
—Is an effective system of positive release operated?
—Are usage dates of Raw Materials adequately recorded?
—Is there an effective system for examination of goods in store, to detect deterioration?
—Are consignments of Packaging Materials identifiable?
—Is an effective system of positive release operated?
—Are usage dates of intimate Packaging Materials adequately recorded?
Hygiene and Pest Control
—Is a copy of the Code of Practice for Good Housekeeping and Hygiene in the possession of the Factory Chemist?
—Does he encounter any difficulty in ensuring compliance with any part of it?
In-line Checks
—Does the Factory Chemist have access to flow-sheets, etc?
—Are facilities adequate for the drawing of in-line samples (e.g. proper siting of sample cocks)?
—Is the Factory Chemist satisfied that in-line samples are representative?
—Is the Factory Chemist ultimately responsible for the accuracy of measuring instruments on the plant (thermometers, recorders, balances, weights, refractometers)?
—Are records kept of checks on their accuracy?
—Is it possible to establish links between raw materials lots, intermediate batches and finished goods 'batches' (for Product Recall)?

Finished Products
—Is a monthly list sent to the Q.A.D. of finished manufacture not
   released for normal sale?
—Is there a system whereby samples of goods in the factory
   warehouse are subjected to re-examination if storage is
   prolonged?
—Are samples examined just before despatch of goods if storage is
   prolonged?
—Is quality of packaging and coding of units and cartons/shrink-
   wraps checked by laboratory, sufficiently frequently?
3. *Special Examinations*
—Are sufficient samples subjected to shelf-life tests?
—Are they properly examined by responsible people?
—To whom are adverse results reported?
—(Mainly for Milk Powder and Dehydrated Soup Factories):
   Is a sample of each product examined monthly for *Salmonella*
   and *Staphylococcus aureus?*
—Are environmental samples examined monthly for *Salmonella?*
   (See LI-08.000–1).
—Is an efficient statistical net weight control system in operation?
—Does Factory Manager see LP forms weekly?
4. *Quality Assurance of Analytical Work*
—Has an internal control plan been established?
   (See PLI 76–8).
—Has it been agreed with Q.A.D.?
—Is it being implemented?
—Are there satisfactory arrangements for regular maintenance of
   analytical equipment, e.g. balances?

APPENDIX II

Examples of Quality Control Systems

QUALITY CONTROL SYSTEM

DATE January, 1978

RAW MATERIALS AND INTERMEDIATE PRODUCTS

SHEET 13 **FACTORY** PETERHEAD

PRODUCT/GROUP RAW MATERIAL

PR 6162C

Material	Sampling Point	Frequency	Taken by	Ex'd by	Test	Method	Specification/ Norms	Other information *Action if outside norms
Hydrolysed Plant Protein PX (Promex)	After delivery	1 sample per delivery	Laboratory Personnel	Factory Laboratory	Moisture Salt	Oven Drying Volhard	No Specification Results still being gathered	GROSS DEFECTS—REJECT CONSIGNMENT MARGINAL DEFECTS—REFER TO HEAD OFFICE FOR DISPOSAL INSTRUCTIONS
Lamb, Raw	"	"	"	"	Moisture Fat	Oven Drying Ether Extraction	H290/P7 September, 1977	
Mushrooms (Canned)	"	"	"	"	General Condition Net Wt. Drained Wt.	Visual On 8 mesh sieve	H292/P9 August, 1977	
Mustard (Thomy No. 4)	"	"	"	"	Moisture	Oven Drying	No specification Results still being gathered	
Peas, Dehydrated	"	"	"	"	General Condition Moisture Soaking Gain	Visual Oven Drying Overnight soak	H300/P17 August, 1977	
Potato, Dehydrated	"	"	"	"	Moisture Soaking Gain Size Defects	Oven Drying Overnight soak Hand Selection	H301/P18 September, 1977	
Red Peppers (Frozen)	"	"	"	"	Size Ash Bacteriological	TVC at 30°C	H297/P14 September, 1977	
Starch VN7	"	"	"	"	Moisture Gel Test pH	Oven Drying Brabender	12–14% No Specification 5·0–5·5	

APPENDIX II—*contd.*

QUALITY CONTROL SYSTEM   **FINISHED PRODUCTS**   SHEET ....1.... **FACTORY** PETERHEAD

DATE January, 1978   **PRODUCT/GROUP** Aluminium Can Line

PR.6162A

Material	Sampling Point	Frequency	Taken by	Ex'd by	Test	Method	Specification/ Norms	Other information *Action if outside norms
Empty Cans	Filling Line	Hourly	Laboratory Personnel	On Site	Coding	Visual		Request adjustment and isolate offending stock to re-inspect
Filled Cans (a) unclosed (for garnish)	Filling Machine	10 cans/ 20 min	,,	,,	Garnish Weight	Tared Can	As recipe	Request adjustment and isolate offending stock to re-check
(b) closed	,,	10 cans/ 20 min	,,	,,	Net Weight	Tared Can	200 g min	Request adjustment and isolate stock for check (100%) through period
Closed Cans	Closing Machine	1 can/head/ hour	Engineer	Seam Examination Room	Seam Quality	Strip and Measure (by hand)	Countersink ≮0·136" Hook lengths ≮0·074" Seam length ≯0·126"	Request adjustment and isolate preceding stock for 100% check of previous hour
		Patrol	Line Fitter Laboratory	On Site	,,	Visual	Seam thickness 0·062–0·066" Overlap ≮50%	

DISCUSSION

Mr. V. Staniforth (H. J. Heinz Ltd) said that in the visual inspection of deliveries of raw materials sample size is important. For instance, to assess the proportion of visual lean in frozen meat, it is necessary to examine entire blocks. Similarly, the inspection of dry goods for extraneous matter might involve the sieving or hand sorting of the contents of an entire bag.

Regular visual examination of machine parts in contact with food for signs of wear or damage could keep to a minimum the amount of production held for examination because of suspected contamination. The organisation involved in isolating and dealing with quantities of goods suspected of having some defect is particularly important. Sometimes a fault is identified during a production run but immediate remedial action cannot be taken. Filling of containers has to be completed, the product isolated, and then suitably dealt with. Visual assessment and tasting should feature prominently in control procedures because they are quick and to the point. Chemical analysis must be carried out and, in addition to routine checks, occasional examinations for such things as lead and tin in the product after storage should also be undertaken.

Mr. C. P. Lester (Unilever) asked how far stacking patterns should be taken into consideration when stationary retorts are used.

Mr. F. Paine (Packaging Industrial Research Association) said that the orderly, usually sequential, use of deliveries of batch identified packaging materials is a practice which could avoid some quality problems, particularly in the use of biological materials, such as paper and board which could vary from batch to batch and during storage.

Mr. D. E. Blenford (Hildon Associates) asked how tasting methods are used and how effective are they. He also asked what systems are used to avoid cans which had been completely filled with sauce when they are required to contain also a solid component.

Mr. D. A. Herbert (Metal Box Co.) recalled that in the paper it was stated that a quality controller should spend more than half his time on the factory floor. He asked Dr. Moss to elaborate on this point.

Mr. J. R. Blanchfield (Bush Boake Allen Ltd) asked the speaker to explain the precautions that had to be taken when a product with a pH below 4·0 is hot filled and not subsequently sterilised in the sealed container.

Mr. A. Dulin (Marks & Spencer Ltd) asked if the use of modern thin-walled cans leads to excessive damage by mechanical handling systems or by rough handling during distribution. If so, was there anything the quality assurance function could do about it.

Mr. I. M. V. Adams (MAFF) asked if the number of cans damaged in retail outlets had risen as a result of some modern selling methods, for example dumper displays.

Dr. E. T. Moss said that stacking patterns in retorts are very important. The temperatures at a number of points in stationary retorts have to be measured to determine the heat distribution pattern and to find the lowest temperature achieved. Heat penetration and processing details have to be calculated using the lowest temperature. Different stacking patterns produced different temperature distribution patterns. The ideal pattern produced a minimum processing time for the maximum retort load. In practice, the pattern which produces the best compromise has to be used.

He agreed that the methodical use of all raw materials including packaging, with release subject to laboratory approval, was very desirable.

He described a device to prevent cans being filled with sauce only. It consisted of a beam of light directed into the can so that the bottom of an empty can would reflect the beam to a mechanism which, if activated, stopped the line. This device was placed on the line immediately after the fillers which dispersed the solid ingredient, such as beans, and thereby detected cans which had not received a portion of solid ingredient.

In his organisation the Factory Chemist is responsible to the Factory Manager, with technical responsibility to the Quality Assurance Manager, who was part of the general administration of the company. It is essential that the Factory Chemist works with his senior colleagues as a team and this means that he spends at least half his time on the shop floor. In these circumstances it is his experience that quality is not disregarded in the interests of productivity. In the very rare event of disagreement over the release of products, the decision is referred to the Quality Assurance Manager.

When products with a low pH are hot-filled, the lid of the sealed can must be heated rapidly by the contents. This always occurs when cans are rolled on conveyors. Glass containers are not similarly handled and they must be quickly inverted to achieve the same effect.

Can damage in the factory is a matter for the engineering staff rather than the Factory Chemist. The quality assurance function can only point out the faults and suggest remedies. When new handling equipment is proposed, Quality Assurance can draw attention to potential dangers and faults and should be involved in the designs and installation of equipment.

We have in the UK a particularly good history of canned food product safety. We have been using canned foods for a long time, have become well informed about them and very familiar with them. The buying public in the UK usually recognises a blown can and rejects it. Notwithstanding the reduction in tinplate thickness in recent years, the number of damaged cans when compared with the total number of cans produced is very small indeed.

14

Quick-freezing Meat and Fish Products

ANTHONY R. ILLES

Technical Adviser, Findus Ltd

INTRODUCTION

In our factories we manufacture a range of products based on fish, meat, and vegetables, but this paper will be restricted mainly to fish and to a lesser extent to meat.
The four basic elements we set out to control are as follows:

1. Product safety.
2. Organoleptic quality.
3. Cost control (i.e. we must ensure that we put in what the specification says in terms of types and amounts of ingredients—no more and no less).
4. Compliance with legislation.

FISH PROCESSING

The nature of processing and the required degree of control vary with the type of raw material used. There are four basic raw materials:

1. Market fish (this is fish which has been gutted and stored in ice and is sold at the fish market as 'fresh fish').
2. Frozen at sea fish (this is fish which has been gutted and quick-frozen at sea).
3. Imported frozen blocks of fillets for further processing.
4. Other imported blocks suitable for direct conversion into the final product.

These materials are dealt with as described in the following section.

Raw Material Quality Assessment
Market Fish
   This type of raw material is by its nature extremely variable. Whatever the scientific basis of quality assessment, in practice a subjective judgement almost immediately prior to the auction sale has to be made. The judgement is based not only on observation of the physical characteristics of the fish but also on an extensive knowledge of the fishing ground, the length of the trip, how fish quality varies with the season and breeding cycle, and even the fish company (some fishing companies offer a more consistent quality than others). The essential things which we look for are the following:

1.   The nature and colour of the eye.
2.   The colour and odour of the gills.
3.   The texture of the skin.
4.   The colour of the bellyflaps.
5.   The resilience of the flesh, which is normally assessed by poking the fish with a finger!

   These characteristics vary from species to species and from fishing ground to fishing ground; there is no doubt that there is a scientific basis for all of this, but the actual assessment has to be subjective and relies mainly on experience.
   From the cost control point of view, it is important that fish which still give the predicted yield of flesh are purchased, and here again it is a matter of considerable experience. The bone structure and hence the yield of, for example, cod can vary considerably from fishing ground to fishing ground.

Frozen at Sea Fish
   There are fewer problems here since the fish is caught and frozen within a short time after catching. Therefore, it is not the age of the fish which affects its quality but the efficiency of gutting and handling (for example, poor gutting can result in the presence of viscera in the gut cavity, which can give rise to serious processing quality problems with defrosted fish). It is easier to define the defects which must be absent and assessment can be made on samples taken from batches of frozen at sea fish.

Imported Fish Blocks
   Here it is really a question of examining samples of blocks for a range of physical defects such as bones, skin, black membrane, and geometry.

Taste Panels
   So far mention has been made only of the assessment of quality based on

physical characteristics, but of course the ultimate test is the taste panel. Having made an assessment based on physical characteristics, the fish is cooked under standard conditions and tasted by a trained taste panel. I would emphasise 'trained', since the object is not to decide if the taster likes the fish but to look for certain specific flavours which are indicative of quality. There are objective methods such as TVB (total volatile bases) or TMA (trimethylamine) which relate to specific levels of chemical compounds, to age, and hence to quality, but these are not practical except in so far as they provide historical back-up information.

Process Control

The basic material used in the manufacture of most prepared fish products is the fish block. Where these are not imported direct they are manufactured. The control of the block manufacturing process is aimed at producing a block which meets all of the requirements in terms of shape, weight, cavities, ice pockets, and physical defects. In processing there is a balance between yield, cost, and quality, or, for example, filleting yields can be improved at the risk of increasing bone content. Similarly, the yield after skinning can be improved, but this may result in a red discoloration which is unacceptable. The level of recovered flesh (mainly recovered from the 'V' cuts which are made to remove pin bones) also has to be controlled in order to protect the texture of the fish block.

The processing of fish into blocks is a wet, messy, and often cold business and does not present any substantial microbiological problems provided that pre-washing is adequate and chlorinated water is used throughout. Control of the processing depends essentially on experience in respect of machine setting (the filleting of fish in a large scale modern factory is done by machine and not by hand). Each species of fish is different in skeletal shape and varies from fishing ground to fishing ground, and, therefore, machine setting depends very much on a knowledge of the type of fish being put through the factory. Having set the machine to obtain the optimal yield, subsequent control depends on regular sampling and physical examination against a standard for defects such as bones and skin. There is no possibility of instrumental in-line control. We are dealing with a highly variable natural raw material; that is not to say that technology has no role, indeed there have in recent times been significant advances in the technology of fish flesh recovery after conventional filleting. This process does require close control of water content and loss of soluble protein, but even here machine setting based on sampling and laboratory results is still the method of control.

It is obvious that there could be significant problems with effluent coming from a factory carrying out the processing just described. Firstly, there is a solid 'offal', which consists of skeletal bones and skin which has to be continuously removed and sent for conversion into fish meal. Secondly, there is a liquid effluent. Water is an essential element in fish processing—for washing, filleting, and skinning—and hence the waste water coming from such a factory carries a considerable biological load. This clearly could be a problem for coastal discharge is not available. Control over this liquid effluent is almost impossible since the biological load will vary with the type of fish, the nature of the flesh, which varies throughout the year, and the fishing ground.

Checks

As was mentioned above, the object is to produce a symmetrical fish block which can be used for the high-speed manufacture of a range of fish products. Where the fish blocks are manufactured within the company or purchased from outside, there are a number of checks which have to be carried out, and these are summarised below.

Physical Dimensions

It is vital that blocks are within the specified dimensions, otherwise there will be considerable problems in the sawing and chopping processes. Furthermore, there are legal considerations of fish content which rely on correct block dimensions.

Cavities

The presence of cavities in a fish block will result in a high level of breakages through chopping and sawing, and here it should be remembered that in the case of fish fingers, for example, we are talking about the manufacture of approximately 2 million fingers per day.

Physical Defects

These include bones, skin, and black membrane, and their presence is assessed by examining a 1-kg sample when defrosted. This is done simply by running the fish through the fingers and picking out the various defects. Here again we meet the problem of applying control in a practical fashion. There are, for example, objective methods for the determination of bone content which rely on enzymatic or chemical degradation of the flesh, but the time and laboratory resources necessary make such methods totally impractical for day-to-day use.

Dehydration

Again, this has to be assessed visually and, if excessive, would result in rejection of the block due to the adverse effect on eating quality.

Other Checks

This category includes chemical analysis for water content and fish/protein content and also examination from time to time for elements such as lead, cadmium, and mercury.

FINAL PRODUCT

Having looked briefly at the actual block, we now come to the various processes used to manufacture the final product. Only one major product will be considered, namely fish fingers (breaded).

Fish Fingers

Having obtained acceptable blocks, it is necessary to stabilise the temperature to a given level. If the temperature is too low, the fish is brittle and will tend to shatter during sawing and chopping, and if the temperature is too high, the fish will tend to deform during these processes. The centre and outside temperatures of blocks are checked by means of thermo-couples, but the main means of control depends on accurate control of cold-store temperature where the blocks can be stored for a set period of time prior to processing.

The blocks are removed from their cartons and sawn and chopped into fingers. The settings of the machines are checked on a regular basis by examination of the fingers for both dimensions and weight. This is particularly important since variation in size of these will affect the fish content of the final product and also may result in light-weight packs being produced.

The raw fingers are then coated in batter and breadcrumbs and fried in order to crisp up the coating. This is a highly delicate process. Batter viscosity is automatically controlled, but actual pick-up depends not only on this but on the amount which drifts off or is blown off prior to coating in bread crumbs. The setting of this air-blow device is one of fine judgement and really this depends on experience in the interpretation of results of weight control checks on the fried product and raw fingers. So, for example, if the fried product weight is drifting down and the raw finger weights are constant, then the air flow would be reduced to allow more batter retention. The essential raw materials of the coating, i.e. batter mix and breadcrumbs, are subjected to laboratory examination before use. The viscosity of the batter at a given concentration has to be within defined limits, such that the automatic controller on the line can cope. The distribution of particle sizes in breadcrumbs is important in order to achieve a good uniform coating and sieve tests are applied. The other raw material is, of course, frying oil. A typical fryer may hold up to 1 tonne of oil and control of oil quality is essential from the point of view of flavour and storage life of the finished product. There is also the problem of the lowering of flash and fire points as the level of free fatty acids increases. This is a safety consideration, although fryers are fitted with automatic CO_2 extinguishers. The pick-up of oil by the product is sufficient under normal conditions to ensure that continuous replenishment with fresh oil avoids any serious problems with free fatty acids, but nevertheless chemical checks are carried out on a regular basis. Again, we have to look to experience in respect of line control. Examination of an oil sample for colour, clarity and odour is often a more rapid and reliable indicator of declining quality than the chemical tests such as free fatty acids or peroxide value. It is interesting here to note that any failure in the catalytic burning unit employed to remove frying smells coming out of the factory is normally detected first by the noticeable smell!

After frying, the fingers are transferred direct to a blast freezer. The required freezing time is normally determined in the light of operating experience, which is backed up by temperature checks on the freezer (rather than temperature checks on the product, since this would be impossible).

Automatic or hand packing then takes place. Any failure in this end of the line can result in total shutdown of the process, since product temperatures cannot be allowed to rise significantly. The final packs are subjected to check weighing and metal detection before shrink-wrapping and despatch to the cold store. We have already seen that in respect of weight control the correct weight results from controls which are applied at an early stage of the process and we are mainly concerned with odd packs which contain less than the required number of fingers. It is, of course, necessary to carry out regular checks on metal detection and check weigher efficiencies.

Microbiological checks are made throughout the process and chemical analyses for fish content are made on the final product. Such tests are largely historical and in-line checks are made by means of a simple strip test which gives a good indication of the fish content. However, as we have seen, control of fish content really depends on the control of cutting weights and batter pick-up. The final check is to cook the product and eat it. At this stage we are not necessarily looking for subtle changes that can be detected by a trained taste panel (as was the case with the raw material fish), rather we are looking for something which is not normal. In this assessment use is made of production personnel, who take part in regular daily taste panels.

MEAT PROCESSING

The major difference between the manufacture of fish products and meat products is that meat is a high-risk raw material in microbiological terms. As far as Findus Ltd is concerned, we take in frozen boneless meat in the form of blocks. The majority of beef is in the raw state. We also take in frozen poultry meat which has already been stripped from the carcase, and the majority of this is in the cooked state. The first element of control is a strict 'block and release system', that is, all meat is automatically embargoed and not released from the cold store to the factory until laboratory examination has been completed. The most important test is, of course, examination for the possible presence of pathogens, particularly *Salmonella*. At the same time a visual examination is carried out on samples in order to establish that we have, in fact, been sent the quality of meat which was ordered. Here again, we have a situation where it is certainly possible to apply objective chemical methods for the determination of fat and even possibly connective tissue, but in practice a visual and physical examination by experienced personnel achieves the desired result.

The raw material meat, having been released from the cold store, is then processed into a wide variety of products. During this processing the separation of raw and cooked meat, together with close attention to general hygiene and temperature control, are the essential elements of control over quality. The raw meat blocks are defrosted and the meat is then either processed as individual joints for eventual slicing, or diced, minced, or chopped for incorporation into a range of cooked meat products.

Temperature checks are an extremely important aspect of control, in respect of both cooked and raw meat. Cooking times and temperatures have to be closely controlled and recorded. It has to be remembered that we are dealing with a fresh food and the quality of the final frozen product (in terms of organoleptic and microbiological quality) is only as good as the fresh raw material being used. There is an over-riding requirement that the temperature of meat and associated ingredients, such as gravies or sauces, are held at either below 5 °C or above 70 °C. These temperatures are continuously monitored by means of built-in thermocouples which give a continuous temperature readout. The reliability of these temperatures is checked at regular intervals by means of portable temperature-measuring equipment.

Unlike a canned product, a frozen product is not sterile and, therefore, microbiological counts are critical and any problem arising in the process is passed on to the final product. Therefore, samples for microbiological testing are taken from intermediate points in the process as well as from the final product. In a similar way to the block and release system described for the incoming raw material, a control system is used for the final product, and this cannot be released for despatch to depots until a full range of microbiological and chemical tests have been completed on samples.

Another major consideration with meat products is meat content, since many products are covered by specific standards in the Meat Regulations. In this respect, control of cooking yield is critical since the meat is normally weighed into the product in the cooked state and, therefore, large variations in cooking yield will give rise to variations in raw meat content by analysis. The main in-line control of meat content is, therefore, cooking yield checks, determining simply by weighing the raw material in and the cooked meat out. The stock resulting from the cooking process is used in a variety of products and not necessarily in the same product as the meat from which it was derived. Again, a comparison can be made with canned products where, for example, 50 % of raw meat put into a can and subsequently cooked is still 50 % raw meat equivalent in the product as sold. Therefore, I think it is clear that the control of meat contents in our kind of processing is much more complex. Meat contents by analysis are of necessity historical and, therefore, cannot generally be used as a means of in-line control.

In a modern prepared foods factory, much depends on the correct adjustment of machines and this adjustment is monitored by means of regular sampling and checking against an agreed standard.

Finally, there are a number of stages in the processing which are common to both fish and meat products, namely packaging, metal detection, weight control, and freezing.

As far as packaging is concerned, we are dealing with vast numbers of cartons, aluminium foil containers, and plastic bags, and the speed of packing is very high and, therefore, checks on the quality of packing material have to be made on a sample basis before despatch from the holding store to the factory. Metal detection is very necessary in view of the large amount of automatic machinery used at all stages of the manufacturing and packing process and any pack rejected by the metal detector is automatically transferred to a locked container, the key to which is held by the Quality Control Manager. This not only avoids any possibility of the pack finding its way into store but also enables a subsequent investigation to take place to establish the source of the metal contamination. Weight control will soon change substantially with the introduction of the so-called 'average system'. It is, therefore, difficult to say anything about this during this transitional period. Last but not least is the freezing process. Both the rate of freezing and the final product temperature on exit from the freezer are critical in respect of product quality. Freezer temperatures are continuously monitored and product retention times are controlled by means of belt speeds. Product temperatures are checked on a regular basis by means of thermocouples as they leave the freezer.

DISCUSSION

Mr. A. L. Dulin (Marks & Spencer Ltd) questioned whether scientific quality control had a responsible enough role in the manufacture of frozen fish products. The principal emphasis in the industry appeared to be on practical experience as the main controlling factor. It should be beneficial to utilise experienced opinion but to check it objectively by quality control assessment—a more balanced approach.

Referring to the recent publicity regarding the wide range of results for fish content found by analysing various packs of fish fingers, he asked why this should be so.

Bone removal was an important factor in view of the relationship between filleting yield, cost, and quality. He asked how bones are removed and the checking methods involved. He noted that the frozen meat process appeared to have a sounder technical control from the raw material through to the finished product than was true for fish. An important aspect of control in that industry was the separation of raw and cooked meat to avoid cross-contamination. In-going meat content was frequently determined on the filling line by checking cooking yields and relating them back to the raw meat. It was questionable whether average or minimum yield figures should be used.

Professor J. B. M. Coppock (Surrey University) expressed concern about the attitude towards the value of laboratory results as part of the control process. It was often claimed that some of these results were too late to have a useful regulatory effect. A similar viewpoint was taken many years ago in the flour milling industry, but today rapid analytical methods can be used for such determinations as moisture and nitrogen and can assist the control function even when applied to a continuous production system.

Mr. J. H. Smith (Unigate Foods Ltd) explained that with some foods, for example cheese, a subjective evaluation of the finished product based on appearance, odour, and flavour was still the principal method for assessing quality. Scientific methods were employed to check the milk quality and stages of its manufacture into cheese.

Professor A. G. Ward (University of Leeds) referred to the assessment of fish quality at the dockside and suggested the practical use of the Torry electrical fish freshness meter which gave good correlation with the Torry quality scale.

Mr. M. Sanderson-Walker (Birds Eye Foods Ltd) commented upon the move in the industry to buy fish blocks processed in other countries, where many processors control the catches. In these circumstances it was easier to establish a quality assurance relationship with the supplier than in the more subjective buying situation at the dockside. He considered that it was possible to correlate results from the Torry freshness meter with the visual assessment of fish and taste and with hypoxanthine content and optical density tests.

Mr. R. L. Stephens (Marks & Spencer Ltd) stressed that progress was being made to procure better quality fish by going back to the source and visiting the processing operations close to the catching grounds. This was a better approach than the buying lottery at the quayside.

Mr. A. Illes, in response to the points raised, emphasised that the fish industry still relied on the trained eye and the trained testing panel using the Torry quality scale to assess fish quality. He reiterated that in a fast-moving fish production process, many decisions had to be based on organoleptic examination which could be confirmed subsequently by chemical analyses. There was certainly a move towards developing rapid analytical methods to assist quality control, such as the determination of nitrogen.

The Torry electrical fish freshness meter is an aid to the experienced quality assessor but has disadvantages in producing inconsistent results. It is temperature sensitive and the location of the meter can be a critical factor, particularly with large bulks of fish.

Filleting efficiency was checked by the hand examination of samples for the presence of bone. The specification quoted a maximum level of bones permitted in a given weight of fish.

He agreed that fish content results could be very variable. Many factors caused this, such as the different species and where and when they are caught. Fish contents of fish fingers were usually 55–62%.

Meat contents can be determined using the Stubbs and Moore method and relating back to the raw meat equivalent, but in process control quicker results were needed and specifications allowed for minimum yield figures for cooked meat below which the calculated meat contents would be unacceptably low.

15

Breakfast Cereals, Biscuits and Cake-Mix Manufacture

R. J. W. ANDERSON

Manager, Nabisco Ltd

INTRODUCTION

This paper is intended to cover only the day-to-day quality control operation in a company manufacturing breakfast cereals, biscuits, crackers, and cake mixes. Within Nabisco Ltd, quality control is the responsibility of the Laboratory Services Department. The work of this Department also embraces vendor appraisal, the preparation of raw material, packaging material and finished product specifications, packaging development and, in conjunction with the company's Legal Department, the interpretation of UK, EEC, and overseas legislation. These responsibilities are carried out on a continuing basis along the general lines indicated in earlier papers in the Symposium and are not discussed further here.

ORGANISATION AND AUTHORITY

The Laboratory Services Department has a staff of 23, ranging from graduates to hourly paid employees recruited from within the factories. The Manager—Laboratory Services reports directly to the Chairman of the company (see Table 15.1). The Department covers production in three factories, one of which operates on three shifts.

Product quality is seen as being the responsibility of everyone within the manufacturing operation and, in order to obtain maximum involvement and effectiveness, the in-plant quality control function has been set up on a two-tier basis. The first tier is a programme of regular quality checks carried out by production line operators and supervisors, and the second tier consists

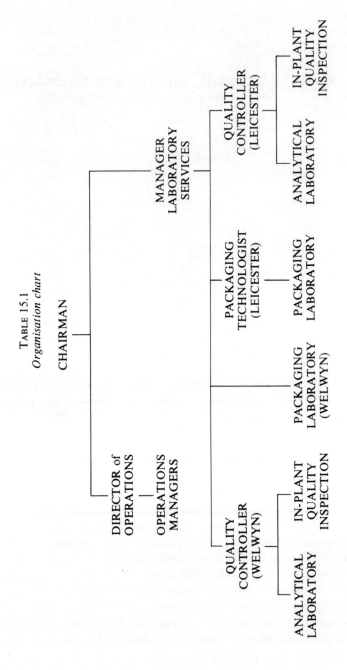

Table 15.1
Organisation chart

TABLE 15.2.
Quality control tests

Stage	Responsibility and frequency
INCOMING INGREDIENTS AND PACKAGING MATERIALS	Laboratory Services (every delivery)
MIXING/COOKING BAKING	Production Operators (10–30 min) Laboratory Services (2-hourly)
PACKAGING	Packaging Supervision (30–60 min) Laboratory Services (2-hourly)
WAREHOUSING DISTRIBUTION	Laboratory Services (monthly)
RETAIL SALE	Laboratory Services (periodically)

of a random series of checks by quality control personnel (see Table 15.2). These random checks by quality control personnel are intended primarily to ensure that the correct standards and procedures are being applied and maintained on each production line. This approach to quality control is applicable only to certain types of product where it is possible for production personnel to make an accurate assessment of product quality themselves without recourse to complex test methods involving the use of equipment. By this approach it is the company's intention to place the prime responsibility for manufacturing product to the correct standards in the hands of those best able to influence it—the production crews themselves.

The Laboratory Services Department has the authority to reject consignments of sub-standard ingredients or packaging materials and to prevent sub-standard products from leaving the manufacturing premises. Within the factories, the Laboratory Services Department acts in an advisory capacity and in the event that sub-standard products are being manufactured or packed, the Department will recommend that the packaging line in question is shut down to avoid unnecessary wastage of expensive packaging materials. Shutting down and re-starting continuous baking ovens and their associated equipment is in itself a time-consuming and costly operation which can result in the manufacture of a significant quantity of unsaleable product as well as having implications in respect of idle labour. It is often more satisfactory to bake a faulty batch of dough and isolate it prior to packing for re-grinding or sale as animal feed than to shut down the operation and dispose of a large quantity of wet, and perhaps very sticky, unbaked dough. For these reasons it is obvious that any decisions about whether or not to shut down a production line when it is producing sub-standard product can only be taken by Production Management, albeit on the basis of advice from the Quality Control Department regarding the seriousness of the fault.

The annual budget of the Laboratory Services Department is £110 000, but the total expenditure on quality control is significantly higher than this when the cost of the involvement of production personnel in the overall quality control programme is taken into consideration.

INCOMING MATERIALS CONTROL

Ingredients

The programme for testing ingredients is based on an assessment of the function of each ingredient in the manufacturing process and the critical characteristics of the ingredients themselves.

The company operates a vendor appraisal system and tailors its acceptance tests to take into consideration the supplier's own quality control programme and the confidence which can be placed in it.

Every consignment of ingredients is inspected and sampled immediately on receipt. This is normally done by laboratory personnel but in certain cases the samples are taken by suitably trained goods inwards personnel. Samples from bulk tankers of fat, flour, and sugar are taken by goods inwards personnel in conjunction with the driver of the vehicle. Prior to off-loading, the vehicle is inspected to ensure that delivery valves, hoses, etc., are clean and capped.

Bulk loads of fat and flour are tested before the vehicles are off-loaded since in many cases the load is to be pumped on top of the previous delivery. Exceptions are made to this rule for deliveries outside normal laboratory hours, but only if an empty tank or silo is available and the material will not be used immediately; in all other circumstances, laboratory staff are called out to check the delivery.

Of the wide range of ingredients used by the company, flours and fats are seen as being the most critical. The millers of cracker flours submit pre-delivery samples of each milling for approval prior to the exhaustion of the previous milling. Once a milling has been approved, samples of each individual bulk load are checked on receipt as an additional safeguard using a Brabender farinograph. The main problems arising with flours are variations in dough strength or water absorption. Adjustments can be made during processing to cope with small variations, but larger variations result in the delivery being rejected. The number of deliveries rejected justifies the workload involved. Once off-loaded on the basis of the farinograph results, moisture and protein are also determined.

Bulk fats are checked for flavour, colour, peroxide value, free fatty acids, and the presence of antioxidants, prior to off-loading. As with flours, sufficient faulty loads are found to justify the precautions taken. High peroxide values and off-flavours are the most common causes of rejection.

All ingredients are examined for appearance, flavour, and the presence of foreign matter. The chemical and physical tests vary according to the nature of the ingredient. Ingredients for cake mixes are subjected to test baking on a laboratory scale prior to approval for use.

While every effort is made to obtain samples representative of a delivery, inevitably problems come to light from time to time while materials are being used, and in such cases laboratory personnel will be notified of the problem by the Production Department and where necessary will undertake a more detailed inspection of a delivery. One of the most common complaints of this nature arises from materials becoming lumpy during storage.

The acceptance tests carried out on ingredients are normally restricted to those parameters most likely to affect the performance of the ingredient. When time permits, more extensive analyses are carried out to check on the other specified characteristics of the ingredients. For example, fats are accepted on the basis of flavour, colour, peroxide value, and free fatty acids, but on an occasional basis iodine value, saponification value, and stability may also be checked.

The analytical laboratories are not equipped to carry out complex analyses and samples are sent every two months to the laboratories of Nabisco's International Training and Research Centre for tests such as trace metals, pesticide residues, aflatoxins, and extraneous matter. Samples requiring microbiological tests are sent out to local laboratories.

Packaging Materials

As with ingredients, the quality control programme on packaging materials is based on an assessment of the critical characteristics of the individual materials and the likelihood of faults occurring.

Outer cases are regularly checked for size, board weight, accuracy of cutting and creasing, print quality, and colour. Occasional checks are carried out on the compression strength of the cases and the absorption of the board surface to ensure that it will be receptive to adhesive. Deliveries are checked to ensure that the cases are dry and clean and have not been damaged by poor palletisation. Faulty creasing and off-square glueing account for the majority of outer case rejections.

Printed cartons are checked regularly for accuracy of cutting and creasing and for print quality. Occasional checks are conducted on board thickness, stiffness, and absorption. Certain products are very sensitive to taint from printing-ink solvents and in these cases odour pick-up tests are performed on the cartons prior to use.

Flexible packaging materials are the most critical as they provide the required barrier against moisture uptake and may also be required to provide a grease barrier. The materials range from bleached Kraft paper for Shredded Wheat, which does not require a moisture barrier, through waxed papers and polythene-coated papers, to cellophane and polypropylene films.

Although moisture barriers and sealing strength are the most important factors on the majority of the flexible packaging materials, few problems are experienced in practice, thanks to the reliability of the suppliers, and it is considered adequate to check these factors on an occasional basis rather than on every consignment. Grease resistance is very important on certain materials and this is checked on every delivery. Other checks carried out include reel width, cut-off length on printed materials, print quality, and freedom from print odours.

Samples of packaging materials are sent regularly to the Research Centre laboratories, where additional checks are carried out on moisture vapour transmission and grease resistance, as well as tests on solvent residue levels and, in the case of PVC, vinyl chloride monomer (VCM) levels.

Problems are experienced in plants from time to time due to excessively loose or tight winding of reels of flexible materials and, for example, poor glueing of the glue lap on outer cases. The incidence of these faults is generally low and the disruption caused to production relatively small, so that it is an acceptable risk not to carry out the very detailed inspection which would be necessary to identify and reject such faulty material prior to its reaching the production line.

PROCESS CONTROLS

Breakfast Cereals

Shredded Wheat is a single-ingredient product made by cooking pre-cleaned wheat, allowing it to temper in bins for a prescribed time and then shredding it. After shredding the product is baked in a continuous band oven and packed.

From the quality control viewpoint, the critical factors in the process are the moisture content of the wheat after cooking, the amount, if any, of wheat which is not fully cooked, and the weight and moisture content of the baked product.

Process operators check for the presence of uncooked wheat and carry out regular weight checks on the unbaked products, the stack height of the baked product and the colour by visual assessment.

The Quality Control Department regularly checks the moisture of the cooked wheat emerging from the cookers and the weight and moisture of the baked product. The finished product is also assessed for shape, shredding quality, dimensions, colour, and flavour. The most common problems encountered include high moisture levels, underdeveloped or flat product, and excessively fragile product. The last two problems relate to a number of factors within the process and the cause is not always easy to establish. Shreddies are produced by a similar process, but are made from milled wheat and have other ingredients added, including invert sugar, malt, and vitamins. As with Shredded Wheat, regular checks are made by the Quality Control Department of the moisture content of the cooked batches.

A sample from every batch is tested quantitatively for the presence of vitamins. A vitamin pre-mix is added to each batch prior to cooking; prior to use, the pre-mix is assayed to ensure that it contains the correct vitamins in the correct proportions and therefore during production it is sufficient to use a single vitamin in the pre-mix as a tracer to confirm the correct addition of the vitamin pre-mix.

After tempering, the product is shredded in continuous strips, baked, and broken into individual Shreddies. Process operators check the piece weight, shredding quality, and colour and the Quality Control Department checks moisture and makes independent checks on piece weight, shredding quality, colour, and flavour. High moisture levels in the finished product can give rise to difficulty in breaking the strips into individual Shreddies.

Biscuits and Crackers

Biscuits and crackers are manufactured by conventional production methods. As previously described, flours are checked on delivery; information regarding the water absorption of the flour is passed to the mixer operators to enable them to adjust the water addition if necessary to obtain the correct dough consistency. Checks are made by the operators of dough temperature and the consistency or 'feel' of the doughs after mixing.

Regular checks are made by the process operators on dough piece weights and on the amount of sugar or salt applied to the products prior to baking.

Crackers are sprayed with vegetable oil after baking and regular checks are made by the oven operators on the weight of the unoiled biscuits emerging from the oven and the weight of oiled biscuits from the oil spray unit. Careful control is exercised over the level of spray oil application as it is critical both to the flavour of the product and to the cost of the product. The operator also checks biscuit dimensions and colour.

Crackers and biscuits which are to be 'sandwiched' pass via a cooling conveyor to in-line creaming machines where a sweet or savoury filling is applied to a biscuit, a further biscuit placed on top of the filling and the completed sandwich passed through a cooling tunnel to harden the filling prior to packaging. The creamer operators check the weights of the biscuits entering the creamer and the weight of a corresponding number of sandwiches so as to determine and control the weight of filling. Where the product is to be packed into a fixed length pack then stack height is also measured and controlled.

The Quality Control Department carries out regular independent checks on biscuit weights and moistures, oil weights, stack heights, cream weights, and product shape, colour, and flavour. Occasional checks are also carried out on pH. The main problems relate to maintaining the weight, shape, and stack height of the product, particularly on crackers.

Cake Mixes

These are produced by blending the dry ingredients, flour, sugar, raising agents, colours, flavours, etc., in a mixer; once thoroughly mixed, fat is added in a pumpable state and mixed in. The mixing time after adding the fat is very critical—undermixing gives a poor dispersion while overmixing yields a lumpy mix and has an adverse effect on the product performance.

After each batch has been mixed, a sample is taken by the operator and passed to the Quality Control Department for test baking. Unlike the other production lines in the factory, the cake mix process operators are unable to make their own assessment of product quality and must rely on the quality control test baker to confirm whether or not a batch is satisfactory. The few problems encountered in cake mix manufacture are normally due to the omission of an ingredient. After packaging further samples are examined and tested by the Quality Control Department to ensure that the correct mix has been packed.

FINISHED PRODUCT CONTROL

Samples of packed product are taken regularly by the Packaging Supervision Department from each packaging line to check the weight of the contents, that the packs are correctly sealed and code dated, and that the quality of the product is satisfactory. The number of biscuits per pack is also checked on packs on which a claim is made of the number of biscuits in the pack.

Random but less frequent samples are taken by the Quality Control Department and checked in the same way for the same factors. The pack weights are checked on a different weighing equipment from that used in the production checks to guard against the risk of the production scales being faulty or incorrectly set up.

All packed products are passed over automatic check-weighers and metal detectors. Whenever possible packs are passed over the check-weighers immediately prior to their being sealed so that any underweight packs can be topped up and re-fed on to the production line. This procedure avoids the wastage of packaging materials and the labour necessary to open underweight packs and re-feed the product. The operation of check-weighers and metal detectors and their associated rejection mechanisms are checked by an engineer at the start of each shift and subsequently at regular intervals during the shift by supervisors using clearly identified test packs. Packs rejected by the metal detectors are blown off the line into sealed bins and are subsequently examined to establish the reason for the rejection.

Samples taken by quality control personnel are set out, along with any relevant comments, in the Quality Control Department. Production and packaging supervision personnel visit the Quality Control Department during each shift to inspect these samples. By this means the supervisors are continually being reminded of the standards which are being sought for the product and have any shortcomings pointed out to them.

The shelf-life of the products is dependent on the correct moisture level being achieved and the packs being sealed correctly. From time to time samples are taken from the production line or from the warehouse and are subjected to shelf-life and transit testing. These tests are carried out prior to launching a new product or making changes to ingredients or packaging materials, and are also carried out periodically on normal production to ensure that products and packs are up to standard.

Shelf-life tests are carried out under accelerated and ambient conditions. Tropical conditions (37 °C/90 % relative humidity) or temperate conditions (25 °C/75 % relative humidity) are used for accelerated tests, the lower temperature being used primarily for 'cream'-filled products. Moisture and weight uptake measurements are made and the product is assessed after 1 month in tropical conditions or 2 months in temperate conditions by a laboratory test panel. The samples stored under ambient conditions are checked regularly during the period of their expected shelf-life for any signs of deterioration.

Simulated transit tests are conducted by subjecting cases of products to drop tests under laboratory conditions and assessing levels of damage to the products and packaging. Breakage assessments are also made on product shipped through the distribution system and then returned to the laboratory for evaluation.

Product is also purchased periodically from the retail trade and fully assessed for product and packaging quality and breakage levels.

Samples of all products are submitted regularly to the company's Research Laboratories for checks on vitamin levels on fortified products, microbiological quality, trace metals, and compositional analysis.

REPORTING AND COMMUNICATIONS

The reporting of the results of quality control tests and the general feedback of information to management is crucial to the success of any quality control programme.

Routine problems arising from quality control checks are reported immediately to the relevant production line personnel and, if considered appropriate, the product being shipped to the warehouse is isolated in a special quarantine area in the warehouse and each pallet marked 'HOLD FOR LAB'. After a suitable interval, depending on the nature and seriousness of the fault, which could range from an incorrect date code to a burned product, the quality control inspector will check again. If the problem is serious and still persists, then the Quality Controller will be informed and if he or she considers it appropriate, the Production Manager will be contacted, irrespective of the time of day or night.

The time scale and the action taken will obviously vary according to the seriousness of the fault, and in practice it is seldom necessary to involve the Production Manager to get corrective action put in hand. It is, however, particularly important with a three-shift operation to ensure that clear step-by-step reporting procedures are laid down so as to ensure that key personnel are informed of problems as soon as possible and that problems arising during the evening or on the night shift are not permitted to drag on until the following morning.

All faults reported are logged on a report sheet detailing the time, the nature of the fault, and to whom it was reported. A copy of this log is passed daily to the Production Manager, who may then check on recurring faults.

On a weekly basis all quantitative quality control results, weights, moistures, pH values, etc., are summarised and circulated to the Production Manager and to the Costing Department, which uses the data for checking yields. Where convenient the data are tabulated in such a way as to highlight any week-to-week trends which may occur.

Each week an informal presentation is made of randomly selected samples produced in each of the factories during the preceding week. This is held each Monday morning and is attended by management, including the Chairman, Marketing and Sales Directors, Brand Managers, Product Development Manager and representatives from the Production Department. In this way all relevant senior personnel are kept informed on a week-to-week basis of the quality of the company's products and of any problems related to product quality. From time to time samples of product of varying ages purchased from trade sources are incorporated in the presentation. The products are scored by the Quality Control Department and the scores recorded to show any trends which may occur. The two-way communication with management on product quality which results from this weekly meeting is undoubtedly beneficial to all parties and plays an important role in establishing the strengths and weaknesses of the products and production processes.

Additionally, at one factory regular weekly meetings are held with production supervisors and operators to review any substandard product produced during the previous week and to establish how the problem arose and what steps may be taken to prevent a recurrence.

CONSUMER COMPLAINTS

One important function in any company is the investigation of consumer complaints and the reporting of the types and numbers of complaints to management so that, wherever possible, corrective action may be taken. This function is primarily in the hands of the Laboratory Services Department, working closely in conjunction with the Sales Department, by whom the complaint letters are received and answered.

Within the production operation normal precautions are taken to avoid complaints of foreign bodies; apart from the use of metal detectors, no glass containers are permitted in production areas and production personnel are discouraged from wearing jewelléry and carrying loose items in overall pockets. Where possible, conveyors are covered and overhead work is not permitted while production is running.

Where a complaint concerns foreign matter or requires detailed investigation, then the sample and the consumer's letter are passed to the Laboratory Services Department, where it is investigated and a report prepared normally within 2 days. If at this stage it is considered necessary or desirable to withdraw the remaining stock from a supermarket or warehouse, then an instruction to this effect is issued and action is taken promptly by the Sales and Distribution Departments. The importance of correct and legible date coding of packets and outer cases cannot be over-emphasised if the product is to be located and identified. On most products, codes are changed each shift but on cake mixes each batch is coded separately so as to minimise the quantity of product to be recalled should a major problem arise.

Once the initial laboratory investigation of a complaint has been completed, the complaint sample or foreign matter is circulated to the appropriate production personnel so that they are made aware of the problem and also to give them an opportunity to suggest a method of preventing a recurrence.

Where specific problem areas or undesirable trends are apparent, the Laboratory Services Department will call a meeting of the appropriate managers or production supervisors to review the problem and discuss solutions. Such meetings are attended from time to time by processing or packaging operatives to ensure that they appreciate the seriousness of the problem.

At the end of each month, a detailed report listing each complaint received is prepared by the Laboratory Services Department and is circulated to management and to the Production, Marketing, Sales and Distribution Departments. This report shows the number of complaints actually received and also the number of complaints per million units sold so as to facilitate comparisons from year to year, bearing in mind that sales volumes may have changed significantly.

Public health or trading standards complaints are dealt with by the Laboratory Services Department in conjunction with the company's Legal Department.

RELATIONSHIP WITH OTHER DEPARTMENTS

Although the *Laboratory Services Department* is administratively completely separate from the *Production Department*, close contact is maintained at all levels and all production supervision personnel spend some time with the Laboratory Services Department as part of their training programme.

The Department works closely with the *Sanitation Department* to ensure that hygiene standards are being maintained and that adequate measures are being taken to control infestation. Close attention is paid to incoming goods which can harbour rodents or insects. Slow-moving materials are regularly inspected for traces of infestation. Both departments liaise with the Engineering Departments responsible for new installations to ensure that these are capable of being cleaned properly and will not give rise to product contamination or infestation problems.

New projects within the company are progressed by multi-disciplinary groups which include Laboratory Services as well as Production, Engineering, Marketing, Sales, and Distribution Department personnel.

Joint visits are made regularly with the *Purchasing Department* to existing and potential suppliers and close liaison is maintained over the timing of deliveries to ensure that adequate time is allowed prior to use to allow adequate testing to be carried out and if necessary replacement materials obtained with minimum disruption to production scheduling.

The *Distribution Department* advises the Laboratory Services Department monthly of the age of the oldest stock of each product in each of its warehouses so that checks may be made on the quality of the product if necessary. The performance of any new pack or major packaging change is carefully monitored jointly with the Distribution Department. Close contact is maintained with *management* and the *Marketing Department* through the weekly product presentation and, in the event of products or packaging deviating from established standards, perhaps in respect of colour, the Marketing Department will be consulted regarding the acceptability of the product. Artwork for new packs is checked by the Laboratory Services Department prior to final approval.

Regular contact is maintained through the *Sales Department* with *private label* and *export customers* to ensure their needs are fully met.

EXTERNAL QUALITY AUDITS

Nabisco Inc. sets out to maintain consistent standards of quality on a worldwide basis. In Europe the company's Training and Research Centre in France provides a back-up to each of the European companies' own technical facilities by performing complex or instrumental test procedures which cannot be efficiently performed in the individual companies' laboratories.

An annual Quality Control Conference is arranged by the Centre in order to provide an exchange of experience between quality control personnel in the various European Nabisco companies and to provide an opportunity to discuss new materials, equipment, and techniques. Quality standards for ingredients, packaging materials, and finished products are reviewed and the Research Centre personnel present comparative reviews of the results of their tests on the samples submitted by each company.

Senior personnel from the Training and Research Centre visit each of the European companies at least once per year to review the company's overall quality control programme and in doing so ensure that it meets fully the requirements and standards set by the parent company.

DISCUSSION

Dr. D. C. Simmonds (Park Cakes Ltd) opened the discussion by agreeing with the emphasis placed by Mr. Anderson on the importance of effective communication. Dr. Simmonds asked Mr. Anderson for further comment on the involvement of the Quality Control Department with product and process development and its need to be concerned with the distribution system.

Dr. Simmonds said he thought a consumer, having bought a product, expected an identical or near identical product when repeating the purchase. In cake manufacture, where the acceptability of the product depends so critically on its appearance, it was therefore very important to maintain a consistent visual standard.

Dr. Simmonds said that he had recently changed his employment within the cake baking industry, from one firm using a very well defined quality control system based on product sampling, to another using a total product inspection system which was still in process of being modified to improve efficiency of the quality control operation. He asked Mr. Anderson to comment on the merits and cost effectiveness of the operation, within his own company.

Mr. C. P. Lester (Unilever Ltd) asked for further information concerning the use of accelerated storage testing and the importance of transit testing when changes in packaging were made.

Mr. D. C. Horner (Northern Foods) noted that little mention had been made of the need to co-ordinate daily the quality problems of a multi-factory operation making identical or similar products on several sites. It was not unknown for raw material rejected by one factory at the time of delivery, to turn up at another, in the hope of acceptance.

Mr. D. E. Blenford (Hildon Associates) said that problems of controlling the quality of products throughout a distribution system arose when some part of distribution was carried out by a third party.

Mr. F. A. Paine (P.I.R.A.) said that accelerated storage tests on moisture loss or gain might be worthwhile, using the Oswin method which utilises the change in electrical properties with moisture content and could give answers in 7–10 days under actual rather than accelerated conditions when moisture loss or gain was the only consideration. Some transit tests in use may be out of date. With the introduction of palletisation the drop test has become less relevant and compression tests have become more important.

Mr. M. Sanderson-Walker (Birds Eye Foods Ltd) said that his company employed field quality controllers to carry out audits in both wholesalers' premises and in smaller outlets but the company was also fortunate in having agents for the larger direct delivery outlets who filled counters themselves and who reported any problems found.

Mr. Anderson in his reply said that the relationship between the Quality Control and the Product Development Departments was a very close one. In his company the Product Development Department reported to Marketing but all new product development was handled through all its stages by multidisciplinary groups (product development, quality control, engineering, production and cost accountancy) with the co-option of specialists as required.

The involvement of the Quality Control Department in the distribution system was also close. Quality Control received a monthly report from the Distribution Department of the oldest stock in the system, so that action required to isolate any product thought to be at risk could be taken.

Inspections of all the storage facilities used were carried out to ensure that the requirements of storage and product handling were met. Quality control audits in the retail trade were also carried out regularly.

The quality control operation of his company had been changed from a product inspection system to its present two-tier system which included process control. This had been effective in reducing waste and therefore improving efficiency but had not necessarily improved the final product quality, of those products meeting the specifications set.

In his experience, accelerated storage tests were a necessity when dealing with long-life products, such as biscuits, but care had to be exercised in interpreting the results. If a product lasted for five weeks in the accelerated conditions (i.e., high temperature) it would withstand any conditions in practice. However, products failing the accelerated test might be perfectly satisfactory for reasonable periods in normal atmospheric conditions.

Transit tests, in the field and in the laboratory, are essential to test all packaging changes. Stacking tests are carried out wherever possible. Consideration must be given to carrying out storage tests in conjunction with transit tests because some events occurring during distribution may adversely affect the subsequent shelf-life of the product.

His company had only one product made at more than one site and so he had not met the problem of reject raw materials being sent from one factory to another.

In his company, quality audits took into account that a large number of products are sold through third parties such as cash and carry stores, so products were bought by the auditors from small corner shops drawing supplies from such sources. If any problems exist in the shops the system picks them up but investigations into their causes are sometimes very difficult, because of the need to trace the history of the product after leaving the factory until it reached the retail outlet.

16

Chocolate/Sugar Confectionery Manufacture

DON BARGENT

Quality Assurance Superintendent, Mars Confectionery Ltd

INTRODUCTION

This paper, as previous papers, is concerned with an integrated food control operation, but with particular emphasis on the responsibilities of the Quality Assurance (Q.A.) Department. The Q.A. Department works in close liaison with almost all divisions of the company, in particular the Research and Development, Production, Marketing, Engineering and Sales Departments.

The organisation and methods, etc., relate to a company producing a wide range of chocolate, sugar, and flour confectionery using continuous processes on a four-shift basis, and although part of a multi-national organisation, the company operates essentially as an autonomous unit. The organisation and control procedures have been developed over a long period to suit our type and style of business. It is not suggested that they are appropriate to all confectionery companies or that they are ideal—indeed, they are constantly being reviewed and improved.

Product development and improvement, market research, plant design, etc., are all done within the company and the brief summary below indicates the departments most concerned in determining the specifications and standards, etc., for the product range.

Raw material specification	R&D—Product Development
Product recipe, composition	R&D—Product Development
Processing equipment	Production Engineering; R&D
Manufacturing procedures	Production; Engineering; R&D

Packaging specification	R&D—Packaging Department
Weights and pricing	Marketing
Quality standards	Q.A.; R&D; Marketing; Production
Analytical standards	Q.A.; R&D
Microbiological standards	Q.A.; R&D
Process control	Production; Q.A.; R&D

The company aim is consistently to produce products which meet the agreed quality standards within legal and safety requirements—at an acceptable cost. The responsibility of assuring quality and safety lies with every associate in the company , the Q.A. Department having the overall responsibility of coordinating the various activities most directly involved. The total effectiveness of the system will be finally judged in terms of consumer satisfaction and sales performance. (Note: *all* employees, managers and non-managers, are associates.)

It is important to remember that we are not selling products that are regarded as an essential part of a normal diet, although they make a nutritional contribution. Our products sell because their flavour, texture, and value give satisfaction to the consumers who, of course, have a right to expect that they are safe to eat.

The Q.A. Department and overall company organisation must, of course, depend on size and product range; the *approximate* data given below set the scene:

1. 16 major products with many size and packaging variants for UK and export markets.
2. 4000 associates employed.
3. Over 2000 million consumer packs produced per annum.
4. The cost of the Q.A. Department is approximately 0.5% of the company turnover.

THE COMPANY ORGANISATION

The outline organisations shown below detail only those areas directly concerned with product development, the manufacturing process and quality assurance.

1. *Manufacturing*—2700 associates.

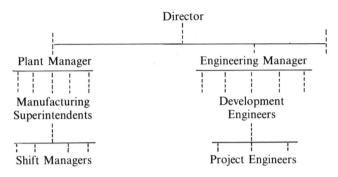

2. *Research and Development*—230 associates.

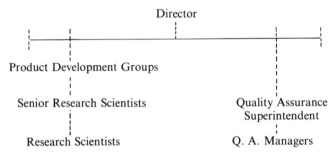

3. *Quality Assurance Department*—90 associates.

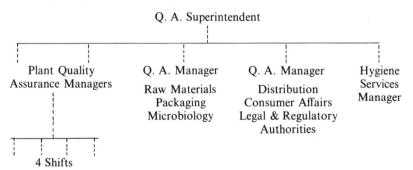

In our organisation, the Q.A. Department is independent of the Manufacturing Departments and of the Marketing Department, but of course works in close liaison with both.

In many other companies the Q.A. Department is within the Manufacturing or Marketing Divisions, but provided it has the necessary authority it can function efficiently in either—the aims and objectives are unchanged.

THE QUALITY ASSURANCE DEPARTMENT

The essential functions of the Q.A. Department in our organisation, very briefly stated, are as follows:

1. To ensure that the raw materials and packaging materials meet the required standards in all respects. The specifications are set by R&D.
2. To provide data and advice to enable the production processes to be controlled *by production*. This implies rapid feedback of information and easily operated lines of communication at all levels.
3. To ensure that all product despatched meets the agreed quality standards with respect to composition, weight, taste, texture, safety, and legal requirements.
4. To monitor the distribution system from factory to ultimate consumer and make recommendations or take action as necessary.
5. To deal with legal and regulatory authorities as required.

The aim of all departments is to prevent the manufacture of any substandard product. Inevitably, however, such product is made on occasion, as often the only way to regain control, when lost, of a particular aspect of the process is to continue running with necessary adjustments. In most instances the product will be scrapped or re-worked before reaching the packing stage. If not, the Q.A. Department will hold such product for re-checking if necessary and decide suitable action(s).

The Q.A. operation is covered in more detail in later parts of this paper.

THE TOOLS FOR THE JOB

The Associates
They must be adequately qualified and trained, accurate, and with a high degree of integrity. Adequately qualified may mean academic qualifications and/or experience in the manufacturing and associated processes. Both types of 'qualification' are needed, one or the other being more important depending upon the individual jobs within the Q.A. Department.

Methods

Standard methods for assessing all quality control checks must be developed, agreed, and documented. This applies to the whole range of inspection processes, from complex microbiological or analytical measurements to subjective evaluation of product appearance. It is particularly important when a number of shift teams are involved in order to standardise the data collected.

A Quality Manual is prepared for each product, including the following features:

1. Checks required, frequency, and sampling procedures.
2. Detailed methods.
3. Why the check is done—a useful discipline to avoid unnecessary tests.
4. Standards for each check, ideally in the form of warning and action limits. The standards for objective measurements are in general numerical values, those for subjective measurements, e.g. product appearance, can be set by examples, diagrams or photographs illustrating limits of acceptability.

The original standards must be set bearing in mind the marketing, legal and safety requirements and the capability of the production line in its normal operating mode (speed, output, manning, variability of raw materials, and processes). If the standards required cannot be met, then of course the company does not yet have a marketable product.

Equipment

The cost of quality assurance and other control functions has been dealt with in detail in other papers.

Equipment must be available to provide accurate and relevant data as and when required by the control operation and within the capabilities of the operators. Furthermore, in order to increase productivity and reduce the overall cost of the total operation, it is important to consider the split in cost between operators and equipment. Each item of equipment must be justified in terms of its overall benefit to the company. It is, of course, easier to justify 'automated' systems when operating a four-shift operation, thus ensuring maximum utilisation of such equipment. A further important point to consider is the elimination of boring, tedious, physically demanding, and repetitive operations, thereby improving the job content of all associates.

THE PRODUCTION PROCESS

For the 16 or so major production lines, the processes necessarily cover a very wide range. However, those common to most products include the following:

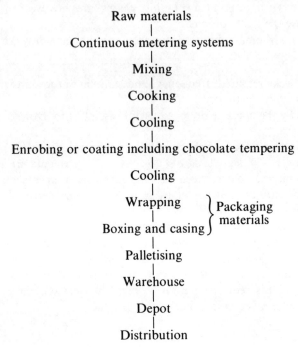

Raw materials
|
Continuous metering systems
|
Mixing
|
Cooking
|
Cooling
|
Enrobing or coating including chocolate tempering
|
Cooling
|
Wrapping   ⎫ Packaging
| ⎬ materials
Boxing and casing ⎭
|
Palletising
|
Warehouse
|
Depot
|
Distribution

THE FACTORY QUALITY CONTROL ORGANISATION

The Manufacturing division is responsible for making the product to the agreed quality standards. Information, advice, etc., to enable this to be done is provided by:

1. Production associates on-line quality inspection systems developed in consultation with Q.A.
2. All Q.A. sections.
3. Other departments, e.g. R&D, Engineering, as appropriate.

The Q.A. Department does not, and should not, have the authority to shut down or make changes to a production process, only to recommend suitable actions. Their ultimate responsibility, and rarely used sanction, is to prevent the despatch of any sub-standard product. The fact that such a system works very efficiently is largely a reflection of the easy and rapid communication systems.

THE QUALITY ASSURANCE SYSTEM

The system being developed is known as P.A.S.S. or 'Product Assurance Surveillance System'. It provides:

1. A rational, systematic, and documented approach for the entire quality assurance programme from raw materials to the consumer.
2. Problem-solving and decision-making guidelines but not instructions—judgement is still required.
3. Identification of critical control points where loss of control may lead to unacceptable product with respect to quality, safety, or legal requirements.
4. Adequate information, when required, lines of communication, and responsibility.
5. Estimation of risks.
6. Test procedures, quality standards, warning and action levels.

Every check or measurement carried out in the total inspection system is aimed at reducing or eliminating the risk of unacceptable product for any reason. The risks involved can be broadly classified into three types, namely safety (S), regulatory (R), or manufacturing (M).

1. *Product Safety*
   S1   Public health—*Salmonella*, etc.
   S2   Physical hazards—extraneous material, e.g. glass, metal, stones, wood, plastic.
   S3   Public health—infestation.
   S4   Raw material tracing to finished product.
2. *Regulatory Requirements*
   R1   Ingredients, labelling.
   R2   Weights and measures.
   R3   Date marking.

3. *Manufacturing Controls*
   M1 Time and mixing speeds.
   M2 Temperature.
   M3 Analytical—chemical and physical.
   M4 Microbiological (excepting S1)—covering raw materials, plant processes, and finished product.
   M5 Flavour.
   M6 Visual.
   M7 Formula control—composition.
   M8 Incoming raw materials and packaging—delivered quantities.

The P.A.S.S. Manual will include the following information for each item checked:

1. Items—e.g. a raw material, process plant, work in progress, packaging, finished product.
2. Risk—risk category S, R, or M.
3. Control—e.g. microbiological test, analysis, appearance, taste, weight, composition, temperature, time, physical properties.
4. Frequency of check—e.g. continuous, once per load, four per shift.
5. Methods and equipment—e.g. visual, balance, gas–liquid chromatography, atomic absorption spectrometry.
6. Action level—e.g. analytical or weight limits, unacceptable taste or appearance.
7. Responsibility—ideally one manager.
8. Action—action required and who must be informed.
9. Documentation—where and who is responsible for recording and filing information.

A typical P.A.S.S. Manual for a product will consist of approximately 70–80 single-sided A4 sheets comprehensively covering all controls to assure satisfactory product to the ultimate consumer. It is not intended to be a document that will be regularly used for reference, but rather a comprehensive summary of all aspects of the control and assurance procedures that are in current use, with facilities for amending, updating, and including new controls as required. In practice it will be sub-divided into many sections appropriate to particular areas of the control operation and used in these areas.

Appendix I illustrates the form of the P.A.S.S. Manual. It is intended only as an illustration and, in order to maintain confidentiality of the company's products and processes, the items quoted do not relate to a particular product, nor are the quantitative data or action levels those actually used.

Raw Materials

Each raw material batch is checked to ensure conformity with the specification laid down by R&D. The specification of course should only contain standards and limits that are *important* to the process operation, product quality, and safety. The method of sampling and frequency of checks depend upon both possible consequences of using sub-standard raw materials and confidence based on past results of a particular material and/or supplier. Appendix I illustrates part of the P.A.S.S. system for a particular raw material, e.g. sugar. It illustrates the principle of the system in use; the actual data covering frequency and action levels have been changed to protect company confidentiality.

A further important part of the system is raw material tracing and sample storage, whereby for each delivery:

1. A unique reference number is allocated.
2. All quality data from vendor, Q.A. inspection and analysis, microbiology, vehicle inspection, etc., is documented under the reference number. Where possible a positive release system is operated whereby the material is not cleared for use until all checks have been satisfactorily completed.
3. Movement of the raw material is traced from warehouse to plant, in-plant store to process, and process to finished product.
4. A reference sample is retained for 1 year in a cold store.
5. A sample of each finished product from each shift is retained for 1 year in a normal air-conditioned warehouse environment.

Packaging Materials

The system is essentially similar to that for raw materials, except that the supplier and order number are used as the unique reference.

Important aspects of quality that would normally be checked include:

1. Solvent retention—gas–liquid chromatographic checks if considered necessary to conform to agreed standards.
2. Dimensions, reel quality, total substance ($g\,m^{-2}$).
3. Colours—to agreed colour standards and limits.
4. Bulk packaging by supplier.
5. Moisture content, stiffness, compression value, etc., as appropriate.

Process Control

Process Data Monitoring

Critical process data, e.g. times, temperatures, pressures, flow-rates, are either continuously monitored or checked at specified intervals.

Intermediate Inspection

In-process sampling is carried out at important stages to determine acceptability of various components with respect to such criteria as density, moisture content, texture, appearance, weight.

The final product composition and individual component acceptability are more easily assured by checking at intermediate stages rather than attempting an 'analysis' of the final product. Furthermore, this procedure enables faster corrective action to be taken.

Microbiological Controls

Microbiological checks are effected on raw materials, materials in-process, plant, and finished product to ensure standards have been met. By the nature of the tests, results are not available until 1–4 days after sampling. Subsequent actions, if any, from these checks comprise:

1. Plant and process are satisfactory—no action required. This is, of course, the result in the majority of cases.
2. Plant and/or process are approaching the warning limits and should be shut down and cleaned.
3. Plant and/or process have deviated from standards. The plant must be immediately shut down and cleaned. The risk and therefore subsequent actions must be determined for each individual case, but would invariably involve a hold of finished product and more extensive sampling.

Certain areas of the processes prior to the 'cooking' stage will support bacterial growth, and particular emphasis is therefore placed on raw materials—operating a positive release system where possible—and plant hygiene. The nature of all our products is that, although they may carry a bacterial load if control has been inadequate, they will not support bacterial growth.

Finished Product Control

At the primary packing stage, product is sampled at specified frequencies and levels to determine:

1. *Weight control* and variation to ensure compliance with both company and legal requirements.

2. *Product defect levels*—subjective judgements with respect to such qualities as shape, gloss, decoration, physical damage, colour, texture, and hardness, as appropriate to the product. It is in this subjective area that it is more difficult to establish standards and ensure uniformity of judgement between different people. Careful training is required, with illustrations or photographs where appropriate.

Packaged Product Quality

Packaged products are checked with respect to such criteria as material registration, seal integrity, pack appearance, box filling appearance, box closure, legibility of shift code, and expiry date.

Note: in order to determine frequency of sampling and size, it is important to determine:

1. What accuracy is required, e.g. weight to 0·1, 0·5 or possibly 1 g.
2. What confidence level is required, e.g. 95%, 99%, etc.

Well known statistical tables can then be used to determine inspection levels. It is, of course, a waste of time, effort, and money to inspect more than necessary.

Taste Panels

The important test of all our products is—what do they look and taste like? Each day a complete range of products made from the previous night are distributed around the company, primarily to management, but written comments are invited from any associate who samples the tray.

The comments are collected and summarised weekly by the Q.A. Department when any significant trends may be further investigated.

Formal taste panels may be convened at any time to investigate particular areas, using a wide variety of well known taste panel techniques, e.g. pairing tests or sequential analysis.

Consumer Protection Devices (CPDs)

CPDs include metal detectors, check-weighers, missing-bar detectors, heat-damage detectors, magnets, and sieves, i.e. devices designed to prevent the inclusion of:

1. Foreign bodies, particularly metal.
2. Defective weights with respect to legal requirements.
3. Grossly defective weight packs, e.g. one instead of two bars in a pack.

4. Severely heat-damaged chocolate products caused by machine stoppages when using heat-seal wrapping materials.

A formalised procedure is laid down for checking that all such devices are operating satisfactorily and to the required sensitivity for metal detectors and check-weighers. The procedure should include frequency and methods of checking and action in the event of a device failure. The first action is invariably to shut down the wrapping machines or equipment until the fault is rectified.

Product made since the last satisfactory check is held for re-checking, again according to laid-down procedures.

Warehouse and Distribution Assurance

The major consideration in these areas is the maintenance of quality standards already achieved in the product. Continuous monitoring of warehouse and depot environments and training of all personnel in the distribution system are key factors in maintaining quality. Posters, booklets, visits, etc., all contribute to assuring an awareness of the important points with respect to confectionery storage and distribution, namely:

temperature and humidity requirements;
palletisation and stacking;
infestation and contamination risks;
stock rotation;
general handling.

Quality assurance can be fully maintained to the level of large wholesalers, but at retail outlets it is more difficult since the company has no title to the goods and no authority with the retailer. Advice via the sales force is used whenever possible.

Hygiene
Microbiological

Microbiological controls were discussed above. In the event of a plant shutdown as a result of microbiological checks or, as is generally the case, plant shutdowns for routine maintenance, specified cleaning programmes are followed. These will include:

1. Items of plant to be cleaned.
2. Degree of dismantling necessary.
3. Renewals required, e.g. plastic pipework.

4. Cleaning materials, dilutions, times, and temperatures to be used.
5. Wet or dry cleaning.

Insect and Rodent Control

The hygiene services section of the Q.A. Department shown above under the Company Organisation provide:

1. Continuous monitoring of the total factory, including warehouse and offices.
2. A routine treatment programme for all important areas, including spraying, fumigation, and traps, as appropriate.
3. A four-shift cover to deal with any problems immediately they are found.
4. Advice and inspection as required or requested by outside depots, customer warehouses, and retail outlets.
5. Advice in the early stages of plant design to avoid subsequent problems with infestation.

Hygiene Training

The Q.A. Department contributes to the overall effort to ensure hygienic operations and good housekeeping. The techniques used include poster campaigns, job involvement meetings, and slide and film presentations, ideally illustrating areas in our own plants.

EMERGENCY PROCEDURES

These procedures are required for, e.g. power failure, steam failure, and equipment breakdowns. Actions required are so diverse, depending on which of the product lines are involved and the nature of the breakdown, that it is impossible to cover this topic briefly.

TRAINING AND MOTIVATION OF PEOPLE

In-plant Q.A. data are designed primarily to help the Production Departments to control their production processes to ensure finished product of acceptable quality. As there are more production operators than Q.A. personnel (approximately 25:1 in this company), and they see the plant and product continuously, it is obviously desirable that they will all have a quality control function.

This approach is encouraged by extensive training of all appropriate production operators using the Q.A. methods, defect categories, documentation, etc. Each production line carries out their own quality measurements, with the Q.A. Department doing a concurrent audit either on-line or in the warehouse. The two sets of results may be compared by well known statistical techniques to ensure that the system is working satisfactorily, and to highlight those areas where further discussion or training is required.

THE QUALITY AUDIT

At intervals field audits are done to determine the quality, age, and distribution of products in retail outlets. Three types of audit are done:

1. A regular monthly audit carried out by the sales force for four selected products, changing each month.
2. A 6-monthly audit covering the entire product range, primarily concerned with the age spread in relation to the declared product shelf-life, but including an overall quality assessment.
3. Special audits for particular products, areas, etc., as appropriate, initiated by the Marketing, Sales, Q.A. or R&D Departments.

MANAGEMENT CONTROLS

Quality Survey Reports

Weekly and monthly (4 weeks) summary reports are prepared and circulated to all senior managers and other managers most directly concerned. They are sub-divided by product and include the following information:

1. Weight control performance—means and variance.
2. Statistical check of conformity with legal requirements.
3. Percentage of product components.
4. Number of checks done.
5. The most important of the analytical and physical properties measured, e.g. acid content, some declared ingredients, hardness values, particle size distribution.
6. Size data, dimensions, distribution, etc.
7. Product defect levels.
8. Packaging defect levels.

9. Expiry date and code dating performances.
10. Trend graphs as appropriate for the most important quality parameters and/or for current problem areas.

The weekly survey reports each of the four production shifts separately as an aid to management control. The monthly survey also includes the results for the previous period and serves as a basis for a regular monthly quality survey meeting attended by senior management from Production, Marketing, R&D and other Departments as appropriate to the agenda prepared by the Quality Assurance Department.

The hourly, shift, and weekly quality assessment control charts are maintained on each of the production lines to ensure easy accessibility at all times.

Recovery of sub-standard Product

In spite of all the controls, at times sub-standard product will be produced. The Q.A. Department has the authority to hold such product and advise the appropriate department of suitable recovery operations, e.g.

re-work
re-pack if packaging defect;
hold for re-check;
sorting if economic, depending on probable yield;
scrap.

Sub-standard Ingredients

As mentioned previously, we operate a positive release system for most of our raw materials whereby all checks are completed before the material is released for production use.

Sub-standard raw materials can arise from (a) those materials that have failed to conform to specification from our test results, and (b) very occasionally materials that give problems in the production process and on re-check are found to be outside specification. No sampling procedure can give a 100% guarantee of acceptability.
Subsequent actions may be:

1. Reject to supplier—the most probable action.
2. Blend with another batch such that the blend conforms with the specification.
3. Examine possible use for a specific product, e.g. slightly discoloured sugar, if satisfactory in all other respects, may be used in a dark-coloured boiled sweet.

Consumer Complaints

In a company producing over 2000 million consumer packs per annum it is inevitable that some defective product will have escaped the total quality assurance net, or have been damaged in the distribution system or retail outlet. Such complaints typically represent 1 complaint for 100 000 packs, increasing in the summer months due to heat damage to chocolate products, chocolate being subject to an irreversible appearance change giving a white 'bloom' effect on exposure to temperatures around 28 °C (82 °F).

Any consumer who complains will be recompensed for the product, including postage, given an accurate explanation of the reason for the defect where possible, and always treated courteously and efficiently with the aim of ensuring their satisfaction and continued custom.

Consumer complaints also act as an extremely valuable guide to defects at very low incidence levels that are detected only rarely or with great difficulty by normal in-plant sampling or in-field audits.

FUTURE DEVELOPMENTS AND NEW PRODUCTS

It is essential that the Q.A. Department is involved as early as possible in any new product, process, or equipment development in order that possible problem areas may be discussed and resolved. This should not merely mean waiting to be informed, but actively finding out about proposed developments. An easy communications environment and regular personal contacts facilitate this process.

APPENDIX I

Illustration of the P.A.S.S. Manual

Plant: Mars, Dundee Road.   Product A.   Process A.   Preparation A.

Item	Risk	Control	Frequency of check	Method used, equipment	Action level	Responsibility	Action taken	Documentation
Incoming Gran sugar bulk	S2	Screens	Once per week	Visual	Reduced flow-rate. Missing, broken or blocked	Production Shift Manager	Maintenance informed and requested to replace or repair	Production shift log. Maintenance shift log.
	R1	Identification. Appearance	Every load	Visual. Organoleptic	Unacceptable appearance or taste	Q.A. Manager (Raws)	Inform Supplies Mgr., Q.A. Superint. and R&D. Reject shipment	Q.A. records
	M3	Analytical R/sugars	Spot checks	Lane & Eynon	$>0.04\%$	Lab. Services Manager	Inform Supplies Mgr., Q.A. Superint. and R&D. Reject shipment if analytical defect will impair finished product Quality or Safety	Q.A. records
		Trace metals	Once per month	AAS	Lead >0.5 ppm Arsenic >1.0 ppm Copper >2.0 ppm Sigma 3 GLC $>0.06\%$			
		Moisture						
	M6	Vehicle inspection	Every load	Visual	Any physical or chemical damage	Receiving warehouse Mgr., Q.A. Mgr. (Raws)	Supplies informed. Any damaged goods rejected	Q.A. files. Receiving warehouse records
	M8	Weight of load	Every load	Weighbridge	Any shortage	Material Services Manager	Supplies informed. Supplies Manager makes appropriate adjustment in vendor contract or rejects delivery	Material services records
	S4	Traceability	Every load	Sample reference library	Consumer reaction. Retrospective analytical results	Q.A. Manager (Fin. goods) Q.A. Manager (Raws)	Refer to tracing records Examine reference sample	Tracing records and Q.A. records

APPENDIX I—contd.

Plant: Mars, Dundee Road.

Product A. Process A. Preparation A.

Item	Risk	Control	Method used, equipment	Frequency of check	Action level	Responsibility	Action taken	Documentation
Sugar storage hoppers	S3	Infestation inspection	Visual	Once per week	Evidence of filth or infestation	Hygiene Services Manager	P.S.M. and Q.A. Manager (Raws) informed. P.S.M. arranges for cleaning as necessary. Hygiene Services Mgr. arranges fumigation	Q.A. records Hygiene services records
Incoming bulk fat	S1	Supplier assurance	Visit suppliers manufacturing units	Once per year	Sub-standard conditions or products	Research Scientist, Q.A. Mgr. (Raws)	Issue report to Supplies Q.A. Superint. R&D seek improvements or reject	Supplier assurance records
	S4	Traceability of deliveries	Sample retained for 1 yr in reference library	Every load	Consumer reaction. Retrospective analytical results	Q.A. Manager (Fin. goods)	Refer to tracing records. Examine reference sample	Tracing records and Q.A. records
	F.1	Identification. Appearance. Taste	Organoleptic	Every load	Unacceptable appearance or taste	Q.A. Manager (Raws)	Inform Supplies Mgr., Q.A. Superint. and R&D. Reject shipment	Q.A. records
	M3	*Analytical* 1. FFA 2. Colour 3. Trace metals	1. Titration 2. Lovibond 3. AAS	Every load Once per month	1. $> 0.1\%$ 2. $> 12Y > 1.2R$ 3. Lead > 0.5 ppm Arsenic > 1.0 ppm Copper > 2.0 ppm	Q.A. Manager (Raws)	Supplies Mgr., Q.A. Superint., R&D informed. Waiver may be issued by R&D if analytical defect will not impair finished product *Quality* or *Safety*	Q.A. records
Lecithin	M1	Stirrer speed	Visual	P.M. shift	< 60 rpm	Production Shift Mgr. Maintenance Shift Mgr.	Repair or replace	Maintenance records
Mixing vessel	M2	Temperature recorder	Visual	Continuous	$40\,°C \pm 5\,°C$		Inform Instruments	Instruments records
	M1	Mixing time	Clock	Every batch	> 5 min > 3 min	Production Shift Mgr.	—	—
Mixer	M4	*Microbiological examination* 1. E. coli 2. Entero 3. Staph. (coag +) 4. Y & Ms	Swab 1. Detection 2. Count 3. Detection 4. Count	Once per week	1. Positive 2. > 500 ft^{-2} 3. Positive 4. > 500 ft^{-2}	Q.A. Mgr. (Raws)	Q.A. Superint. R&D informed. Waiver may be issued by R&D if microbiological defect will not impair finished product *Quality* or *Safety*	Lab. services record. Q.A. files. Q.A. tracing records. Microbiology records

DISCUSSION

Mr. E. Best (Rowntree Mackintosh Ltd) said that quality assurance was needed to establish consumer trust in a particular brand or company name and to improve long-term sales. Quality assurance was considered as a profit-making operation despite the difficulties of return-on-investment calculations. He asked whether 0·5% of turnover was a reasonable investment in quality assurance.

Although the Product Assurance Surveillance System (P.A.S.S.) appeared to have much flexibility it was very complex and the dangers of becoming slaves to the system and perhaps losing sight of the real objectives must be avoided.

He asked what influence the guarantee printed on the label had on the incidence of consumer complaints, how the company exercised control over product recall and whether Mr. Bargent considered that performance tests on the plant were a necessary supplement to laboratory tests in certain circumstances.

Mr. A. Turner (Cadbury Typhoo Ltd) asked why there appeared to be some choice in whether the production department conducted their own tests or had them done in the laboratory. He also asked what potential value records had in respect of court cases, particularly in relation to potential defences of 'all due care and diligence' and 'an inevitable consequence of the process'.

Mr. H. W. Houghton (Schweppes Ltd) explained the difficulties in identifying all potential causes of product recall and the emotive problems involved in classifying product faults into the categories requiring the various levels of procedure.

Mr. K. Anderson (Brooke Bond Liebig) agreed that plant performance tests were of value, particularly in multi-line production, because the final product and performance were the result of a complex interaction between the people, the process, the ingredients, the machinery and the packaging material.

Mr. P. O. Dennis (Brooke Bond Liebig) said that while 'all due care and diligence' and 'an inevitable consequence of the process' could always be pleaded as mitigating factors, in some instances they were statutory defences. For example Section 3(3) of the Food and Drugs Act 1955 says 'it shall be a defence for the defendant to prove that the presence of such (extraneous) matter was an unavoidable consequence of the process of collection or preparation'.

Mr. D. Bargent said in reply that the cost of a Q.A. department at about

0·5 % of turnover, although high, was regarded as appropriate for his particular industry and company, which considered consistent high quality as vitally important to its long-term success and a factor that should not be sacrificed for any short-term benefit. He did not suggest that the level of expenditure indicated was appropriate for all food manufacturers.

P.A.S.S. was a collation of all the existing control and assurance systems, many of which had been operating for years. It was not revolutionary or necessarily new in concept. The manual was divided into sections containing Q.A. procedures relevant to the subjects of each section. The implementation of the procedures by each function constituted the total assurance system.

In his company the product recall system had never been seriously tested at the higher levels and he hoped that a real need would never arise. The system had several different categories with various courses of action depending upon the seriousness of the problem and possible consequences to the consumer. Every case had to be judged against these criteria and the appropriate action taken. He stressed that:

(a) An organised plan of action must be available, updated annually to take account of any changes.

(b) Speed of action is vital, sometimes minutes count.

(c) Total honesty with any outside agencies that may be involved is essential.

(d) The need for adequate records of raw materials, process, quality checks etc., and product tracing procedures as far as possible along the distribution chain, certainly to the forward end of the depot, was imperative.

Consumer complaints for similar products in different parts of the world are illustrated by the following:

Country of sale	History of guarantee panel	Complaints/million bars
UK	30 + years	10
US	2 years	1
Holland/France	None	0·1

The country of manufacture had no significant effect on level of complaints; bars produced in Holland and sold in the UK followed the UK complaint level and *vice versa*. Differences in national consumer attitudes and activity and the guarantee panel history are considered to be the major factors in determining the level of consumer complaints. Damage in the distribution system, particularly in warehouses and retail outlets, accounts for about half of the total complaints caused primarily by heat and damp damage. It was agreed that education of the retail trade in the correct way of handling stock helped, but much more was required.

The practice of production operators carrying out their own instrumental process checks was encouraged as far as possible according to the nature of the tests and equipment required and the capability, interest and willingness of operators. This involved the production personnel in the Q.A. system and gave quick results directly to the people who needed them.

Records of the use and efficiency of consumer protection devices, e.g. metal detectors, can be very useful in negotiations with Regulatory Authorities, representing evidence in mitigation that all reasonable precautions had been taken.

Performance in the plant is the acid test for packaging materials. Laboratory or pilot plant tests are useful sorting procedures, but will not necessarily guarantee that the material will work in the normal production environment.

17

Concluding Remarks

A. G. WARD

Procter Department of Food Science, University of Leeds

Many words were circulated in the preprinted papers prior to the Symposium—most of them useful—and many more have been spoken at it. Little purpose would be served by a summary of the various papers, each of which is concerned with some particular approach to food control. It is even difficult to pick out specific points for comment, because control involves the interaction of so many factors. Each person who has attended the Symposium will select for his own use the particular aspects that relate to his interests. Almost alone of those taking part, I have no direct experience in food control within the industry, but in recent years I have been involved in intensive discussions on the subject with leading practitioners, several of whom have given papers at the Symposium. So, looking at the subject from some distance, I have picked out five points for further consideration, which are likely to be significant in the immediate future.

1. The size, mode of operation, technical competence, and skill in applying food control of firms in the food industry vary widely and similar variations can be observed within the distribution network. The planning of complete food control systems, as described in the Symposium, is largely confined to the bigger firms and to a proportion of medium-sized companies. But many small firms lacking such systems persist and will continue to be commercially viable—many indeed being highly profitable. Some, such as the flourishing small bakeries, are based on skilled practices, with direct control of quality by the craft operative. They provide welcome variety, often with high standards of quality, and have a worthy place in the future of the industry. But there are also small firms that maintain profitability by cutting corners, taking risks, and

277

exploiting the limitations of enforcement. The abuses which result from such an approach are exposed from time to time by the law or by the media and reflect discredit on the whole industry. Indeed, doubts are raised about the viability of the 'self-regulating' approach, which is the ideal of progressive food firms, offering as it does both a fair deal for consumers and flexibility for the industry. It will be necessary for the food industry and the IFST to be fully aware of what is happening in this respect and to seek appropriate action. As has been made clear at the Symposium, wide differences in standards occur also in the distributive network, where poor conditions and bad handling often result in quality losses in foods which have been manufactured to high standards. The disclaimer that once the food has reached the distributor the control function of the food industry ceases cannot be maintained. Ignorance of precise conditions during transport, storage, and display must be overcome by surveys. Statutory date marking, now impending, and the possible application of strict product liability to foodstuffs will further emphasise the responsibility of the manufacturer for the product into the hands of the consumer, no matter by which route it travels. Changes necessary to meet this responsibility require a new approach by many involved in distribution, but it is unlikely that any initiative for change will come from within the more backward areas of the wholesale and retail trade. Indeed, legislative pressure may be the only means of producing action effective throughout the distribution network.

2.   A frequently neglected subject in food control is the attitude of consumers to products with a high degree of uniformity, as compared with those with an element of variability. Such variability needs to be restricted so as not to give unacceptable products. The success in recent years of the small baker illustrates a consumer wish to avoid monotony in foods, whereas the steady decline in consumption of uniform, plant-baked bread refutes previous industrial assertions on this subject. In my view this is not a subject for argument but for practical investigation. It seems to me likely that there are many foods, such as baked beans, vinegar, and flour, which the consumer expects and prefers to be always the same if under a single description and brand name. Others, of which bread and cheese are typical, are more enjoyed if some variation within bounds is provided even from a single source. With modern control systems there should be no great problem in imposing variation on

a product line, while retaining limits which leave the extremes still acceptable. The concept of controlled variability applies with particular force to the provision of whole meals (i.e. whole courses of meals). Lack of recognition of this in the past has adversely affected the acceptability and commercial success of several systems of catering, including some examples produced by the food manufacturing industry. Airline catering illustrates this, with particular emphasis on the adverse reaction to uniform, packaged presentation.

3. A few words are needed on nutritional quality and its control in manufactured foods—a subject not greatly discussed at the Symposium. Nutritional science has been largely successful in indicating minimal levels of nutrients required in the diet to avoid risks of deficiency diseases. When government proposals for reinforcement of particular foods with specific nutrients have been made, the food industry has normally willingly cooperated as long as the proposals have a reasonable basis of established need, are practicable for manufacturers, and do not create new hazards in the product (e.g. sharply reduced shelf-life). Enforcement of nutritional standards has in the past taken account of real difficulties in ensuring even distribution (e.g. nutrient additions to flour). The prevention of avoidable losses of nutrients during manufacture and storage is receiving increasing attention but is still an aspect of control and process design requiring additional emphasis.

Nutritional science is, however, far from being in a position where much positive guidance for healthy eating can be given with certainty. Indeed, the extent of human variations in response to particular food intakes has been inadequately assessed. These circumstances dictate caution for government and industry alike in accepting nutritional guidelines as a basis for action. Humans have thrived on the most varied diets and it may be that the power of adapting human needs to what is available is a key aspect of human nutrition. Food control in the sense of imposed diets (except in illness or for babies under 6 months of age) should at present be avoided and responsibility for choice left firmly with the consumer.

4. The present food control procedures represent, in most respects, an advance on previous practices—or lack of practices. This apparent completeness gives them a certain degree of inertia, resisting change. But, apart from internal forces requiring change, external factors will not allow a static attitude in the food industry. These

include (a) imposed changes in raw materials, (b) legislative changes, including any, such as new defences, arising from the revision of the Food and Drugs Act 1955, (c) changing consumer attitudes, especially from women in employment, and (d) technological developments in equipment and control systems, especially those allowing increased control 'in-line'.

It will be increasingly difficult to separate 'quality control' and 'process control' or, in Andrew Bolton's words, 'quality control' and 'quality assurance'. A new generation of food controllers, some arriving armed with the new electronic control skills, will have to carry through the changes. These controllers will need all those arts that affect human relations to which various speakers have referred.

The M.F.C. itself must serve as an agent of change by the attitude it encourages, particularly by means of the Part III Examination and the Dissertation. Candidates should be challenged to provide solutions to the new problems as they arise—as used to be the practice in Cambridge Mathematical Tripos examinations. The Dissertation is an ideal way of allowing a candidate to show the originality of his thinking.

5. My final point affects the attitude of senior management in the food industry to food control and to those engaged in its practice. Leading firms have passed beyond the phase of regarding control as a limited operation, requiring only care and diligence, unsuitable for top-grade entrants. It is recognised by such firms to be the core of effective operation and a vital factor in commercial success, interacting with all other activities. But the old attitude persists, especially in some well established sectors where processes change only slowly (e.g. parts of the dairy industry). So control staff are recruited with only limited training and academic background (e.g. 2-year diploma students). Such staff lack the power, status, and incentive to bring about the necessary changes. Their work does not develop their initiative and they may inoculate their successors with the view that food control is a dull, restricted subject. So efforts are needed, in the interests of industrial prosperity and of consumer safety and satisfaction, to ensure a proper attitude to the control operation in all food companies. We must also change the views which students acquire of control work—often, unfortunately, from their experience of vacation or sandwich employment.

In conclusion, we should look to the future role of the IFST in fostering developments in food control. Its main current contribution, which may well in the end prove decisive, is the establishment of the Mastership in Food Control. The careful planning of further Symposia when developments make this appropriate, perhaps supplemented by short 'courses' to which firms are more willing to send junior members of staff, is a second task for the Institute. Thirdly, it should consider the establishment of working parties to tackle the nursing of new developments through their early stages. Although this forms an ambitious programme for the Institute, the success of the present Symposium, which owes so much to the organising group and to the guiding hand of Peter Dennis in the preparation of the papers, augurs well for the Institute's ability to play a leading role in the future of food control.

Institute of Food Science and Technology of the United Kingdom

THE CODE OF PROFESSIONAL CONDUCT

The Code is binding on all members of the Institute and shall be subscribed to by all applicants as a condition of membership.
The institute requires each member:

(i)   To promote the aims of the Institute.

(ii)   So to conduct himself or herself as to reflect credit upon the profession.

(iii) To use all proper means to maintain the standards of the profession and to extend its usefulness and sphere of influence.

(iv) To respect any confidence gained in his or her professional capacity.

(v)   When making statements or recommendations in a professional capacity to do so objectively and fairly.

(vi) To take legitimate steps through proper channels to ensure (or assist in ensuring) the wholesomeness of any food with which he or she is concerned.

(vii) To avoid unwarranted statements that reflect upon the character or integrity of other members of the profession.

(viii) To recognise his or her responsibility for the professional guidance of subordinates under his or her immediate control.

(ix) To support fellow members who may find themselves in difficulties on account of their adherence to this Code and the Institute in its efforts to protect them.

Most of the requirements are the subject of guidelines published by the Institute and state the principles and practices to be followed in order to adhere to the Code.

Index